THE VAGABOND PAPERS

REVIEWS OF THE PREVIOUS EDITION

'The best writing about Australian urban conditions in the 1870s …
One of the great documents of the Victorian Age.'
Financial Review

'Straightforward and unsentimental …
candid revelations of the seamy side of life.'
Times Literary Supplement

'The best reporter of the high and low society of our grandparents.'
ABC Books for Comment

'Now much that was dark is all too poignantly clear.'
The Age

'A really useful contribution to the history of Sydney and Melbourne.'
Sun News-Pictorial, Melbourne

'Straightforward, sceptical, sardonic.'
The Australian

'Magnificent social history.'
Ballarat Courier

'A valuable contribution to our understanding of life in those days.'
Launceston Examiner

'An important source of early Australian history.'
Economic Record

'Terrible times they must have been. But they do make lively reading.'
Adelaide Advertiser

'The Vagabond's influence was real and resulted in
important investigations and reforms.'
The Bulletin

The Vagabond Papers

— EXPANDED EDITION —

JOHN STANLEY JAMES

('The Vagabond', 'Julian Thomas')

EDITED AND WITH AN INTRODUCTION BY

MICHAEL CANNON

First published in 5 vols by George Robertson 1877-78
Abridged edition published by Melbourne University Press 1969
This expanded edition published 2016
Main text set in 11/12 pt Linotype Georgian
New material set by Cannon Typesetting in 11/12 pt Adobe Caslon Pro

© Copyright 2016
All rights reserved. Apart from any uses permitted by Australia's Copyright Act 1968, no part of this book may be reproduced by any process without prior written permission from the copyright owners. Inquiries should be directed to the publisher.

Monash University Publishing
Matheson Library and Information Services Building
40 Exhibition Walk
Monash University
Clayton, Victoria 3800, Australia
www.publishing.monash.edu
www.publishing.monash.edu/books/vp-9781922235985.html

Monash University Publishing brings to the world publications which advance the best traditions of humane and enlightened thought. Monash University Publishing titles pass through a rigorous process of independent peer review.

Published in association with the State Library of Victoria
328 Swanston Street, Melbourne, Victoria 3000, Australia
slv.vic.gov.au

Front cover: image John Stanley James, 'the Vagabond', probably photographed in Virginia, c.1875.

National Library of Australia Cataloguing-in-Publication entry:

Creator:	Vagabond (John Stanley James), 1843-96
Title:	The Vagabond papers / edited and introduced by Michael Cannon.
Edition:	Expanded edition.
ISBN:	9781922235985 (paperback)
Series:	Australian history
Notes:	Includes index.
	Includes 'The Vagabond in Virginia' by Robert G. Flippen, 1959- and 'The Vagabond in New Caledonia' by Willa McDonald, 1957-.
Subjects:	Vagabond, 1843-1896.
	Virginia--Social life and customs--19th century.
	Melbourne (Vic.)--Social life and customs--1851-1891.
	New South Wales--Social life and customs--1851-1891.
	Queensland--Social life and customs--1851-1891.
	New Caledonia--Social life and customs--19th century.
	Australia--Social life and customs--1851-1891.
	Australia--Description and travel.
Other Creators/ Contributors:	Cannon, Michael Mongague, 1929- editor, writer of introduction.
Dewey Number:	994.03

Printed in Singapore by Markono Print Media Pte Ltd

EDITOR'S NOTE ON THE NEW EDITION

That eccentric but lovable scribbler who became famous as 'The Vagabond' would have chuckled to see how successfully he evaded both his admirers and his pursuers. Whether writing in Europe, America or Australia, he always kept on the move. Always skipping from one hotspot to the next, always (from the age of thirty or so) pretending to be someone else.

I thought I had done fairly well in the 1969 edition of this book to have tracked down his real name, birth place, and so on. But considerable gaps remained. The first mystery was his sojourn in Virginia, USA, where he claimed to have married a rich widow but gave scant details.

Then, a few years ago, another enthusiast got in touch with the Melbourne Press Club to say he had discovered many of the Vagabond's peculiar activities in Virginia, and the probable reasons why he had fled the country under a false name. That led to a serious reassessment of the man, as outlined by Robert Flippen in the pages which follow.

As though by coincidence, another Vagabond admirer, Dr Willa McDonald of Macquarie University, Sydney, had begun writing articles in scholarly journals about the significance of our hero's works. These fill the second major gap in the 1969 edition—an examination of the Vagabond's reportage of conditions in New Caledonia.

There will always be more to discover about our subject and his wanderings, for there is a bit of the Vagabond in all of us. My hope is that this expanded edition of his life and work will stimulate new interest among readers and historians, and cause new enthusiasts to delve even deeper into his remarkable story.

The articles selected for this edition have been reprinted in the form in which they appeared in the original *Vagabond Papers*, except for cuts made to save space. These have eliminated most of the philosophical homilies which probably yielded the Vagabond personal satisfaction as well as a penny per extra line, but they are mostly irrelevant today. Their excision has been indicated by the usual three dots. In all other respects the punctuation and spelling have been left as in the original edition. A few notes have been added to explain asides on contemporary events and personalities which may not be found in the usual reference works.

No particular pattern is apparent in the order in which the material first appeared in book form. For this edition, the articles selected have been rearranged so that they fall under general subject headings. Some articles have been retitled in order to make the subject more obvious to today's readers: in such cases the original title is given directly underneath. No doubt there will be differences of opinion on the selection of some articles and the elimination of others, but the riches of the Vagabond's work are such that several different worthwhile collections could have been made. His travels throughout south-eastern Australia, for example, are contained in a separate volume entitled *Vagabond Country* (1981).

I must acknowledge my gratitude to the multitude of librarians, academics, editors, publishers, merchandisers and reviewers who made possible the publication of this work. Special thanks are due to the La Trobe Library staff for their assistance with many of the illustrations.

If only the Vagabond could live again in our times, I am sure he would express deep gratitude to all the staff at Monash University Publishing for their work in bringing his words before the public once again. What, I wonder, would he say about our lives today?

M.C.

CONTENTS

Editor's Note on the New Edition	vii
The Vagabond in Virginia, USA	xv
The Vagabond in New Caledonia	xli
Introduction to the 1969 edition	1

PART ONE   DOWN AND OUT

1	A Morning at the Hospital	19
2	The Outcasts of Melbourne	27
3	A Night in the Model Lodging-House	41
4	Sydney Common Lodging Houses	46
5	The Waifs and Strays of Sydney	51
6	Sixpenny Restaurants	61
7	Pauper Funerals	66

PART TWO   LIFE IN PRISON

8	Six Hours in a Dark Cell	77
9	A Month in Pentridge	84
10	Gately the Hangman	101

PART THREE   MIDDLE CLASS MORALITY

11	In a Fashionable Church	107
12	A Suburban Church	112
13	At a Bazaar	119
14	"Sabbath-Breaking" in Sydney	124
15	Sydney Theatres and Bars	130

PART FOUR   COLD CHARITY

16	A Day in the Immigrants' Home	139
17	Three days in the Benevolent Asylum	149
18	At the Sailors' Home	168

PART FIVE   MANLY SPORTS

21	A Brutal Football Match	207
22	Boxing with Skin Gloves	210
23	Bare Knuckle Bouts	214

PART SIX   THE DEMI-MONDE

24	The Theatre Vestibules	229
25	The Magdalen Asylum	236
26	The Protestant Female Refuge	249

A 'Vagabond' Bibliography   257
Index   267

ILLUSTRATIONS

Idealised lithograph of 'The Vagabond' From a portrait by G. C. E. Foley	xix
'A Mansion Completed in Ten Weeks' *Farmville Mercury*, 19 August 1875	xxi
'Stanley Park' mansion on its original site *Photograph by Robert G. Flippen*, 1999	xxvii
Advertisement for Stanley Park Academy *Farmville Mercury*, 12 August 1875	xxix
Advertisement for English & American Bank *Farmville Mercury*, 13 May 1875	xxxiii
Auction of personal belongings of Mr and Mrs James *Farmville Mercury*, 27 January 1876	xxxix
'The Vagabond' in middle age From a lithograph by 'Leo' (J. H. Leonard)	xlv
'The Vagabond' in later years From a photograph by Ateliers of Melbourne	liii
Down and out *Melbourne Punch*, 6 March 1879	17
Workmen bring an accident case into the Melbourne Hospital *Australasian Sketcher*, 17 December 1881	20

The Melbourne Hospital again   23
Melbourne Punch, 15 October 1868

Honorary help   25
Melbourne Punch, 6 September 1877

Yarra Bankers   28
Melbourne Punch, 19 December 1878

Larrikins of the period   32
Melbourne Punch, 4 May 1876

Melbourne larrikins   35
Melbourne Punch, 30 March 1876

How 'Money' is made   39
Melbourne Punch, 5 September 1872

Late arrivals at the Model Lodging House   42
Australasian Sketcher, 13 May 1876

Melbourne cab driver and his passengers   45
Melbourne Punch, 13 July 1876

The Sydney Soup Kitchen   48
Australasian Sketcher, 4 June 1883

The social joys of a Melbourne street arab   53
Illustrated Australian News, 5 August 1885

Scene in a larrikin school   59
Melbourne Punch, 5 October 1876

Waiting for breakfast at a sixpenny restaurant   63
Illustrated Australian News, 21 December 1881

King Fever and his victims   68
Melbourne Punch, 9 June 1864

Life in prison   75
Australasian Sketcher, 1 November 1873

ILLUSTRATIONS   xiii

The 'silent system' at Pentridge Gaol   81
Australasian Sketcher, 4 October 1873

Gaol sentences for rich and poor   88, 89
Melbourne Punch, 3 March 1870

Middle class morality   105
Melbourne Punch, 29 June 1876

The Rev. Charles Strong   109
Australasian Sketcher, 29 January 1881

Dr John Edward Bromby   114
Weekly Times, 1 August 1874

Fancy Fair at the Town Hall   121
Illustrated Australian News, 21 December 1881

Returning from Botany   125
Illustrated Sydney News, 31 December 1853

Sydney at night, after the close of the theatres   133
Illustrated Sydney News, 17 April 1880

Cold charity   137
Illustrated Australian News, 11 July 1868

Picking oakum at the Immigrants' Home   144
Illustrated Australian News, 11 July 1868

Casuals in the Immigrants' Home   147
Australasian Sketcher, 19 June 1880

The Benevolent Asylum, Melbourne   154
Illustrated Australian News, 8 August 1868

Free concert at the Benevolent Asylum   165
Illustrated Australian News, 8 August 1868

The Sailors' Home   173
Illustrated Australian News, 31 October 1878

Inside a Hornbrook Ragged School　182
Illustrated Australian News, 20 February 1884

The 'Erald Angels　189
Melbourne Punch, 31 October 1878

Effect of state education on neglected children　192
Melbourne Punch, 23 January 1873

Manly sports　205
Australasian Sketcher, 18 June 1881

A bare knuckle fight of earlier days　217
S. T. Gill etching (detail), La Trobe Library

The demi-monde　227
Illustrated Australian News, 1 September 1893

The Theatre Royal, Melbourne　230
Broadside, La Trobe Library

Seven o'clock outside the Theatre Royal　233
H. Glover: *12 Hours Road Scraping in Melbourne* (Melbourne, n.d.)

Theatricals of the period　238
Melbourne Punch, 12 October 1871

Landlords and tenants　244, 245
Life, 18 April 1889

Humane proprietor of sewing machines　253
Melbourne Punch, 15 May 1873

The Vagabond in Virginia, USA

By Robert G. Flippen

At the conclusion of the American Civil War, Virginia was rendered a vanquished land, having withstood the brunt of nearly half the battles fought during 1861 to 1865. From the ensuing havoc, arose a defeated people seeking to establish a new social order and system of labor in concert with the newly emancipated Negroes.

Adversity for some provided opportunity for others, as the decade following the war brought two waves of migration to Southside Virginia. The first originated from the Northern States, led by those whose motivations and desire for supremacy were transparent and resented. Referred to as 'carpetbaggers', very few were ever accepted among the people of the South.

In 1868, a second wave began to arrive, consisting of Englishmen recruited by the Virginia Immigration Society. They were welcomed into the area and regarded as instrumental in helping to revive the economy. These settlers sought to colonise an area south of the James River, comprising the counties of Amelia, Appomattox, Buckingham, Brunswick, Charlotte, Cumberland, Halifax, Lunenburg, Mecklenburg, Nottoway and Prince Edward.

Successes in assimilation were often used as testimony in the effort to encourage further waves of English immigrants, which consisted of gentlemen farmers, retired military officers, some lawyers, clergy, builders and engineers.[1] That they chose Virginia to settle was largely attributed to 'the traditional attachment of the English for Virginia.'

John Stanley James was one of these immigrants who settled in Farmville, Virginia. He would later achieve great notoriety in Australia as a prolific journalist who assumed the alias of 'Julian Thomas', writing under a pseudonym, 'The Vagabond'. His articles about everyday life in Melbourne and its institutions were printed in the columns of the *Argus* newspaper. The subject matter was often devoted to topics not normally discussed in the era, such as the treatment of prisoners, or the condition of inmates confined in lunatic asylums, the fallen young women in the Magdalen home, even the fare at sixpenny restaurants and the patrons who dined there. His anonymity as the author created wide speculation as to his true identity. So popular were his articles that many were later consolidated into book form, comprising five volumes known as *The Vagabond Papers*, first published in 1877 by George Roberston, a Melbourne bookseller and publisher.

This article is intended to introduce James to the American public, and particularly those in Virginia where he attempted to settle. What motivated him to leave behind a wife and family, palatial new home, his students and career, to seek refuge on a distant continent and assume a new name? For readers in Australia, it is hoped that this will bring new understanding, in learning where James came from and why he chose to leave Virginia in 1875, ultimately arriving in Melbourne 'sick in body and mind, and broken in fortune'.[2] He would soon engage in his unique style of immersion journalism, later recognised with his induction into the Melbourne Media Hall of Fame in 2012.

Before he became notorious as a freewheeling observer of Australian life, the English-born immigrant John Stanley James experienced a spectacular rise and fall in Virginia. Yet so humiliating was his downfall that he never revealed the details. Despite the hundreds of first-person newspaper articles he later wrote, which cemented his fame, only brief hints were ever given of his earlier experiences in America.

James is thought to have arrived in the United States from England, travelling steerage class aboard the White Star Line's s.s. *Adriatic*.[3] The luxury liner was launched in October 1871, and its maiden voyage took place in April 1872. While in transit, James wrote a series of descriptive letters detailing how passengers fared in the steerage passage between Liverpool and New York. The letters were supposedly published simultaneously in the *New York Tribune* and *London Daily News* and were said to have 'caused an extraordinary sensation on both sides of the Atlantic'.[4]

By 1873, James was working with Joseph Arch, an English agricultural labor activist and future Member of Parliament. An article in a Virginia newspaper from December 1873 noted that James had been appointed to supervise 'the interests of Joseph Arch to recruit English colonists to Virginia', and was soliciting monetary contributions from the public to help defray the cost of immigration. Their hope was to reduce the passage amount from $25 to $5. The paper's editor remarked, however, that there was 'an abundance of people here' who needed employment, and felt little responsibility to subsidise foreigners. He declared, 'If Englishmen want to come here and take their chances, let them find their own passage money. They are not so essential to our happiness as to warrant us to pay their passage hither, nor any part of it.'[5]

During the severe slump which was affecting the whole American economy, James probably found it difficult to obtain more than a little freelance journalistic work to supplement whatever Joseph Arch could pay him. In the fifth volume of *The Vagabond Papers* (1878), he recalled how he used to travel with the eccentric photographer Eadweard Muybridge, posing for him against colorful backgrounds to help make photographic studies for sale. This seems to fit in with the photographer's 'missing' few months early in 1874, a period when even his keenest biographers have been unable to track his wanderings with assistants who helped to carry his bulky photographic equipment. After that experience, as James noted, Muybridge returned to San Francisco, discovered his wife's infidelity during his absence, shot her lover dead, and was freed by a sympathetic jury.

In early March 1875, James arrived in Farmville, a small town in Virginia, as a visiting correspondent representing the *London Labor News*. He was accompanied by General James R. Slayton, editor of the New York journal *South*. Slayton penned an interesting account of their journey to Farmville, which was published using the nom de plume 'Rambler'. Their journey began in the State capital Richmond, a clue that James may have been living in that area at the time. After taking passage westward along the Richmond & Danville Railroad, they disembarked in Burkeville, Nottoway County, for several hours before they changed cars to a connecting line, the Atlantic, Mississippi & Ohio Railroad. As it was midday, the pair set out to find a meal:

> We had hardly touched the platform when we were saluted by a colored runner, who wished to take us to the railroad eating house to dinner and after consultation, we had determined to follow him, when the arrangement was interrupted by the appearance of runner No. 2, who informed us that that nigger was a fraud and a cheat, that the hotel was a one-horse concern where you were charged seventy-five cents for a much poorer meal than Col. Flippen sold for fifty cents; and taking our valises, he strode toward the opposition house, with Mr. James and myself in the rear. We found good food at the table, and plenty of it; but it was cooked in such a manner that one would have the dyspepsia if forced to live on it a month. But this is the fault of all Southern hotels; too much lard is used to make the fare either healthy or

palatable. After dinner, we occupied our time, a part of it, in conversing with the citizens, many of whom are new comers from England . . .⁶

Upon reaching Farmville, they were greeted by a delegation of citizens led by local editor Joseph Andrew Horner St. Andrew, and escorted to their accommodations at the Randolph House, Farmville's main hostelry.

Next day, 9 March, they received an enthusiastic welcome from members of the Farmville British Association, who gathered at the Court House for a reception in their honour. The two addressed the assembly regarding recruitment of English settlers and proposed establishment of the Southside Virginia Immigration Society. The text of their speeches was printed in the local newspaper. In the transcript of James's address, he revealed the apparent reason he left England, saying:

> I am a plain, modest man; many of the cherished institutions of our native land were too much for me and so I have fled to these hospitable shores, making my home here, where I trust that this great country may remain ever governed by the people for the people.⁷

James also mentioned his prior association with Joseph Arch and the English farm labor reform movement.

On 10 March, Slayton and James journeyed seven or eight miles south of Farmville to visit Hampden-Sidney College and the Presbyterian Union Theological Seminary. There they noted the schools were flourishing with superior facilities. It was perhaps this visit to Hampden-Sidney College that provided the most overt reference to James's time in Farmville. In the Second Series of *The Vagabond Papers* (1877), James wrote of visiting the College. Here he met its venerable headmaster, Robert Louis Dabney, and heard his views on State-sponsored education, all unfavorable, to say the least:

> The foremost and most celebrated of these critics is my old friend, the Rev. Randolph [sic] L. Dabney, D.D., professor and principal of the Union Theological Seminary, situated at Hampden-Sidney, near the Court-house of Prince Edward County, Virginia. Now, Dr. Dabney is a scholarly gentleman of rare attainments, but as a clergyman he is of the Church militant. He has the blood of chivalrous cavaliers in his veins, and his heart is in his State, and opposed to the reconstruction of the peculiar institutions formerly prevalent in "Dixie."

Idealised lithograph of the Vagabond,
from a portrait by G. C. E. Foley.

James continued:

> A high-toned Southern gentleman and hospitable host is Dr. Dabney. I have been his guest, and experienced all the charm of his intellectual conversation. We had much in common; but still, on the public school question, I am forced to admit that his testimony isn't worth a cent. First because it is of the North, and Dr. Dabney has not "accepted the situation," but hates the North and its institutions worse than Lucifer. Second, the "Civil Rights Bill" establishes perfect equality in schools, churches, theatres and railroad cars, and if the State Schools become an institution in the South, the negro boy may sit down at the desk by the side of the heir to valueless acres and princely blood. This is an abomination in the nostrils of our professor, who is already burdened with a negro representative in the State Legislature; and so he takes up his pen to prove the system is all wrong and a vicious one . . .[8]

Before the end of March 1875, James, with the encouragement of other local settlers, had decided to live permanently in Farmville, with the purchase of ninety acres of land known as 'Lake Hill' for $1,700. Alfred Moth, cashier of the local English & American Bank and one of the earliest colonists in the area, acted as agent. James intended to 'erect a fine residence on the hill' which offered impressive scenic views of the surrounding countryside.[9]

The mansion which Mr and Mrs James planned to build was insured for $2,200, so their total investment may have been about $3,900, a very subtantial sum for those times. James was notoriously impecunious, so most of the money must have come from his wife's pocket, perhaps some of it from his new friends on the Bank Board, since they were courting him to settle in the district.

James came to Farmville assuming the persona of a man of letters and was known as 'Dr.' J. S. Stanley-James. His community involvement would become extensive and freely chronicled in the local newspaper. Known as *The Farmville Mercury*, the newspaper was published by another English immigrant, J. A. H. St. Andrew. The printing press was located in a shed in the backyard of his Beech Street home in Farmville and managed by his brother-in-law, Robert Battersby.[10] St. Andrew had previously published *The Southside Virginian* in Chase City. Having sold it to John J. Ashenhurst, he purchased *The Farmville Commonwealth*, which he renamed *The Farmville Mercury*. Both newspapers were focused in their emphasis on English colonists by aiding in their assimilation.

A Mansion Completed in Ten Weeks.

As an instance of the enterprise and go-a-headishness of our town, we refer to the fact that the elegant mansion of Dr. Stanley James, in Stanley Park, has been put up and ready for occupancy inside of ten weeks. The architect and builder, Mr. F. Harper Twelvetrees, had peculiar difficulties to encounter in getting his materials on to the ground and otherwise, but nothing prevented the rapid progress of the work. The mansion is splendidly situated overlooking a magnificent expanse of country. Mr. Twelvetrees states that in fulfilling his contract he was greatly indebted to O. T. Wicker, Esq., who supplied the tin work; Mr. S. H. Boileau, plasterer, and Mr. E. T. Rodgers, painter, for their promptitude and dispatch. The whole work reflects honor on our business men.

After the Vagabond married Mrs Caroline Lewis, they moved to Farmville, Virginia, and purchased ninety acres of land adjoining the town. Here they constructed a two-storey mansion featuring an observation tower that provided spectacular views of the countryside. The elaborate structure named 'Stanley Park' was ready for occupation in only ten weeks.
Farmville Mercury, 19 August 1875

Because St. Andrew was also invested in the English colonisation effort, James's activities were given frequent attention in the columns of all of these papers.

April 1875 began with James on a whirlwind speaking tour of Southside Virginia. Accompanied by General Slayton and St. Andrew, the three would traverse Prince Edward, Charlotte and Mecklenburg Counties over horrid road conditions, arriving in Chase City on 2 April. That evening they addressed a Board of Settlers convened at Chase City Academy. A transcript of their speeches in a subsequent issue of *The Southside Virginian* emphasised completion of a railroad to Chase City, with advertising and a substantial modern hotel as essential to the economic development of the area. James began his address with a humorous reference to the poor road conditions by alluding the famous encounter between Henry Stanley and Dr David Livingstone in Africa, saying he did not know much about the roads in Ujiji, but if they were anything like the roads leading to Chase City, 'I am not at all surprised that Livingstone remained so long lost to the world . . .'. It was at this meeting that James declared he was a naturalised American citizen, and encouraged all the new settlers to seek a path to U.S. citizenship.[11]

As he was in the process of relocating from Chase City to live in Farmville, J. A. H. St. Andrew attended a meeting convened in his honor on 5 April at the Colored Baptist Church of Chase City. There he gave a heartfelt farewell to the colored people of the community. St. Andrew advised them of the necessary traits for success such as honesty, virtue, temperance, religion, politics, etc. He was followed with brief remarks from General Slayton and J. S. Stanley-James, who closed by commenting that 'the colored people of Chase City were in a far better position, relatively, than the agricultural laborers of England'.[12] They were paid for their labor and could, through thrift and pluck, acquire land and exercise a vote, and in this regard, they were 'far better off' than their European agricultural counterparts. On 6 April, the three proponents of English immigration ventured to Wylliesburg to meet with the Charlotte County Immigration Society. After a resolution of welcome was passed, all three men spoke strongly against repudiation of the State's debt as contemplated by the Legislature.

In Farmville, work continued on the formation of the nascent Southside Virginia Immigration Society. James accrued more responsibility in its operation by serving as Corresponding Secretary. His duties included the composition of letters of solicitation to various corporate officials and personages, and promotions which included advertisements in newspapers from as far away as Minnesota, New York, Pittsburgh, Baltimore, Cincinnati, Des Moines and Indianapolis. He also served on the committee drafting the organisation's Constitution.

James announced this Constitution on 10 May 1875 to an assembly of English colonists and their supporters in Buckingham Court House, Virginia. There he stressed the need for a railroad to be constructed in order to open the interior of the County to development. He also encouraged current settlers to sell parcels of land to those newly arrived, and recommended that the English & American Bank in Farmville process all transactions.[13]

Many contributions to the area have been made by English settlers, but the construction of Episcopal churches has endured the test of time. Most notable was the Johns Memorial Church in Farmville, which stands today on High Street across from the rotunda of Longwood University, then known as Farmville College. Another was in the Spring Creek vicinity of Prince Edward County, called St. Anne's. Here, a modest church edifice was dedicated on 10 June 1875 amid great fanfare as James and many of his compatriots attended the consecration service. The site was chosen because there were a number of immigrants in the vicinity, forming a distinct colony known as Clarendon. The colony was named in honour of the Earl of Clarendon, a friend of Thomas Homer, another English immigrant and the colony's principal proponent.

Clarendon was developed along the same plan that was used to some success in Chase City. A general store had been opened and a local Grange Hall was under construction as a meeting place for farmers to exchange ideas and agricultural practices. Tradesmen such as wheelwrights, blacksmiths and professionals such as teachers were encouraged to settle and achieve immediate employment. Separate public schools were planned for both white and Negro children, while ten acres were set aside for Negroes to live on. Thomas Homer proposed to have alternate building lots donated to future immigrants as an incentive to settle there.

Though Episcopalians were quite common in Prince Edward County before the American Revolution, not one church for their worship was established in the following century. It was hoped that the consecration of St. Anne's would spark an Episcopal revival in Prince Edward and beyond. St. Anne's was indeed the culmination of an international effort, as funds were solicited and raised from as far away as England. All manner of items such as furniture, prayer books and embroidered covers were contributed. Some generous ladies of New York donated an organ and a Miss Trickett, of England, donated a marble font.

News of the Right Rev. Bishop Johns's arrival to consecrate the new church helped to swell the throng of worshippers. The Bishop arrived at Prospect Station along the Atlantic, Mississippi & Ohio Railroad, and was escorted the five miles to the site by J. A. H. St. Andrew, Henry Jacob and Thomas Homer, whereupon the service began. *The Farmville*

Mercury published the order of proceedings, but noted the concluding communion service was dispensed with as the Bishop had to leave on the next mail train from Prospect.[14]

After the service, all were invited to nearby 'Oakland', the estate of Thomas Homer, for a repast and entertainment. A game of cricket followed, in which John Stanley James was reported to have 'showed some excellent play.' Accompanying James was Walter N. Powys, a cricketer of world renown who was known as a 'mollyduker' because he was a left-handed batsman who also bowled left-arm roundarm fast. Discussion after the game suggested a challenge would be made to the Richmond eleven to play the Prince Edward team. In one of his articles on cricket, James claimed he was the founder of the Richmond (Virginia) Cricket Club and that they paid Negroes twenty cents an hour to field balls while the whites did nothing but bat and bowl.[15]

James and Powys also shared a keen interest in wildlife, as James was a contributor to *Forest and Stream Magazine*, reporting on experimental importations of game such as rabbits, pheasants and partridges into Virginia. Walter Powys returned from England in late 1874 after participating in an important cricket match with the Cambridge team, bringing with him thirty-two pairs of English rabbits. Half of the rabbits were of a distinct breed, black in colour, which originated in Hawkstone, the seat of Lord Hill. They were said to resemble crows milling about in a distant pasture view. Powys also brought two pairs of English pheasants and released all into the wild on his property located about five miles from Farmville. An old English tenant farmer congratulated Powys on his feats of athleticism, but chided him saying, 'Future generations will curse the name of Powys for introducing the rabbit into Virginia.'[16] In the Fourth Series of *The Vagabond Papers* (1877), James recalled this encounter between neighbours in greater detail and added, 'I remember that we had a good laugh at this prophecy, and I replied that, unless rabbits took a fancy for tobacco plants, they could not do us much harm.'

A more robust effort in the importation of animals was achieved by J. M. and Farnsworth Taylor, who purchased land in the Blacks and Whites (Blackstone) section of Nottoway County. J. S. James, who served as the agent, reported that the brothers had imported select stock horses and cattle as well as various breeds of pointer dogs. Their intention was to establish a hunting resort and guided hunting excursions on the James and York Rivers. The International Association for Protecting Game and Fish was organised in 1875 and John Stanley James was one of six serving on an advisory committee for Virginia.[17]

Throughout his later writings in the South Pacific, James mentioned Masonic items of interest, but never admitted to being a member of the secretive fraternal order. Research at the Grand Lodge of Virginia revealed that he was indeed a member of Farmville Lodge No. 41 Ancient Free and Accepted Masons. His name appears on the membership roll for 1875.[18] A clue to this affiliation is found in a mention in *The Farmville Mercury* stating 'Brother Dr. Stanley-James' has a rare and ancient book on Freemasonry published in 1754, entitled *The History of Freemasons*, by Brother J. Scott of London. The article continued to give details found in the book such as where Lodges were located at the time and the persecution of its members in the past, and concluded with 'Brother Dr. Stanley-James expresses his willingness to lend this rare work to any "Gentile" who may be curious as to Masonry, if the same will first show his fitness to understand it by joining the Craft.'[19] James's name would later be expunged from the Lodge's roll of Master Masons on 24 February 1876 for failure to pay dues.

The former slave plantation purchased by Stanley-James comprised a ninety-acre tract bordered by the Town of Farmville corporate line to the east, the Atlantic, Mississippi & Ohio Railroad to the south, Buffalo Creek to the west, and the Appomattox River on the north. Construction of a grand mansion built in the Anglo-Italian Gothic Villa design and dubbed 'Stanley Park' was completed in less than three months. The architect and builder was another English immigrant, Frederick Harper Twelvetrees. An article entitled 'A Mansion Completed in Ten Weeks' noted that the builder had experienced difficulty in transporting materials to the site. No doubt this was due to the steep incline leading to the residence. Various subcontractors cited for their 'promptitude and dispatch' were praised as an example of the enterprise and 'go-a-headishness' of the community's business leaders.[20]

In 1980, as a university student returning home to Farmville on breaks, I would ramble on the banks of the Appomattox River westwards along an abandoned rail bed built ninety years earlier for the Farmville & Powhatan Railroad. Emerging from a shadowy canopy of forest growth through an ancient and forgotten section of Farmville, there suddenly appeared a pasture and, above, crowning a tall hillside, the ghostly image of 'Stanley Park' mansion. I was drawn to its unusual Gothic design. Cows were then kept on the pasture, and the house itself used for storage of farm implements and spare parts. I knew the owners, and was able to walk inside the house, with its well-preserved plaster walls, and climb the stairs to the fourth floor. There, the panoramic view of the countryside gave me a new perspective of the area's geography. It was a perfect refuge for a young romantic, who then and there vowed to unravel the mystery of the deserted mansion.

The house included a number of unique architectural features; most visible was the tower occupying the third and fourth floors. There were three chimneys with nine openings framed by simple mantles. The first floor featured six rooms with two large bay windows on the north and east sides. Hidden sliding pocket doors enabled two rooms to become a great room perfectly suited for dining or entertaining. A narrow servants' staircase wound from the first to the second floor, which included three large bedrooms. Due to the location on a hill, a lightning rod system was installed, crowned with copper trees and a weather vane. Behind the house was a small two-room structure that probably served as a summer kitchen and servants' quarters.

An unattributed description of land near the 'Stanley Park' property was given by James in 1886, included in his chapter entitled 'The King of the Cannibal Islands':

> How well I remember standing on a bluff looking over the Appomattox, the river winding a silver streak through the valley, the slopes green with tobacco plants, the distant woods tinged with lovely shades of blue and red. Below us hundreds of negroes, the men all in black, the women with many a streak of colour in the bright kerchiefs around their necks and twisted on their heads. A stone's throw on the bluff above them, unknown Confederate and Federal dead were buried together. Here we had fought one of our last fights with Grant. So short a time, and yet in events so long! Randolph, of Roanoke, on whose land we stood, loved not slavery; he released his bondsmen at his death; but I think, if possible, his bones would have turned in his grave if he had heard the excited preachers on the bank urging the negroes against sin, and to lead a new life—namely, to avoid whisky-drinking and to vote the Republican ticket. Whilst our political masters applauded on one bank, girl after girl walked into the stream up to her armpits, and was dipped three times in the name of the Trinity, emerging in an ecstasy, shouting, amidst a chorus of "glories," "I am saved . . ."[21]

James intended not only to reside here, but also to operate a private school known as 'Stanley Park Academy'. The first session was scheduled to commence on 1 September 1875 for a select number of boys under sixteen years of age. The course of study included English, with particular attention to grammar and writing, Latin, French, Mathematics, fencing with foils, etc. Private lessons were available for adults as well as vacancies for a few boarders. The *Mercury* referred to an advertisement for Stanley Park Academy stating 'Literature and tuition have always gone hand in hand and the Doctor is only resuming an old *role*.' The role referred to his claim of association with Shrewsbury College in England. The editor of the *Mercury* offered encouragement,

'Stanley Park' on its original site before being rebuilt by Gordon Johnson and Alecia Daves-Johnson on their farm in Prospect, Virginia, about 20 kilometres away.
Photo by Robert G. Flippen, 1999

stating that 'Dr. Stanley-James will give students the opportunity of becoming proficient in drilling and fencing accomplishments, far too much neglected in the present day. We shall certainly call round to see the first grand assault at arms. The very idea makes us feel young again.'[22]

The final mention of Stanley Park Academy appeared in the 9 September edition of the *Mercury*, as the editor reported, 'Dr. Stanley-James opened the session on Monday under very encouraging circumstances.' It is not known how many students, if any, were actually enrolled in the curriculum. However, it is quite certain that the first session did not reach a successful conclusion, due to the disappearance of John Stanley James around the end of September or the beginning of October 1875.

Why did this man who came to Farmville just six months before leave suddenly without any notice? Up to this point, James's coverage in the local media fancied him as somewhat of a favourite in the community. He was welcomed and encouraged to settle in the district. But the sudden cessation of varied newspaper items about him casts suspicion on what must have transpired. Given his frequent coverage, had he died, surely there would have been a lengthy obituary extolling his many virtues and talents and lamenting his early demise. Likewise, had he simply relocated because of another opportunity, there would have been an article lamenting how much he would be missed.

There is, however, nothing to be found in the columns of the *Mercury* to explain his sudden disappearance. What made his fall from grace in the Farmville community so grievous that he would depart for Australia, there to assume a new identity as 'Julian Thomas'? There appears to be not a single, but a series of misfortunes that led to his hurried departure.

First and foremost would be James's association with the English & American Bank in Farmville. The bank was established shortly after the English colonisation movement began and served the immigrants as well as the community at large. Although the financial panic of 1873 had resulted in one of the nation's worst depressions, the English & American Bank weathered the financial crisis, confidently advertising 'no panic on hand at present.' Indeed, by 1875 the bank was generating good profits for its shareholders, declaring a generous dividend of fifteen per cent.

As a demonstration of his new prominence, James was elected to the bank's Board of Directors in April 1875. The following week he was elected as Honorary Secretary of the Board. His tenure on the Board can easily be tracked by the bank's weekly advertisement in *The Farmville Mercury*, as the names of Directors were prominently displayed therein. His name appeared in advertisements starting on 13 May 1875 and

STANLEY PARK ACADEMY,

FARMVILLE.

PRINCIPAL:

Dr. J. S. STANLEY-JAMES,

(formerly of Shrewsbury College, Eng.)

A select number of boys under 16 years of age will be received by the Principal to educate with his own children.

The course of study includes English, (with special attention to Grammar and Writing,) Latin, French, Mathematics, Fencing &c.

Private lessons given to adults.

Vacancies for a few Boarders. Terms very moderate.

Session commences September 1st.

Address as above.

aug 12, 1875.

One of the Vagabond's first actions on moving into 'Stanley Park' with his new wife and her children was to establish Stanley Park Academy and profess that as Principal he was 'Dr. J. S. Stanley-James'.
Advertisement in Farmville Mercury, 12 August 1875

ceasing with the 9 September 1875 edition. It is difficult to determine exactly what caused his removal from the Board, but clues may be found in some of his writings in Australia just two years later:

> I was a bank director myself, once, but I failed in the business. In truth I was anything but a success, and quarreled with my comrades at the board because they would not lend money to my personal friends. People would come and implore me to get their bills discounted for a few hundred or thousand dollars. I could never resist such appeals; and when the board, quite properly, refused to advance money on valueless security, I often scribbled my name on the back of a bill and made myself responsible. After losing a few thousand dollars at this game, I came to the conclusion that Nature never intended me for a usurer.[23]

Second, one of the more mysterious aspects of James's life was his brief marriage to Caroline Lewis James. As told by J. B. Cooper, an Australian historian who was a close friend of James in Melbourne, Caroline was 'a rich Southern lady', the widow of a planter from Richmond, Virginia. Cooper also wrote that James mentioned she 'had a family—and also the temper of a Southerner' and that they agreed to separate, whereupon James left for Australia.[24]

It is not known how or where the two became acquainted, but given the huge mortality rate for young men during the Civil War, it is little wonder that a 30-year-old James would arouse the interest of women upon his arrival in Virginia. His literary skill and ability as a raconteur, coupled with his recent participation in the Paris Commune of 1871, could understandably make him an attractive catch in the eyes of a wealthy widow.

There are a few vague references to James's marital status in the *Mercury*, namely a mid-August 1875 issue that noted 'Dr. Stanley-James and family are now settled in their new residence at "Stanley Park".' Also the advertisement for Stanley Park Academy noted, 'A select number of boys will be received by the Principal to educate with his own children.' It is yet unknown how many children Caroline had prior to her relationship with James, or if she had a child by him. In the Third Series of *The Vagabond Papers*, James would later make a passing reference to 'the only widow I ever loved'.

As to why James and Caroline parted, one can only speculate, but the reason may again be financial, as the quondam bank director learned a hard lesson about assuming financial liability for others. The money he lost may ultimately have been exacted from Caroline's purse, resulting in a resentful and irreconcilable difference. The sequence of events causing

James's removal from the bank's Board of Directors and the subsequent failure of his marriage to Caroline would suggest that the two disasters were closely associated.

Two documents are on record in the Prince Edward County Clerk's Office in Farmville relating to James and Caroline. The first is dated 28 August 1875, and is apparently the result of their determination to separate. It states that J. S. S. James was desirous of making some provision for his wife Caroline L. James, and that 'in consideration of the natural love and affection' for his wife as well as the 'further consideration of five dollars cash in hand paid to J. S. S. James', he gave to her 'Stanley Park', the property, the house and its contents.

It is significant that the document purported to free Caroline of further financial obligations, stating that the property was 'hereby conveyed for the sole and separate use and benefit of the said Caroline Lewis James, and for her sole and separate support and maintenance during her life, free in all respects from the debts, contracts and control of the husband, the said J. S. S. James'. The builder, F. Harper Twelvetrees, was named Trustee and bound to administer any of a number of scenarios of succession or disposal.[25]

Also found in the Clerk's Office is a Memo of Articles of Agreement between F. H. Twelvetrees as Trustee for C. L. James and W. F. Paulett. The latter agreed to lease the 'Stanley Park' property for seven years, starting 1 January 1876 and concluding 1 January 1883, for the sum of $300 a year. The terms pertained to the use and maintenance of buildings, an insurance requirement of $2,200, and the conservation of trees by permitting only dead wood to be cut for firewood. No 'colored persons' were to occupy the dwelling house excepting the servants of a white family residing therein. Only farming was to be performed on the property, and no business was to operate on the premises.[26]

Finally, an increasingly contentious series of letters and editorials appeared in the *Mercury* between 16 September and 7 October 1875, printed under the title 'The Anglo-Virginians'. In his prior speeches and writings, James often urged the British colonists to become American citizens. His zeal for American nationalism, however, was not shared by all of his fellow immigrants, rather many sought to remain colonial, embracing Virginia as English subjects while rejecting the Federal government's Republican administration of President Ulysses S. Grant. It was in this exchange of ideas in the *Mercury* that John Stanley James would ultimately be accused of insensitivity to and hatred of England, the land of his birth.

The editor, J. A. H. St. Andrew, began 'The Anglo-Virginians' editorial by praising Queen Victoria and noting the reverence and affection for her position as felt by the English colonists of Virginia:

It is not hard for Virginians to understand that British settlers should cherish a love for the Queen and country they have left behind. The glories of England in peace and war, in literature, arts and sciences are joint heritages of both citizens and settlers. In the State so closely allied to the Old Country in manners, maxims, laws and ideas the people have learnt to honor England's Queen as truly as do England's sons. "It is a dirty bird which fouls its own nest," says the old proverb, and we believe that Anglo-Virginians will be none the less devoted to their new allegiance because they fondly remember their ancient loyalty. The Virginian who does not love Virginia is no true Virginian, and the British settler who was devoid of affection to the land of his birth would be deserving of the fate which Scott described in the burning words:

> "Living, shall forfeit fair renown,
> And double dying, shall go down
> To the vile dust from whence we sprung
> Unwept, unhonored and unsung."[27]

Apparently stung by the 'dirty bird' reference, James responded in the following issue by quoting extensively from a letter written by Anthony Trollope, the prominent English author, who had toured the Colony of Victoria in Australia. His letter was reprinted in many newspapers of the time, and James made known that Trollope's views were also his own. The subject was the plight of English farm laborers, and how their counterparts in Australia, Canada and the United States fared much better than in England:

> What man of wealth in England can justify to himself the difference of position which he sees and feels between himself and the poor hedger and ditcher, whose limbs are racked with rheumatism as he works, up to his knees in mud, on an onion and a lump of bread and cheese? . . . *look even upon that great question of loyalty to the mother country as one of second rate importance.* That question of bread and cheese—or rather, as it exists in the Colonies, of beef and mutton—with all the concomitant comforts which follow the first great comfort of a sufficient diet . . .

ENGLISH & AMERICAN BANK,

FARMVILLE, VA.,

Authorized Capital, - $100,000.

CHAS. BUGG, President.

W. W. H. THACKSTON, Vice Pres't.

ALFRED MOTH, Cashier.

Directors:

R. M. Dickinson,
N. E. Venable,
J. S. Stanley-James,
O. T. Wicker,
W. W. H. Thackston,
Thomas Homer,

Edgar Allan,
Chas. Bugg,
H. R. Hooper,
S. H. Bliss,
A. G. Powell,
Albert Hurd.

The above Institution does a General Banking business, issues Certificates of Deposit, and has in connection therewith the Savings Bank feature, receiving deposits from 25 cents upwards. Interest allowed on time deposits of 5 per cent. per annum.

Checks sold on the principal cities, and collections made and remitted at fair rates.

apr 10—1y.

In May 1875, the Vagabond was elected as a director of the English & American Bank in Farmville, Virginia. Other prominent residents and business leaders are listed in this advertisement.
Farmville Mercury, 13 May 1875

James's quotation of Trollope's views continued:

> *Of what account is the wealth of twenty thousand if twenty million be in need? What consolation can a sense of his country's glory give to a man whose children cry for bread?* To those who have enough, and twice more than enough, patriotism and the pride of power, and the enduring honour of a great nationality are luxuries indeed. With a full stomach and easy limbs, and a knowledge that nothing is wanting for the morrow, he may revel in the memories of Blenheim, Trafalgar and Waterloo; *but, unless a country can feed its people, and educate them, and treat them that life shall be a source of enjoyment and not of pain, such memories are but of small moment* . . . We are doing, perhaps all that can be done at home, but at home it is slow work. Throughout these Colonies, and perhaps more especially here in Victoria than elsewhere, the work is not being done slowly. The working man eats and drinks and holds his own, and looks you in the face; and, though he serves you—as one man must always serve another, he is not your slave. If this be so—and I think that no one who has travelled through these Provinces [the Australian colonies] will deny it . . .

The text quoted by James and printed in italics, were points he clearly wished to emphasise in reply to St. Andrew's editorial. It was probably the writing of Anthony Trollope, with his positive descriptions of life in Australia, that ultimately influenced John Stanley James, the future 'Vagabond', to leave Virginia for that continent. James closed his communication by flippantly declaring, 'Respectfully submitted to the English residents in Virginia, in spite of the vulgar proverb, "It is a dirty bird &c."'[28] Was he apologising for his own misdeeds?

In the next weekly issue of the *Mercury* dated 30 September 1875, the editor devoted an entire column in response to James's quotations from Anthony Trollope. He began by questioning the relevance of Trollope's observations, noting that immigration proponents had for years advocated settling in Virginia, and that 'Englishmen of the right *calibre* can do better in every respect here than at home', and that loyalty and honor were sentiments shared by Virginians and Englishmen alike.

Just as James had previously referred to Trollope's observations, St. Andrew quoted from another prominent English writer, Arthur Clayden, in an effort to contradict the arguments of Trollope and James. Clayden, a prior associate of Joseph Arch, wrote *The Revolt of the Field* in support of the National Agricultural Laborers' Union during Arch's tour of Canada in 1873. Clayden would emigrate to New Zealand in 1877 and take up farming there. In drawing a comparison between laborers in England and those in the United States, St. Andrew conflated selected writings of Clayden, who asserted that the condition of farm laborers in England had greatly improved in recent years. He added quotes from an unnamed labor union advocate in the *New York Herald*, to claim the American workman, particularly in the Northern States, was not much better off than slaves in the South before the Civil War. A contrast of immigration philosophies became apparent when St. Andrew wrote, 'Virginia does not invite laborers, but small capitalists.'[29]

Indeed there existed a fundamental difference between the immigration efforts of Joseph Arch, with which John Stanley James was first identified, and the English colonists of Southside Virginia. Arch and James concentrated on improving the lot of English yeomen farmers by introducing them to new lands in Canada, America, Australia and New Zealand. There they were able to start life anew, free from the burden of the time-honored system of labour found in England. These ancient traditions tended to entrench the yeoman into an agricultural quasi-caste system from which extrication was difficult, almost impossible. Most of the English settlers who came to Southside Virginia were of a different sort: they tended to be derived from the professional and retired military classes, very few of whom were actual farmers, but they embarked upon the avocation optimistically, almost as a manifestation of adventurist spirit.

St. Andrew also took James to task for his perceived lack of English patriotism by asking:

> Does Dr. Stanley-James despise the man who feels a thrill of loving affection when he speaks of "My own my native land"? If the Doctor *does not*, there is nothing for him to argue with the *Mercury* about. If he *does*, we decline all argument. The man who loves not the land of his birth—be he Virginian, English, Scotch, Irish or German—places himself outside of the pale of argument. He is welcome to his solitary position.

The response of John Stanley James to St. Andrew's accusations was swift and tempered with anger:

> Sir—In your article in to-day's issue of the *Mercury* [30 September 1875] you do not attempt to dispute Mr. Anthony Trollope's assertions, but turn the tables upon me, who only quoted them. At the present moment my time is far too valuable to waste in a newspaper controversy. I know that I shall never convert *you* who are above all English, and I also know that as I now attack one of your pet prejudices, you will be sure to have the last word. Nonetheless, as you throw out a challenge to me, I will avow my faith, and if I stand alone, so be it!

James continued to dissect the editor's use of Clayden's beliefs and those of a trade union advocate to make his point, as two cases that were unrelated and not analogous:

> Why quote these opinions then? The apparent reason is to prove that England is a better country to live in than America. And it is in this that I disagree with you; I love Virginia more than I do England. If Great Britain is so rich and prosperous, and such a beautiful country to live in, what inducement is there for anyone to come here? I believe otherwise; I believe America, and particularly that State in which I have made my home, Virginia, to offer greater advantages for prosperity and happiness than the land in which I was born. I love this State, I love the people, I love Virginia more, and therefore I love England less, for I cannot serve two countries. And cannot you understand that all this may be without "hatred of the Old Country"? The one question is, which shall I be, an Englishman or a Virginian? If I loved England most I would remain an Englishman and *remain in England*. I do not, therefore I am here and a Virginian . . .

James concluded his letter with a postscript taunting the editor:

> Here is a conundrum—Many Englishmen settled in this State have children born in England their "motherland," but who will be reared and brought up as Virginians. Now is their "first instinct" (that of "every honorable heart"—*vide* your article) to be love for England or love for Virginia?[30]

This correspondence from James was his last submission for publication in *The Farmville Mercury*. It was dated 30 September and published in the 7 October 1875 edition, so it is reasonable to conclude that, when writing it, he had yet to leave Farmville. Perhaps realising the consequence of this letter among his colonial peers, he probably left for Australia shortly before its publication. In the short span of a single month John Stanley James lost the prestige and power of a bank director's position, his wife and adopted family, a newly constructed home and, finally, the respect of the local newspaper editor, the very individual who had invited James to visit Farmville just six months before.

A special meeting of the Southside Virginia Immigration Society was convened on 23 October 1875, with J. A. H. St. Andrew, the Society's Vice-President, presiding. The Secretary, J. W. Womack, read the notice convening the meeting, and after a quorum was determined to be present, a motion was presented by Colonel J. P. Fitzgerald and seconded by Dr W. W. H. Thackston 'that the office of the Corresponding Secretary had become vacant by reason of the continued absence from Farmville of the member elected to that position.'[31] It seems that the Society was so embarrassed by James's disappearance that the *Mercury* refused even to name him in its report.

On 28 January 1876, an auction was held at 'Stanley Park' with H. J. Crute conducting the sale. A sizeable advertisement in *The Farmville Mercury* listed many high-quality items being offered for sale. Featured was the household furniture of walnut and mahogany, including an 'elegant English solid mahogany writing bureau'. Also sold were walnut chairs, a cane-bottomed rocker, horsehair sofa, mahogany sideboard, toilet service, bedstead, washstands, extension table, lamps, large cooking stove, and even the servant's bed and mattress.

Lot 27 in the auction catalogue included James's own garments, comprising 'a splendid assortment of English clothing', made by fashionable tailors in the latest styles and best materials. There were 'two handsome Dress coats, elegantly faced and lined with silk, a fine Ulster overcoat, pantaloons, vests and coats in great variety'. Also sold were items that probably belonged to Caroline, such as 'pure gold jewelry, including heavy Albert chain, bracelets . . . and ladies' dresses sold in parcels.'[32] The inclusion of her jewels and clothing in this sale suggests that she was left in a dire financial condition. With 'Stanley Park' leased for occupation to W. F. Paulett for the next seven years, it is not unreasonable to conclude that Caroline Lewis James had left Farmville and perhaps moved to where she previously lived, most likely Richmond.

It is difficult to establish the route that James took to get to Australia. It seems possible he left on a ship from Norfolk, Virginia, first arriving in Sydney before reaching Melbourne. It is also possible that he travelled on the recently-completed transcontinental railroad across the United States and its territories, before boarding a ship in San Francisco bound for Australia. In any event, when he disembarked, he did so having assumed a new alias, that of 'Julian Thomas'. He would, it appears, live the rest of his life attempting to hide the shame he incurred in Virginia while simultaneously achieving fame in Australia as 'The Vagabond'.

NOTES

[1] 'The Second Coming of the English to Virginia', *University of Virginia, Alumni Bulletin* Vol. IV, No. 3, November 1897, 60-72.
[2] Preface to *The Vagabond Papers*, First Series, George Robertson, Melbourne, 1877.
[3] 'Mr. Stanley James', *The Farmville Mercury*, 25 March 1875.
[4] 'J. S. Stanley-James, Esq.', *The Farmville Mercury*, 1 April 1875.
[5] 'Mr. Arch's English Laborers', *The Daily State Journal*, Alexandria, Virginia, 6 December 1873.
[6] 'Life in Virginia', *The Farmville Mercury*, 1 April 1875.
[7] 'Speeches of Gen. James R. Slayton of New York and J. S. Stanley-James, Esq. of England, Delivered at the Court House, Farmville, March 9, 1875', *The Farmville Mercury*, 18 March 1875.
[8] 'Ragged Schools', *The Vagabond Papers*, Second Series, George Robertson, Melbourne, 1877.
[9] 'Land Sale', *The Farmville Mercury*, 18 March 1875.
[10] Bradshaw, Herbert C., *History of Farmville, Virginia (1798-1948)*, *The Farmville Herald*, 1994, 305.
[11] 'Board of Settlers—Public Reception of Gen. James R. Slayton, of New York and J. S. Stanley-James, of London', *The Southside Virginian*, 8 April 1875.
[12] 'Mr. St. Andrew's Farewell to the Colored People of Chase City', *The Southside Virginian*, 15 April 1875.
[13] 'Grand Immigration Meeting—Buckingham C. H. All Alive', *The Farmville Mercury*, 20 May 1875.
[14] 'Clarendon Colony, Prince Edward County—Consecration of St. Anne's Church by the Right Rev. Bishop Johns', *The Farmville Mercury*, 17 June 1875.
[15] Cannon, Michael, Introduction to *The Vagabond Papers*, Melbourne University Press, 1969, 4.
[16] 'English Colonization in Virginia', *The Farmville Mercury*, 15 April 1875.
[17] 'The International Game Protective Association', *The Farmville Mercury*, 24 June 1875.
[18] *Grand Lodge of Virginia Proceedings*, 1875, 132-3.
[19] 'Freemasonry', *The Farmville Mercury*, 16 September 1875.
[20] 'A Mansion Completed in Ten Weeks,' *The Farmville Mercury*, 19 August 1875.
[21] 'Thomas, Julian', *Cannibals and Convicts, Notes on Personal Experiences in the Western Pacific*, Cassell, London, 1886, 21-2.
[22] 'Stanley Park Academy', *The Farmville Mercury*, 2 September 1875.
[23] 'A Peep at the Blacks', *The Vagabond Papers*, Fourth Series, George Robertson, Melbourne, 1877, 57.
[24] Cooper, J. B., 'Who Was "The Vagabond"?', *Life*, 1 January 1912.
[25] Prince Edward County, Clerk's Office, Farmville, Virginia, Deed Book 31, 549-50.
[26] Ibid, 662-5.
[27] 'The Anglo-Virginians', *The Farmville Mercury*, 16 September 1875.
[28] 'Anglo-Virginians', *The Farmville Mercury*, 23 September 1875.
[29] 'Anglo-Virginians', *The Farmville Mercury*, 30 September 1875.
[30] 'Ango-Virginians', *The Farmville Mercury*, 7 October 1875.
[31] 'Southside Immigration Society', *The Farmville Mercury*, 28 October 1875.
[32] *The Farmville Mercury*, 27 January 1876.

STANLEY PARK, FARMVILLE, VA.

H. J. CRUTE, Auctioneer,

By instructions will sell by auction, at the above address, on

FRIDAY, JANUARY 28TH, 1876,

a new and splendid stock of Household Furniture; Superior Assortment of Clothes made from the best English Goods, Crockery, Glassware &c.

CATALOGUE:

Lot 1. A fine Extension Walnut Table.
2. A magnificent Mahogany Sideboard.
3. Half dozen Walnut Chairs, cane bottomed, with Rocker.
4. Half dozen cane bottomed Walnut Chairs.
5. One Walnut Horsehair Sofa.
6. An elegant English Solid Mahogany Writing Bureau.
7. Four handsome Lamps.
8. A magnificent Mahogany Wardrobe.
9. A very fine Walnut Bedstead.
10. A new and excellent Spring Mattress.
11. A beautiful Walnut Bureau and Mirror.
12. A fine marble-topped Wash Stand.
13. An elegant Toilet Service.
14. do.   do.   do.   do.
15. A large and useful Mahogany Clothes Chest.
16. One child's Bed and Mattress.
17. do.   do.   do.
18. One elegant Walnut Bureau and Mirror.
19. A Wash Stand.
20. Servant's Bed and Mattress.
21. Large Cooking Stove with Furniture, nearly new.
22. Large Kitchen Table.
23. A small Pine Table.
24. Brass Kettle.
25. Crockery, Glassware &c. to be sold in parcels.
26. A Miscellaneous assortment of Wash Tubs, Buckets, Boards, Boxes, a splendid Revolver, Sad Irons, Bottles, Jars, Wheelbarrow, Saws, Axes &c. to be sold in parcels.

CLOTHING.

Lot 27. A splendid assortment of English Clothing, made by fashionable tailors of the latest styles and best materials, including a fine Ulster Overcoat; two handsome Dress Coats, elegantly faced and lined with silk; Light Brown Overcoat; Thick Brown Overcoat; Pantaloons, Vests and Coats in great variety; Shirts, Drawers, Ties and other articles to be sold in parcels.
28. A collection of pure Gold Jewelry including heavy Albert Chain, Bracelets &c., &c.
29. Several Ladies Dresses &c., to be sold in parcels.

☞ SPECIAL NOTICE. ☜

MR. CRUTE begs his patrons to take notice that the sale will commence punctually at 11 o'clock. TERMS CASH.

☞ MR. CRUTE invites gentlemen to call at McKinney Bro. & Co's., and examine the Dress Coats mentioned above.

The Vagabond's prosperous life in America came to an abrupt halt in the autumn of 1875. After he fled to Australia under a false name, his wife was compelled to vacate 'Stanley Park' and auction most of their belongings. She sold her own mahogany and walnut furniture and her clothing, as well as her husband's 'splendid Revolver', 'fine Ulster Overcoat', a great variety of 'Pantaloons, Vests and Coats', and even her 'Servant's Bed and Mattress.'
Farmville Mercury, 27 January 1876

The Vagabond in New Caledonia

By Willa McDonald

Half a century before George Orwell's essay 'A Hanging', John Stanley James wrote a compelling piece of journalism about the execution of New Caledonian Kanaks by the French military. The killings—including the shooting by firing squad of a thirteen-year-old boy—were the end result of a series of incidents that began with the slaughter of pigs owned by a French settler. James wrote an eyewitness account of the execution that angered the French colonists, shocked his readers and left no-one in doubt as to where his sympathies lay.

Known at the time as 'Julian Thomas', James was sent to New Caledonia in 1878 by the *Sydney Morning Herald* to cover what became known as the Great Revolt by the indigenous Kanaks. He spent several months in New Caledonia embedded with the French colonial forces. His journalism from the troubled settlement attempted to transcend the language of colonialism and provided vivid first-hand reports of the conflict. Like others writing literary journalism in the nineteenth century (for example, the Americans Mark Twain and Stephen Crane), James brought all the techniques of imaginative storytelling to his work, not to avoid factuality but with the intention of enhancing the impact and 'truthfulness' of the reporting.

In the process, his writing betrays the struggle of the literary journalist, whose presence as part of the narrative promotes claims of independence through subjectivity and, at the same time, objective authority because of the writer's direct encounter with real events. It also raises the question, still relevant today, of whether literary journalism, with its emphasis on immersion and its use of literary techniques, offers an alternative approach to reporting the 24/7 news cycle—one that fosters accuracy, truthfulness and social justice.

When James travelled to New Caledonia at the beginning of the Kanak uprising, the country had been annexed by the French for twenty-five years. About 16,000 convicts were upon the island at the time of the Great Revolt, including 4,500 Communards who were deported to the Ile des Pins (one of four detention centres), after the failure of the Paris Commune in 1871. The substantial convict population on New Caledonia was augmented by settlers, whose numbers greatly increased after the discovery of precious metals (such as nickel and copper) in the 1860s.

In the process of settlement, the Europeans ignored Kanak ownership and took much of the best farming land as their own. Despite fences erected by the Kanaks to protect their crops, European-owned cattle wrecked the yam and taro beds, as well as the irrigation channels. There were a number of smaller rebellions in preceding years, but when the fertile river valley, which was home to several villages of tribes led by Chief Ataii, was taken by the French to extend the La Foa penitentiary, Ataii led a major revolt. The rebellion began around the villages of La Foa and Boulouparis but soon spread to other parts of New Caledonia, resulting in a year-long war (see Bullard, Ferraro, James and Toth).

The Revolt was of interest to residents in the fledgling British settlement of Sydney because of both the geographic proximity of New Caledonia (which was fewer than 2000 kilometres to the north-east (about five days sail away) and the broad cultural, historical and political similarities shared by the two colonies. James claimed he was the first reporter to go to New Caledonia when he sailed on the *Gunga* on 20 July 1878. One of his obituaries states that he was the only journalist allowed to visit the Ile des Pins (*Zeehan & Dundas Herald*). He was certainly the perfect choice for Hugh George, the general manager of the *Sydney Morning Herald* to send to report on the uprising. George had been James's employer at the Melbourne *Argus*, and when he moved to Sydney, James followed him. James not only spoke French, having spent some time in France in his youth as a reporter for the English press, but his articles as 'The Vagabond' for the *Argus* had proved his abilities as both intrepid researcher and absorbing storyteller. The articles were very popular with Melbourne readers the year before, while also being controversial, drawing letters to the editor and prompting enquiries in response to his observations of the goings-on in the institutions he visited (McDonald, Cannon).

Despite his tendency to embroider the facts of his own life, James seems to have been meticulous with the information in his journalism. Throughout all the controversies, it appears no-one was ever able to demonstrate that James had his facts wrong, although many resorted to criticising his immersive methods and style of reporting (McDonald,

Cannon). In his first report from New Caledonia published in the *Sydney Morning Herald*, James alluded in an anecdote to the value he put on factual accuracy, saying 'It is true there was a talented Irishman on board, who was a continual delight to me . . . and told me most interesting things about New Caledonia, not necessarily true, and therefore not to be published . . . (*Sydney Morning Herald*, 3 September 1878).

An early feature concerning the New Caledonian Revolt carried by the *Sydney Morning Herald* on 18 July 1878 demonstrates the type of story published by the paper without a reporter in place to cover the war. While it gave an overview of the events, it was clearly written by someone resident in the capital, gathering information second-hand about the rebellion in the interior, compiled by telegraphic dispatches:

> By the *Lochlee* sailing vessel which left here this morning at 9am for Sydney, I wrote details of a terrible revolt of natives in the districts of Ourail [sic] and Boulapari [sic] distant 60 and 90 miles from here . . . On the 25th the first intimation of the outburst reached Noumea. It was reported that a 'poste' of five gendarmes on the River Foa, near Ourail, had been attacked, and all the five men murdered. Soon a general murderous assault upon the 'colons', farmers, and every white resident in the neighbourhood of Ourail was telegraphed . . .

Further dispatches carrying datelines were included in that one lengthy account, finishing with:

> July 7, 9am—The mail leaves in an hour. The latest news is that yesterday eighty-four houses of the natives were burnt near Boulapari. So the captives were taken and executed. All remains perfectly quiet throughout the other parts of the colony and everything is progressing to the complete satisfaction of the authorities.

The report shows the influence of the telegraph in the development of 'news' language—'factual, denotative and functional language'—which would go on to underpin the formalisation of principles of objectivity in journalism in the twentieth century (Maras, 28). While it traces an overview compiled from various bits of news reaching the Noumea correspondent, there is patently much that is not included in the details of the report. Colourless and emotionless, it openly promotes the agenda of the French colonisers and discourages engagement by the reader at anything more than a superficial level.

The 'distance' of the language used in this instance is most likely to have demonstrated to Hugh George the need for a journalist who could more fully describe and explain the war to his readers. He lost no time in despatching James, who sailed for New Caledonia twelve hours after the first news of the uprising reached Sydney (*Cannibals & Convicts*, 48). His assignment was to breach the interior and provide factual, eyewitness accounts, using first-rate storytelling skills, to bring the events and issues alive for the paper's readers.

The day after his arrival in New Caledonia, James had an interview with the colonial Governor Orly, who gave him letters of travel authorising him 'to go everywhere and see everything' (*Cannibals & Convicts*, 69). He was also introduced to Lieutenant-Colonel Alex Wendling, commander of the French forces in New Caledonia, with whom he would travel to Boulouparis.

The arrangement with Wendling was manipulated by the French to their own ends. Wendling, without James's knowledge, intercepted all his communications with Noumea and kept his telegrams from being sent to Sydney. Nor did James receive important telegraphic dispatches giving him crucial information for his reporting. Instead, he was kept busy each morning marching strenuously up and down the hillsides. Once James realised Wendling's daily marches were a planned distraction, he refused to participate, packed his belongings and moved on to La Foa, where he joined the French forces active there as embedded correspondent under Commandant Henri Rivière. It was not until his return to Sydney that James discovered his reports had never been sent. He rewrote them for publication in the *Sydney Morning Herald* in September and October 1878, later collecting them in his book *Cannibals & Convicts* (68-70), Cannon 9-10).

Prior to his travel to New Caledonia, James's literary journalism revealed an investigative reporter who wrote from a discernable set of moral values. His writing as 'The Vagabond' clearly showed a journalist willing to side with those who were the weakest in the power equations of colonialism. He once said, 'In my callow days I was a rebel, and from Garibaldians to Fenians I have ever since had a sneaking fondness for those in arms against constituted authority' (Quoted in Anderson, 16). His teenage years spent alienated from his authoritarian father, including six months spent on the road living as a tramp after an incident of fighting at his school, led him to use his journalism to question power and authority and to side with the poor and disadvantaged. At the same time, his writing shows a man who was politically and socially conservative, immersed in the racist and bigoted attitudes of his time.

Despite his general sympathies with the underdog, James's work can be uncomfortable to read. Take, for example, this 'humorous' sentence from the first instalment of his eight-part series in the *Argus*, 'A Month

A lithograph depiction of the Vagabond by 'Leo' (J. H. Leonard), probably done in Melbourne in the 1880s, to judge by his increasing portliness and baldness.

in Pentridge Gaol': '. . . I am sure Providence never meant white men to work in this climate; they should only look on, and cuss the niggers.' Another example comes from his story 'A Morning at the Hospital', where he describes the patients in the waiting room and includes: 'There is a little Jew boy who is forward and disgusting in his conversation . . .'. In a later article in the Pentridge series, he comments: 'With Chinese patients who complained or looked ill this course [extra treatment] was always pursued, as until these have been under treatment for a day or two you cannot tell if they are seriously ill or not' (No. VI, 14 April 1877). James's first major dispatch from New Caledonia, published in the *Sydney Morning Herald* on 3 September 1878 (under the name 'special commissioner' to distinguish him from the 'resident correspondent'), begins: 'It is seldom that any other nationalities but English-speaking ones are seen on the wharfs of Sydney. Our Chinese brother is of course excepted. He, like the poor, is always with us, and like poverty we look upon him as a disagreeable necessity . . .'

In spite of his coarse bigotry, in his reports from New Caledonia, James increasingly expressed empathy for the Kanaks. In his report on the executions later published in his book *Cannibals & Convicts* (which story was originally published in the *Sydney Morning Herald* on 3 September 1878 as an extract from a private letter), James found a way to connect with the humanity of the Kanaks. As a literary journalist, when he took the time to closely observe and describe the investigations and subsequent killings, he could no longer hide in blithe stereotypes, but was forced to deal with the scene in front of him, and with his own reactions to the events as they unfolded.

James's report of the Kanak executions began with an allegation that Kanaks had killed an ex-convict called Brière, an employee of a French settler. The day before the murder, a pig belonging to the settler had been speared. In retaliation, the settler's men (all ex-convicts, including Brière) had fired on a group of natives killing two, a man and a woman. It appeared that Brière's death was in revenge for the native deaths. On hearing of the killing of Brière, and before drawing conclusions, James resorted first of all to common sense, cynicism, and his journalistic training, to investigate. His first thought was the possibility that the Kanaks had been framed:

> While M. Rathouis obtained all the particulars of the case, I listened patiently and at last asked, 'But do you know that the Canaques did this?' 'It must be they; for both legs were cut off —taken to eat, no doubt!' I was not so sure of this. I remembered that this was a settlement of ex-criminals, and it seemed to me that private revenge could at that time easily satisfy itself, while the odium would be thrown on the natives.' (*Cannibals*, 87-8)

James thought through the possibilities as he made his own enquiries. As he learned more, and it did indeed appear likely that Kanaks had conducted a revenge killing, he went on to suggest the ex-convict may have invited it by rendering 'himself personally obnoxious to the natives'. With M. Rathouis, the French investigator, he attempted to visit Baptiste, a Kanak chief, for more information. 'I much wished to get the intelligent Canaque's view of the question,' he commented, but was disappointed in his quest when they discovered Baptiste and his men had fled their village in the face of the encroaching French forces.

Nevertheless, James was not content to convey in his story the untested view of the colonial military. Unlike his hosts, he was still intent on finding out the facts of the event. Not long afterwards, a messenger arrived, causing much consternation in the settlement with his claims that he had been attacked by natives on his journey. James, not satisfied with the cursory questioning of the French military, conducted his own investigation, closely questioning the man and eventually deciding that, 'he was lying, or exaggerating through fear'. Said James, 'He might have seen a few natives; but that was all' (*Cannibals*, 89).

The French administrators came to no such conclusion. Consequently, a group of five Kanaks, who had already been imprisoned for a month without trial for crimes not listed in James's account, were brought before the Commandant. In the heightened atmosphere following the messenger's claims, Rivière ordered them to be marched to the place of Brière's death where they were to be shot, and their bodies burnt as a warning to their friends. Said James in his later article, 'It ordained an act illogical, unjust, and useless in its results.'

The more James investigated, the further his sympathies lay with the Kanaks. Hartsock (2001, 151) has described empathy as an essential characteristic of literary journalism, so far as it avoids 'reinforcing difference and [shows] commonalities instead'. Although James's writing begins with all the coarse racism of the day, as the passage below illustrates, as he continued to write he could not help but be confirmed in—and display—his contempt for the killing of the five Kanaks. James began his recounting of the scene before him with a physical description of the prisoners, using the techniques of close observation and description in the retelling of a scene that typify literary journalism:

> The prison doors were opened, and five natives were brought forth. Four were handcuffed in pairs; and they were all joined by a stout rope. The last was a boy of only thirteen; the others of ages ranging from twenty-five to forty. All were quite naked except one, who had still the striped jersey worn by the boatmen of the port. Round his neck the boy had a small key suspended by

a piece of string. I wondered whether he had ever possessed a box, or only wore it as an ornament. Another wore a garter adorned with shells; another had a string of beads around his neck. Their woolly hair had been dyed red by lime; some rude combs were stuck therein. They were splendid specimens of humanity; not large men, but with beautifully formed limbs. Two had broad noses and thick lips, but two had almost European features, one being very handsome, with fine eyes, which fixed themselves on mine inquiringly. He seemed to seek a friend, and it might be that he saw the sympathy which was in my soul. In colour, these men were light brown; in each the brain was well developed. They were of a race far superior to the Australian savage (*Cannibals*, 90).

One can hear in James's language a multiplicity of layers. There is the effort of expressing the writer's subjectivity, of creating his persona, and in writing from a nuanced point of view, while achieving enough distance from the subject to give a sense of accuracy and credibility. There is the paradoxical claim to authority from the journalist's presence at the scene—the eyewitness account. And there is the issue of demarcating identity and difference in order for the writer to make sense of the scene for the reader. Yet, this extract also exemplifies the impossibility of objectivity—in the sense of impartial reporting—in the colonial relationship. Relevant here are Spurr's comments that the body is the sign by which the indigenous person—particularly the colonised indigenous—is most commonly represented. As Spurr (1993, 22) notes, descriptions of the 'primitive'

> proceed from the visual to various kinds of valorization: the material value of the body as labor supply, its aesthetic value as object of artistic representation, its ethical value as a mark of innocence or degradation, its scientific value as evidence of racial value or inferiority, its humanitarian value as the sign of suffering, its erotic value as the object of desire.

James's summation of the physical appearance of the Kanaks encompasses many of Spurr's categories—aesthetic appreciation, scientific, humanitarian and erotic value. At the same time, in this preliminary passage he conveys his mastery over these men, both acknowledging and reinforcing the notion that what he is gazing upon is inferior. He conveys the common understanding with the reader that the scene is bizarre and strange to rational, Western eyes. There can be no doubt he is part of the colonisation process which is violently appropriating land, people and culture to itself and imposing its own colonial order. In this passage, he demonstrates the arguments of later writers such as Fanon and Said who showed that language was a primary and essential tool of colonisation, as effective as any weapon in subjugating native populations.

Yet, James also goes further. As his article continues he moves closer towards a genuinely empathic position. While much of the rest of the article is still racist in our modern view, he begins to repatriate the prisoners—who have lost all their humanity in their looming execution—to the category of 'people' by at first likening at least two of them to Europeans and drawing attention to their intelligence and their amicability, while distancing them from the Australian first peoples familiar to his readers. Spurr notes: 'The sympathetic humanitarian eye is no less a product of deeply held colonialist values, and no less authoritative in the mastery of its object, than the surveying and policing eye . . .' (20). Yet, while James cannot escape his position as part of the colonising military force, his developing empathy also cannot be confused with mere pity. By the end of his article, the reader is left in no doubt that the Kanaks have been repatriated to the category of human being.

Why did James take the approach of beginning with a more 'objective' stance and only slowly building empathy? Perhaps the answer lies in his audience. James was writing to white readers—migrants and ex-convicts in the new colony of New South Wales—readers of the *Sydney Morning Herald* who no doubt largely held the local Aboriginal people as dangerous, as curiosities, or in contempt. It should be remembered that until recently, the Australian colony was held at law to be *terra nullius*—or vacant land—the Aborigines not legally existing in New South Wales, let alone holding any rights as prior owners. It was into this atmosphere of prejudice and violent misappropriation that James was writing. It seems likely that his instincts as a storyteller led him to begin his description of the Kanaks with words and ideas that could be absorbed by his readers at home—and with which he himself was comfortable and largely agreed. In Spurr's terms, the language he chose to refer to those five males was meaningful because it entered 'a familiar web of signification' for his readers. Writing over 100 years later, Spurr noted, 'The journalist is literally on the lookout for scenes that carry an established interest for a Western audience, thus investing perception itself with the mediating power of cultural difference' (21).

Without excusing James of his racism, and without elevating him beyond the colonial attitudes in which he was solidly entrenched, this rendering of the Kanaks via the body nevertheless could be interpreted as his method of establishing a preliminary connection with his readers, perhaps the only shared vocabulary available between them when speaking of native peoples. This notion is supported to an extent in James's further descriptions of the executions. He goes on to say:

> For six miles we toiled through the blazing sun. It was hard work and it seemed to me cruel to drag those poor wretches out thus far to kill them. I watched them curiously as we marched along. The boy alone had a timid, curious look. I wish that the young savage with the handsome face and the fine eyes would not look at me with those glances of intelligence. To my dying day they will haunt me . . .

At this point in the story, James is making it clear that his own conscience is aroused, and, he would hopefully intend, so is the reader's. He continues:

> Our prisoners were told to sit down. Did they know what they were brought hither for? The boy had broken off a small branch of the niaouli tree, and was beating off the mosquitoes from himself and his next neighbour. The rest talked in low tones. What were we waiting for? In a few minutes there was a call to attention. Down the path from the other side a body of men marched. It was a column of the garde nationale of Moindou, headed by M. de Laubarede.

James continues to describe the scene, gradually allowing more of his personal observations to intrude, drawing the reader's attention to the injustice he felt he was witnessing. At the same time, he uses small details to create characters and make the scene real for the reader:

> And they? Did they understand . . . One would hardly think so. The boy carelessly brushed away the mosquitoes, one smiled, the others were impassible as before. 'Have you anything to say?' asks M. Varnauld. They shook their heads, and replied 'rien'. For a few minutes they were allowed to talk to each other, and then they were marched a few yards farther on into the camp of niaouli trees.

The executions themselves are described as follows:

> The orders were given clearly and quietly. There were five trees in line; to these they were bound. The boy was first uncoupled and taken to the tree, his hands tied behind him, and a bandage placed round his eyes. Then the others must have known the fate in store for them! But they did not wince or take any notice. One by one the process was repeated, the surveillant and a convict, who appeared to take brutal delight in the work, "officiating". There was not the slightest resistance or murmur from the prisoners. The last was my handsome friend. Released from his fellow, he remained for a

couple of minutes perfectly free and unshackled, and again looked at me with those wistful eyes. Why did he not make one effort for life and freedom? If he had started, I would have bet that in the bush none of our rifles could hit him. I almost felt mad with the man, and my lips found words which he would not understand. 'Par ici' cried the surveillant—the Canaque was looking at me. 'Sacré nom de Dieu!' said the man, rushing forward, seizing the prisoner's wrist, and giving him a torrent of abuse for not being in a hurry to go to be killed. . . M. Varnauld gave the order. . . And the victims against the trees?—four stood up erect, with chests inflated, and every nerve and muscle strung, ready to die like warriors. The boy alone had his head sunk on his breast. The word was given—a discharge—and three bodies slid softly to the ground. "The doctor to the ground," shouted M. Varnauld. I accompanied him. The other two bodies sank down. There was not a word nor a groan. The coup de grace was given to three who yet lived by the revolver of the surveillant le nommé Brière and the pigs of Boyer were avenged. "Blood for blood!"

While restrained by real events (unlike the fiction writer), by virtue of his sympathies and his role as journalist, James has power over the scene as a whole. This extends to the colonial forces and their actions, as he reconstructs that scene for readers from the security of his own gaze. Reminiscent of George Orwell's 'A Hanging', James has constructed the scene in such a way as to leave the reader in no doubt as to his sickened disapproval of the event. He has done that by seducing the reader into an 'insider's' view of the incident—a view that draws the Kanaks themselves into the scene—into the view—as active participants, despite the seeming passivity of their responses to their captors. He creates a feeling, not of charity so much as of empathy for the fates of these people, showing that the condemned behaved with highly valued human traits—dignity, intelligence and compassion. This is confirmed and consolidated in the next scene where, repulsed and disturbed, James reflects on the sight before him:

It was a new and not a pleasant sensation to see these bodies dragged along the ground. Rigor mortis not having set in, the flesh presented a horrible flabby, quivery appearance. A convict with glee took a red handkerchief from the head of one of the deceased, and another tried to remove the jersey, but was ordered to desist. Dragged to the pile of wood, the bodies were thrown on, and some straw having been lighted, and other fuel heaped up, a fierce blaze went up to heaven. The smell of burning flesh is not nice and I retreated to a distance, to smoke and moralise.

Nor does James hold back his opinions when he describes the return to the French camp:

> Shortly we formed column and marched back to dinner with what appetite we might. At table M. Varnauld said, "They died bravely enough." One of the mess retorted, "Oh! they are only brutes; they don't believe in a future, and so have no fear!" Then I—"Monsieur, we are taught in the classics that the highest virtue known to the ancients was to die as these men died. Again, in the glorious revolution of '89, when your 'noblesse' went to the scaffold" (he was a Breton Catholic and a Legitimist to whom I spoke), "their chief pride was that they died with sangfroid. They had not more courage than these poor Canaques. Let us be just. They perished like heroes, and I drink to the dead." (*Cannibals*, 91-3)

James, an English migrant to Australia, was not subject to the same conflicting loyalties to his hosts as a French reporter would have been. Nevertheless, he was a white man immersed in the racism and the cultural assumptions of superiority inherent in colonialism—one who had benefited from migrating and who was participating at least to some extent in the displacement of Aborigines in his inherited homeland. Yet, despite the racism of the time, it is clear from James's writing that he thought his first duty in Noumea was to the journalistic norm of truth-telling, rather than to his own whiteness—his European heritage—or to that of his hosts. Nevertheless, his report confirms the conflicts with subjectivity and meaning with which he was instinctively struggling as a literary journalist. He is, at least in the beginning of his story, both an accomplice to the colonial system of dominance and control, and dominated by it. He begins by both rendering the Kanaks as objects and striving to be objective in his account, succumbing at least initially to the stereotypes of his day. Yet, ultimately, James's article ends on a different note. One that is appalled by the treatment of these Kanaks at the hands of their colonial oppressors.

James's writing was, and continues to be, effective. His immersion in the story allowed him to write with greater empathy and truthfulness about the subject than a more traditional approach to writing news might have allowed. When his dispatches finally appeared in the *Sydney Morning Herald* in 1878, his reports left his Sydney readers disturbed and the French authorities displeased. Henri Rivière was particularly angered, accusing James of ungentlemanly behaviour in the abuse of his hospitality (McDonald, Cannon). By the time his book was published eight years after the war, James was confirmed in his sympathies with the Kanaks and against the French in the conflict.

The toll taken by his hectic life can be seen in this photograph of the Vagabond taken by Ateliers of Melbourne, probably in the 1890s.

REFERENCES

Anderson, Hugh, 'Vagabond Journalist', *Walkabout*, February 1968, 16.

Anonymous, Resident Correspondent, 'Revolt and Massacre at New Caledonia', *Sydney Morning Herald*, 18 July 1878, 7.

Boynton, Robert S., *The New New Journalism: Conversations with America's Best Nonfiction Writers on their Craft*, Vintage Books, New York, 2005.

Bullard, Alice, *Exile to Paradise: Savagery and Civilization in Paris and the South Pacific, 1790-1900*, Stanford University Press, Stanford, 2000.

Cannon, Michael (ed.), *The Vagabond Papers*, Melbourne University Press, 1969.

Ferrero, Chantal, 'When Black is Transparent: French Colonialism in New Caledonia, 1878-1914', *Wansalawara: Soundings in Melanesian History*, ed. Brij Lal, Working Paper Series, Pacific Islands Studies Program, Center for Asian and Pacific Studies, University of Hawaii at Manoa, 1987, 119-156.

Hartsock, John, *A History of American Literary Journalism: the Emergence of Modern Narrative Form*, University of Massachusetts Press, Massachusetts, 2001.

James, John Stanley ('Julian Thomas', 'The Vagabond'), *Cannibals & Convicts: Notes of Personal Experiences in the Western Pacific*. Cassell & Company, Melbourne, 1886.

—— Newspaper Entries:

'New Caledonia: En Voyage', *Sydney Morning Herald*, 3 September 1878, 5-6

'The War' (extracts from letter), *Sydney Morning Herald*, 3 September 1878, 6.

'The War in New Caledonia: Headquarters Camp at Bouloupari, August 1', *Sydney Morning Herald*, 4 September 1878, 7.

'The War in New Caledonia: Headquarters Camp at Bouloupari, August 8', *Sydney Morning Herald*, 9 October 1878, 7.

'The War in New Caledonia: The Causes of the Revolt, Noumea, Sept. 27', *Sydney Morning Herald*, 12 October 1878, 9.

'The War in New Caledonia: The Past and Present Situation, Noumea, Sept.27', *Sydney Morning Herald*, 22 October 1878, 7.

McDonald, Willa, 'A Vagabond: The Literary Journalism of John Stanley James', *Literary Journalism Studies* 6.1 Spring (2014), 65-81.

Maras, Steven, *Objectivity in Journalism*, Polity Press, Cambridge, 2013.

'Obituary, Melbourne', *Zeehan & Dundas Herald* (Tasmania), 7 September 1896.

Sims, Norman, (ed.), *The Literary Journalists*, Ballantine Books, New York, 1984.

—— *Literary Journalism in the Twentieth Century*, Oxford University Press, New York, Oxford, 1990 (reissued by Northwestern University Press in 2008).

Spurr, David, *The Rhetoric of Empire: Colonial Discourse in Journalism, Travel Writing, and Imperial Administration*, Duke University Press, Durham, London, 1993.

Toth, Stephen A., *Beyond Papillon: The French Overseas Penal Colonies, 1854-1952*, University of Nebraska, Lincoln, 2006.

Wolfe, Tom, and Johnson, E. W. (eds.), *The New Journalism*, Harper & Rowe, New York, 1973.

INTRODUCTION

A respectable solicitor should not have bred such a son. Joseph Green James, sitting in his cosy solicitor's office at Wolverhampton, Staffordshire, part of the mortar in the pedestal upholding the majesty and hypocrisy of the English law, had to enjoin his clerks to fear God and balance the ledgers, while his own son, his damnable son, was wandering around the countryside dressed in rags, preferring the company of vagrants and beggars to the comforts of his own home. What was to become of the boy, John Stanley James, born 15 November 1843, already a vagabond at the age of twelve? He would run, and keep on running, and forsake his respectable family, and fabricate a romantic new background for himself, and finish his life in Australia as the brilliant, ever-restless writer concealed under the pseudonym of 'the Vagabond'. Wherever he went, James would carry with him the burden of a sensitive, proud nature, deeply affronted but not quite overcome by the sanctimonious virtues of his home and the more rugged virtues of the English boarding-school system. Not until he was nearly middle-aged could he bring himself to write about the incidents of his childhood and the crisis which caused him to run away from school:

> "Fagging" and bullying were then much in vogue, and I suffered from both. I fought the "cock of the school" for an hour, until I was in a far worse condition than many a pugilist after a prize fight. The only result was that I was severely punished by the head-master. Then my soul grew hard within me, and I only thought of vengeance. In a short time I was again called on to "fag" by my tormentor. I refused, and the bully persuasively twisted my arm. After he had tortured me for a few minutes he let me go, and then, flying to primal man's first means of offence, everywhere provided by nature, I seized a sharp stone. The missile struck my antagonist fair on the temple . . . I was seized, and taken before the masters, and then locked up in my room. For two days I remained here, fed on bread and water. The head-master once visited me, and in a

severe lecture intimated that —— would die, and I should be hanged. At least if he did recover I most likely would be handed over to the police, and endure public ignominy. I hardened my heart. The sense of the injustice of things in this world, which the very young perhaps alone feel, made me defiant. What did I care if my tormentor died? Care? I hoped he would die! . . . So on the third night I dropped from the window by the aid of the sheets, and before morning was in a large town fifteen miles off . . . And when, three days after my absconding, I read a handbill describing my appearance and offering £100 reward for my recovery, I looked on this as an endeavour to capture a criminal, and not as the frightened efforts of the head-master to undo his foolish work. For long months he thought I had drowned myself, and the school suffered considerably through the scandal.[1]

Significantly, James had no thought of heading for home. There was little warmth or understanding for him there. So he sold his good clothes, bought some 'common, rough garments', and started to tramp across England. He slept in 'villages, market-towns and cities', frequenting threepenny and sixpenny lodging-houses used by hawkers, vagrants and beggars. In the 'indiscriminate mixture of humanity in the dormitories' he found 'much that was disgusting', but he remembered the rough comradeship of the men with an affection that was its own bitter commentary on the icy nature of his home.

James does not explain why he returned temporarily to his family. No doubt starvation, a keen weapon against a growing boy, drove him there. Shortly afterwards we find him completing his education at Walsall High School. In this short-lived reconciliation, he even consented to become articled to his father and began clerking on a high stool. It was too good to last. As soon as his frame had filled out, James did the natural thing for a person of his affectionate, emotionally-starved nature and fell passionately in love. His father did the natural thing for one of his cold temperament and forbade the liaison. According to the historian J. B. Cooper, who was a close friend of James in Australia, 'Father and son had a serious and life-long disagreement about a lady, and the son, in consequence, left his home'.[2] Apparently this would have happened about 1860 or so, when James was seventeen or eighteen.

James fled to London, where he managed to keep starvation at bay by copying legal documents. He lodged with a policeman, whose tales of his experiences on the beat intrigued James. The young man began to feel that most irresistible of vocations, the urge to retail the troubles of others to the largest possible audience. He began to write crime news

[1] See first paragraphs of 'Sydney Common Lodging-Houses,' in *The Vagabond Papers*, fifth series.
[2] John Butler Cooper: 'Who Was "The Vagabond"?' *Life*, 1 January 1912.

for the London newspapers, and made a precarious living as a freelance journalist for several years. It was an ideal training ground for the man to come.

By about 1866, when he was twenty-three, James had seen and suffered enough of the low life of London. To recuperate, he took a job as a booking clerk on the London & North Wales Railway. He spent his days off walking around Wales, bathing 'at every watering place on the coast', fishing, climbing Snowdon, and falling in love again.[3] By 1868 he had been promoted to the rank of station-master at Llandudno, North Wales. This modest approach to middle class success was the signal for him to resign and return to the raffish life of a Grub Street freelance. When war was about to break out between France and Germany in 1870, James hurried to Paris to report events, but automatically found himself in sympathy with the revolutionary party plotting to depose Napoleon III. In later years James wrote wryly:

> We were pure patriots, animated by the highest of motives, no doubt; *mais au reste* many of us were young, and, sooth to say, though denouncing the frivolity of Parisian life, we found dinners *au premier* on the Boulevard des Italiens very pleasant, and the song and dance as attractive under a despotism as under a free rule.[4]

James was arrested as a spy, and imprisoned in the Mazas gaol for about six weeks until released on the representations of the British Embassy. He returned to Fleet Street to find his articles on French affairs in great demand for the first time.

Soon after the Franco-Prussian War ended, James went to Warwickshire to report on the formation of Joseph Arch's National Agricultural Labourers' Union and its attempts to raise the starvation wages of its members. The local squire, Sir Charles Mordaunt, had responded by evicting several families from their cottages. In typical fashion, James ignored the public meetings and statements of opposing factions, and went to see the cottages for himself. He described the 'leaky roofs, the cracked walls, the defective sanitary arrangements, the disgraceful manner in which both sexes were crowded together at night' in a fashion which stirred the deepest feelings of his respectable readers.[5] The farm labourers' strike was defeated after great suffering, the 'wretched hovels, bad fare, disease, ignorance, and immorality' became

---

[3] James wrote at length about his Welsh experiences in 'St. David's Day,' in *The Vagabond Papers*, third series, but failed to mention his railways career.
[4] 'My Prison Experiences,' in *The Vagabond Papers*, fourth series (Melbourne 1877).
[5] Fuller details of his observations are given in the introduction to 'A Country Race Meeting,' in *The Vagabond Papers*, third series.

worse than before, but due to journalists like James the urban radicals had been made conscious that pauperism was not merely an industrial phenomenon.

On the crest of the wave, James returned to Walsall to renew relations with his family. The result was quite the opposite to what his sentimental nature longed for. Acccording to J. B. Cooper, he 'met with a chilling reception. The rebuffs, or fancied rebuffs, he received angered him for life. The old feud with his father was revived.' In a passionate reaction, James decided to forsake his family name, to sail for America, and to begin life afresh. He was just thirty years old, and had twenty-three more years to live.

John Stanley James boarded the boat in England, and 'Julian Thomas' disembarked in America. Friendless, unknown, unable to claim the modest fame of Stanley James as his own, 'Julian Thomas' failed to break into the competitive world of New York journalism. We get some hint of the methods by which he survived: in 'The Waifs and Strays of Sydney'[6] he recalls how he posed as a model for a photographer named Muybridge and appeared in scenic photographs 'in half the albums in America'. There is however no hint of the events which led up to his most notable experience, in which he claimed to have married 'a rich Southern lady', the widow of a planter in Richmond, Virginia. Inquiries in that city have failed to elicit any further details or even confirmation of the alleged marriage. According to J. B. Cooper, the quondam Mrs Thomas 'had a family—and also the temper of a Southerner'. They agreed to separate, said Cooper, and 'Julian Thomas' sailed for Australia. The Vagabond later claimed, in an article on cricket, to have started the Richmond (Virginia) Cricket Club, 'where we paid negroes twenty cents an hour for fielding, and never did anything but bat and bowl'. But then he also claimed to have fought in the American Civil War, which took place when he was actually a railway clerk in Wales. So consistently did he claim to be of American birth that he may even have begun to believe it himself and to build the 'fact' into the painful construction of his new identity. The psychological stresses of this process were considerable; Cooper records two suicide attempts in Australia from which the Vagabond drew back at the last moment.

What was his name when he arrived in Sydney? The *Bulletin* (17 October 1896) had him nearly pinned down as 'Sydney James', who 'quartered himself at what was then the Civil Service Hotel' in Sydney before travelling on to Melbourne and adopting the name of 'Julian Thomas' once again. He arrived, 'sick in body and mind, and broken

[6] *The Vagabond Papers*, fifth series.

INTRODUCTION   5

in fortune', in the last quarter of 1875.[7] From then on his activities can be traced with a fair degree of accuracy. Almost penniless, he was forced to pawn his best clothes and eke out his funds by frequenting the cheap lodging houses, sixpenny restaurants and charitable institutions which were soon to yield him much more than food and shelter. It seems almost certain, however, that his first journalistic work was done for *Melbourne Punch*. This lively journal began publishing a series of 'Notes on Current Events, By a Vagabond' on 21 October 1875—soon after 'Julian Thomas' arrived in Melbourne—and dropped the series late in 1877, soon after he left again for Sydney. These short notes on events of the week displayed close familiarity with American events and personalities, and also reflected 'Thomas's' particular blend of liberal, conservative, free trade and anti-church views. Their polemic was of a high order:

> If a body of men were to dump a load of night-soil in the middle of Collins-street, the nuisance would be promptly removed, and the authors of it punished by law; although it would be only locally offensive. Yet here we have a number of persons in Ararat dumping a David Gaunson in the middle of the Legislative Assembly, and while all good citizens in every part of the colony are holding their nostrils at the noxious thing, no attempt is made to remove it, or to punish those who are responsible for placing it where it is[8]

but the often anti-Semitic and anti-Negro views expressed do not make particularly pleasant reading today.

By one means and another, 'Julian Thomas' kept himself afloat until the beginning of April 1876. Then, at the age of thirty-three, came the turning-point in his career, best described in the words of Hugh George, at that time the all-powerful general manager of the *Argus*:

> I came into the office (ARGUS) late one night, to have a final look over some AUSTRALASIAN proofs. While I read, a row began outside—stormy talk between the night attendant and an evident intruder. It got loud enough to bring me out. The explanation was—"This man insists on seeing the editor, and I tell him that's impossible without stating his business." I asked, "What is it you want?" And the man replied, "I'm a journalist, and if this is the first-chop paper I take it for, that ought to be enough." "Come into my room," said I. When he got under the light his general get-up did not indicate prosperity, but he had eyes in his head, and they met mine in a way I liked. I took him short, however. "Now, what is it?" "I want to know if there is any show for a man who is a journalist on this paper." "It depends altogether on what sort of a journalist that man is." "That makes it easy, boss. He's the best (rather unquotable) journalist in this city."

[7] According to the preface of the first series of *The Vagabond Papers*.
[8] 'Notes on Current Events,' *Melbourne Punch*, 30 November 1876. Gaunson was a leading criminal lawyer of the day.

The audacity of that took me. I said, "Journalism does not seem to have brought you much wealth; in fact, I should judge that a sovereign would not come amiss to-night." "You're a white man! Shake!" We shook, and he left with a promise to let me have some copy the next day. The copy came to hand. That man was "The Vagabond," and his engagement was the most profitable contract in that department I ever made for the ARGUS.[9]

'Thomas's' first article for the 'first-chop paper' was 'A Night in the Model Lodging-House', published in the *Argus* on 15 April 1876 and reprinted in the *Australasian* a week later. It bore the same pseudonym, 'By a Vagabond', as the *Punch* articles. The sketch, reprinted fairly fully in the first part of this edition, is a straightforward enough account of the Vagabond's experiences when forced to seek a sixpenny shelter for the night. Immediately it became the talk of Melbourne. There was an obvious reason for its success. Plenty of reports had been published about the plight of the unemployed and the semi-employed, but at that date no skilful writer had actually lived the life of a down-and-out and come through the experience with his objectivity and good humour unimpaired. The technique was often imitated afterwards, but most of those who tried it had a comfortable billet to flee back to when they had had enough. The difference was a crucial one. In rare cases like that of George Orwell, where poverty was his normal way of life, the experience provided, as with the Vagabond, the basis for his best work.

There was, I think, another and more subtle reason for the popularity of the Vagabond's articles. His style of writing was quite the reverse of sensational. There were a few scandalous revelations which led to public inquiries and helped to spread the Vagabond's fame. But his normal method was the straightforward, sympathetic, never sentimentalized description of his experiences and observations. Thus it was not just a matter of writing from the vantage point of what he called 'the inside track'. Somehow the Vagabond repressed his volatile nature, and wrote a cool, unemotional statement of the survival techniques of a man who had almost no money and no home of his own.

Readers' reactions were anything but unemotional. With a thrill of horror the Victorian middle class subscribers to the *Argus* read his almost clinical accounts of what happened to people who slackened their striving for respectability, who abandoned their belief in the importance of money, or who were merely unlucky in the battle of life. When 'The Outcasts of Melbourne' was published a month later, with its description of the life of the vagrants, criminals and prostitutes of the city's back alleys, the lesson was seen to apply to the whole family. Stray once from the path of virtue, the lesson warned, and this

[9] *Lone Hand*, 1 August 1907.

was what happened to you. Work hard, be good, and God would protect you from the terrors of the streets. In such an ironical way, the experiences of the Vagabond became one of the chief props of middle class morality, which was not his intention at all. Yet perhaps his achievement was sufficient. If he had gone on to attack the structure of laissez-faire capitalism which bred the dreadful slums where his vagrants and prostitutes lived, the *Argus* could not have published his articles. Such was the curious interplay of circumstances which led to the production of one of the great documents of the Victorian age. We have bush-and-mateship epics aplenty, but the Vagabond's work gives us one of the very few first-hand accounts of the nature of low life in Australian cities as the era approached its apogee.

After the initial success, other articles followed rapidly. The Vagabond had no sooner spent 'A Day in the Immigrants' Home' than he was inviting his readers to dine in 'A Sixpenny Restaurant'. He lived for several days as an inmate of the Benevolent Asylum and the Sailors' Home. He worked as an attendant at Kew Lunatic Asylum and spent 'A Month in Pentridge'. Furious controversies arose as the Vagabond, his voice never raised beyond an occasional temperate rejoinder, reported what he saw and overheard. Did a well-known doctor perform lithotomy operations with his pocket-knife when proper surgical instruments were available? A public inquiry gravely established that the doctor had merely boasted, in front of his patients, that he could do the job with his pen-knife.[10] Were elderly inmates of the Benevolent Asylum purposely starved to death in a primitive form of euthanasia? The authorities heatedly denied it, whereupon 114 inmates wrote to the committee supporting and expanding the Vagabond's observations.[11] Were the bodies of pauper children thrown into a common grave at the Melbourne General Cemetery and interred without benefit of clergy? The cemetery chaplain said it was not so,[12] whereupon J. H. Stanton, a citizen of note, testified that he had recently seen a weeping mother running through the cemetery trying to keep up with a wagon going at 'a fair trot'. Bumping from side to side was a coffin containing the body of her child, which was dumped into a grave without ceremony.[13]

When they failed to challenge seriously the factual basis of the Vagabond's articles, some public authorities and even journalists envious of his success began to attack his methods. The Vagabond admitted, in the preface to the third series of *The Vagabond Papers*, that his 'mode of writing, and of obtaining information, is considered highly irregular, if not absolutely immoral', but added that he was

[10] *Argus*, 22 and 25 November 1876.
[12] *Argus*, 27 December 1876.
[11] *Argus*, 21 and 30 June 1876.
[13] *Argus*, 8 January 1877.

'perfectly content' with the approbation of the public and the conductors of the *Argus*.

By the end of 1876, public interest in the elusive Vagabond was at its height. Nobody could tell what guise he would appear in next. The managers of public institutions trembled lest they should be entertaining him unawares. When a rumour spread that he caught a particular train to the city each day, people flocked to the station to have him pointed out to them. An actor dressed as a 'Vagabond' was the leading character at the Christmas pantomime. *Melbourne Punch* saw nothing incongruous in continuing to publish the Vagabond's 'Notes of the Week' alongside satires like 'Three Weeks in a Nunnery'[14] in which the Vagabond got a job as cook to the Mother Superior in order to discover whether she ate meat on Fridays. Another *Punch* satire unveiled the Vagabond as J. J. Casey, radical newspaper owner and former Minister for Lands.[15]

Many people believed that the real Vagabond was a person of noble birth, who assumed his incognito to slip out of Government House unobserved and perform his errands of mercy among the deserving poor. In the words of the *Bulletin*,[16] public curiosity was excited 'almost to a point of frenzy' by 'grandiose suggestions and tantalising hints' about the importance and social rank of 'the Great Unknown'. The same journal admitted that the Vagabond achieved 'perhaps the most emphatic and best-merited success ever attained in Australian journalism', but claimed that his popularity had turned his head: 'the real man proved to be of florid style, rather apt to magnify than to depreciate his claims to homage and admiration . . . greedy of the admiration which his recent performances entitled him to . . . It was rather the effusive swagger of Redmond Barry, insistant [sic] on exacting recognition of the utmost of his claims'.

As 'Julian Thomas' claimed the fruits of his work, his apparently true identity gradually became known. There was considerable public disillusionment when the notion of the handsome prince from Government House evaporated. Stanley James smiled behind his double disguise, and embroidered the tale of his American origins even more outrageously. The *Melbourne Bulletin* (27 October 1882), awarding him an unearned doctorate, claimed that 'Dr. Thomas' was 'a native of Virginia, an English public schoolboy, and graduate of a Southern University, an officer in the Confederate States Army . . . with intervals of fighting during the Commune, and for South American Republics'.

Just as the steam was beginning to run out of the Vagabond's work for the *Argus*, his friend Hugh George decided to accept an offer to

[14] 30 November 1876. [15] 23 November 1876.
[16] 17 October 1896.

become general manager of the *Sydney Morning Herald*. He invited 'Julian Thomas' to go with him and write the same sort of articles about Sydney life and institutions.

The Vagabond was farewelled at a testimonial dinner on 17 August 1877, his fellow members of the Yorick Club speeding him on his way with a purse containing 308 sovereigns and their appreciation of 'an eminently unconventional character'.[17] He stayed in Sydney for only a few days, the first article for his new employer being his 'Impressions of Sydney' published on 25 September. At the same time, however, 'Julian Thomas' was completing a final secret assignment for the *Argus*. In October he suddenly appeared in Cooktown, determined to visit the Palmer River goldfields and, as he put it, to 'settle the Chinese question'. He was driven by police-inspector Clohesy in a buggy along the dangerous road to the diggings, and watched the thousands of Chinese immigrants fossicking for gold. On 11 October 1877 he telegraphed from Cooktown to the *Argus* an article stating that the Chinese were 'law-abiding, quiet, and harmless', and claiming that the anti-Chinese agitation had been fomented by a few storekeepers who feared the effects of competition from their Chinese counterparts.[18] A large public meeting held at Cooktown a few days later endorsed the Vagabond's opinion that the government's new £10 capitation tax on Chinese immigrants would prove 'fatal to the prospects of Cooktown'.[19] In later years, after visiting China, the Vagabond recanted his views,[20] but for the moment he was leading a powerful section of public opinion. A further meeting addressed by the Vagabond at the Brisbane School of Arts was attended by the Governor and several leading sugar planters, some of whom hoped that the Chinese would provide a pool of cheap labour to operate their plantations if the trade in kanakas was finally banned.[21]

Back in Sydney for Christmas, the Vagabond began his long-awaited series of articles on low life in Sydney. For some reason they made little impression. Perhaps the residents of Sydney accepted their slums as an inevitable part of city life, unworthy of special mention, unlike Melbourne where most citizens walked by with gaze averted from the human debris around them. Hugh George therefore sent the Vagabond to New Caledonia to investigate a native rebellion against French colonial rule on the island. He sailed on the *Gunga* on 20 July 1878,[22] landing in Noumea a few days later. For weeks almost nothing was

---

[17] An illuminated address presented to the Vagabond on this occasion survives in private possession in Melbourne.
[18] *Argus*, 12 October 1877.   [19] *Argus*, 24 October 1877.
[20] *Occident and Orient* (Melbourne, 1882).
[21] *Sydney Morning Herald*, 7 November 1877.
[22] *Sydney Morning Herald*, 9 August 1878.

heard from him. When he returned, it was discovered that the French authorities had suppressed most of his telegrams. He rewrote his experiences, which, when published in the *Sydney Morning Herald* during September and October 1878, gave the public one of the first and most damning indictments written against French colonial rule in the Pacific. His eyewitness account of the murder by French soldiers of five natives, including a boy of thirteen whose 'soft-eyed gaze' haunted him for years, shocked Sydney readers much more than the description of their own slums. The French reply was to attack the Vagabond's ungentlemanly behaviour in 'abusing the hospitality of the military mess'.

There followed one of the inexplicable gaps in the Vagabond's career. We know that he began investigating spiritualism, publishing the results in a rare pamphlet entitled *Mediums and their Dupes; a Complete Exposure of the Chicaneries of Professional Mediums, and Explanation of So-called Spiritual Phenomena.* In another pamphlet published in reply, entitled *Vagabonds and Their Dupes*, Harold W. H. Stephen congratulated the Vagabond on his 'jolly face and manner', his 'alluring *insouciance*' and 'charming audacity', but likened him to Baron Münchhausen, who told so many fantastic tales of his adventures that he began to believe them himself. It was a shrewd hit, but we do not really know what the Vagabond made of it. All that is certain is that he left journalism for a considerable period and took to occasional public lecturing in Queensland. Not until five years later did he write about his experiences during this period, and even then struck a plaintive note which had an obvious personal application. 'The question is not as to a man's name, but what he does', wrote 'Julian Thomas'.[23] In the same reminiscence he related that in October 1879 his first lecture at Charters Towers was 'such a success, financial and otherwise', that he was persuaded to repeat the performance at Townsville and down the Queensland coast. At towns further inland, however, 'people would not come and listen to me' so the Vagabond amused himself 'with the gay doings in the bars and saloons . . . The drinking which went on was magnificent in its greatness'. The miners heard that he was in town and 'a crowd of anti-vagabonds' set out to murder him. After he had been knocked about severely the publican locked him in a room for the night with 'a bottle of three star' for company.

Then 'the dear chief [presumably Hugh George], who had been strongly opposed to my lecturing' asked the Vagabond to return. He drifted back to Sydney, but could not settle down to regular journalism again. About this time he wrote that he was 'cursed with a perpetual

[23] *Argus*, 5 and 12 July 1884.

unrest', and that for vagabonds like himself, ' "Domestic happiness"—home, wife, children—. . . can never be ours'.[24] His contribution of occasional articles to the Sydney *Daily Telegraph* and other journals late in 1880 and early in 1881, attacking British colonial rule in Fiji, indicates a permanent breach with the *Sydney Morning Herald*.[25] One day in 1881, so he wrote on the first page of *Occident and Orient*, he was walking down George Street when he met a friend called 'M.', whose identity is nowhere revealed. ' "Do you want a trip to China?" said M. to me one Friday afternoon'. The Vagabond immediately assented and four days later set sail with 'M.' on a collier called the *Woodbine*. His only luggage was a toothbrush, a few pounds of tobacco, a small rifle, a pack of cards, and oilskins. He also took along his Newfoundland dog 'Noble', renamed 'Bo'sen' during the voyage. The Vagabond spent nine months travelling to China, Japan, British Columbia and California on the slow collier, returning to Sydney from San Francisco as a passenger on the *Australia* late in 1881. Many of his articles on the voyage and on conditions in countries bordering the Pacific were published in the *Argus*. Some were reprinted in book form as *Occident and Orient*. The preface, dated 'Darlinghurst, February 1882', was dedicated to Thomas Talbot Wilton, a coal mine owner, 'the truest friend I met in New South Wales'. A second volume was announced as being 'in the press' but apparently never appeared.

In Darlinghurst, the Vagabond lived in poverty again. According to Cooper, he was found by the actor-manager Alfred Dampier 'in a miserable lodging, ashamed to come out by day, and apparently in the clutches of a harpy'. Dampier persuaded him to set to and write a play. The result was *No Mercy*, a complex melodrama whose hero, not surprisingly, was described as 'a beggarly scribbler for the press'. Dampier staged the play at the Theatre Royal in Melbourne on 14 October 1882, bringing the Vagabond back to Melbourne to receive the curtain calls for 'author, author!' The *Argus* reviewed the play cautiously, but the *Age* snorted: 'It would be difficult to imagine how a more unreal or unnatural story could be concocted',[26] and soon it closed down. The Vagabond's only other play, entitled *England and Russia or The White Hand*, was performed at the Royal Princess Theatre, Sandhurst, on 15 April 1885.

Dampier and the Vagabond were gloomily touring the country with *No Mercy* in 1883 when an attractive offer arrived from the Union Steamship Company. The Vagabond was to go to New Zealand and write a tourist handbook for them. He got as far as a town on the

---

[24] *Occident and Orient*, chapter 1.
[25] Some of these articles were collected into *South Sea Massacres*, published at the *Australian* office, Bridge Street, Sydney, in 1881.
[26] *Age*, 16 October 1882.

west coast of New Zealand when a peremptory telegram reading 'Meet me in Sydney' arrived from Frederick Haddon, editor of the *Argus*. The Vagabond tore up his contract with the Union Company and boarded the first boat to Sydney. Haddon instructed him to go to the New Hebrides, investigate the methods used to recruit natives for work on the Queensland sugar plantations, and return if possible on a 'blackbirder' to observe conditions during the voyage. The Vagabond landed on Tanna in the New Hebrides group in the middle of September 1883. While he was there the island's native chiefs presented him with a petition to be forwarded to Queen Victoria, asking her to annex the island before the French. The Vagabond boarded the labour vessel *Lizzie* for the 34-day trip to Townsville, arriving there early in November. The result of these adventures was a series of articles published in the *Argus* from December 1883 to March 1884, which generally defended the methods of native recruitment used by Australian captains. These and his earlier articles on the South Seas were later combined into the book *Cannibals & Convicts* (London, 1886). His defence of the kanaka trade did not particularly suit the *Argus* editorial policies, but, as he wrote in the preface to the second series of *The Vagabond Papers*, 'I must write the truth as I see it, and my only endeavour is to be impartial.'

The Vagabond tried hard to return to his old round in Melbourne, being invited by the city police magistrate, Joseph Panton, to inspect Pentridge again but this time as an honoured guest. The Vagabond had barely written 'Pentridge Revisited' for the *Argus* than he was again sent north, to see what should be done with the tragic *Argus* expedition in New Guinea which was competing with the *Age* exploration party led by George Ernest ('Chinese') Morrison. The *Argus* expedition, which left Port Moresby in July 1883 under the unsteady command of 'Captain' W. E. Armit, a man twice dismissed from the Queensland police force, had already resulted in the death of its scientific leader, Professor William Denton. The Vagabond arrived in Port Moresby on the schooner *Elsea* in March 1884. He immediately decided to wind up the *Argus* camp, auctioned its entire contents to the natives for £120, and returned to Melbourne vowing 'to roam no more'.[27]

The Vagabond succeeded in settling down to nearly three years of extremely productive work for the *Argus*. According to Cooper he was being paid a retainer of £100 a year and £2 a column for his articles— an average return of between £6 and £9 a week. He travelled throughout the colony to write his delightful 'Picturesque Victoria' series, breaking off for a few months to write 'A Winter Tour in Queensland' in 1885 but

[27] *Argus*, 14 and 28 June 1884.

INTRODUCTION   13

returning to his Victorian series until April 1886. In that month he sailed
on the *Rome* as *Argus* representative at the Colonial and Indian Exhibition in London. By 18 May 1886 the Vagabond was sending back
articles from London. In July and August he accompanied about a hundred distinguished Australian visitors on a tour through the British
Isles which led to a new series of articles entitled 'Australians At
Home'. Towards the end of 1886 he sailed from Liverpool on the
Parisian, returning through Canada and writing another series for the
Argus on the events of that trip. On 9 April 1887 the second part of
his article 'To Manitoba' was published, after which the Vagabond
abruptly disappeared from the columns of the *Argus* for ever. No convincing explanation of the breach has ever been given. The most likely
reason seems to be that on the same day, a journalist named Francis
Myers, writing under the name 'Telemachus', resuscitated the 'Picturesque Victoria' series for the *Argus*. The Vagabond had already claimed
in an earlier article that the name of the series was indissolubly linked
with his own pen-name, and no doubt regarded the *Argus* action as a
deliberate affront. Despite the great amount of underpaid work he had
done for the newspaper, there was nobody among the *Argus* controllers
to support him. His old mentor Hugh George had died the previous
year at the Australian Club in Melbourne with the new *Argus* general
manager Lauchlan C. Mackinnon by his bedside,[28] but Mackinnon was
not the man to stand any tantrums from his hired journalists. So the
Vagabond left, and began yet another new phase of his life as a contributor to David Syme's *Age*. A fortnight after the Vagabond's last
Argus article, a colorful description of Eight Hours' Day entitled 'The
Carnival of Labor' appeared in the *Age* under the Vagabond's name. A
few weeks and a few articles later, he was suddenly off again—sent by
Syme back to the New Hebrides. The Vagabond sailed on the *Cintra*,
arriving in Noumea early in June 1887. His articles, published at intervals over the following five months, were the sort of strong meat
favoured by the radical controllers of the *Age*. Among other things,
the Vagabond charged the New Hebrides Company with 'slavery pure
and simple'. The company's planters, he claimed, bought natives for
£10 a head but gave them no contract rights like those which were
supposed to be enjoyed on the Queensland plantations. In the New
Hebrides, he charged, irons and the lash were used on both men and
women who refused to work for their owners.

Back in Melbourne late in 1887, the Vagabond filled in a few months
with odd articles and reminiscences entitled 'From My Note Book'.
Syme then sent him to France to look at preparations for the Paris
Exhibition of 1889. He sailed on the *Cuzco* early in May 1888, and on

[28] *Argus*, 14 May 1886.

arrival wrote an entertaining series of 'Parisian Sketches'. Paris in autumn, he decided, was his favourite city—after Melbourne. The Vagabond returned on the *Ionic* late in 1888, and soon was hard at work again on a series of 'Country Sketches'. Stout now and middle-aged, he rattled 'Across the Australian Alps' in Crawford and Co.'s four-horse coach, and continued 'Across the Main Divide'.[29] Hard work for a hard master, even in an Australian autumn. Then Syme had another arduous Pacific assignment for him—this time to Samoa and Tonga. The Vagabond sailed on the *Wainui* from Auckland on 3 July 1889. On Samoa, civil war was thought to be imminent between rival native chiefs backed by Britain on the one side and Germany on the other. The German puppet chieftain backed down while the Vagabond was on the archipelago, but not before great distress and famine, with many deaths, had occurred among the population. After sending off his despatches, the Vagabond sailed on to Tonga. The so-called 'Friendly Islands' were shaking with controversy over the actions of a former Wesleyan missionary, the Rev. Shirley Baker, whom the native King George I had appointed as his prime minister. The Vagabond's articles supported Baker's policies. In Melbourne, the Wesleyan *Spectator* suggested that Baker had bribed the Vagabond with money from the Tongan treasury. On his return, the Vagabond successfully sued the *Spectator* for libel, but was awarded only one farthing damages.

His career as a journalist was practically over. Ephraim Zox, the parliamentarian, found him a job as secretary of the Royal Commission on Charities in 1890-2. After that he continued to write occasional articles, mainly for the *Leader*, but descended rapidly to the hack work of helping to compile illustrated supplements on country towns. Most of the sparkle and verve which had distinguished his work was gone. Half-blind, choking asthmatically in his squalid room in Princes Street, Fitzroy, the Vagabond struggled on to the age of fifty-three. On the night of 3 September 1896 he wrote his last article for the *Leader*, but it was never printed. He went to bed, and at some time during that lonely night died of cardiac asthma. He left no will, no money and few possessions. But his name and fame had survived. On the afternoon of 5 September, Princes Street was jammed with vehicles and people anxious to join his funeral cortege. Among the hundreds of wreaths was one from the Neglected Children's Aid Society 'with deep regret from the little ones in the Home', and another from Lady Janet Clarke as a 'last tribute of respect to one whose able pen has helped to make many lives more cheerful'. The Vagabond was buried in the Melbourne General Cemetery, where a monument simply identifies him as 'Julian Thomas, "The Vagabond"'. Practically everything else which

[29] *Age*, 20 and 27 April and 4 May 1889.

was thought to be important in his era has rusted away, but the best of the Vagabond's work lives on, perhaps one day to inspire a successor to sacrifice most of the things which the world values for the sake of running on 'the inside track'.

M.C.

Melbourne
June 1969

PART ONE

Down and Out

1

A Morning at the Hospital

I am only an out-patient at the Melbourne Hospital. Inside the walls I believe that everything is lovely, the arrangements perfect, the patients well cared for, the nurses patterns of Florence Nightingale (may her name for ever be honoured in the land), and the doctors, practising together in brotherly unity, totally devoid of professional jealousy, strive with all the learning of science and skill of special training to combat our enemies disease and death. However, I am glad that I am only an out-patient.

I, a few months back, on a Tuesday afternoon, first made my way to the hospital. A friendly policeman directed me to the out-patients' ward, situated at the back of the establishment in Little Lonsdale-street. However, I made a mistake, and walked into the courtyard through the open gates, and into the casualty ward. Here "a case" was waiting, and there appeared to be a gathering of surgeons, as for a consultation. To one I applied as to where or how I could obtain needful advice and medicine as an out-patient. He was a right pleasant gentleman, and I hope he has a good practice. Taking out his watch (and, perhaps, if he reads these lines he may remember the incident), he said, "Well, you're rather late to-day, I think, but if you'll go through the other room and ask the clerk, he'll tell you all about it and put you right," and he kindly showed me the road. But my courteous informer was not well up in the ways that are tortuous before one can obtain relief as an out-patient. There were two clerks or attendants at the table, one decidedly Irish, the other with a leaning that way. "You want some medicine, do you? You're too late to-day; you must come again on Friday," was the reply, so I went on my road . . . On the Friday I presented myself again. "Where's your ticket?" Now no one had said anything to me before about a ticket, and I had thought that this was a free hospital. "You must be recommended by a subscriber." "Sir,"

Workmen bring an accident case into the Melbourne Hospital

said I, "being a stranger here I know no subscribers; what am I to do?" "Oh, shure any of the big hotels or shops will give you a card," was the reply; if you make haste you can pass before the committee to-day." So behold there I was, a vagabond indeed, walking up Elizabeth-street soliciting a ticket for the hospital. At many establishments at which I shamefacedly put the question, "Do you subscribe to the hospital, sir?" I was, although unsuccessful, politely answered. At last I struck the establishment of a certain merchant. His clerk, a timid little gentleman, said, "Yes, we have cards for the hospital. You had better wait till Mr. —— comes in." So I sat on a barrel in the warehouse, and waited half an hour. The merchant at last made his appearance— a man of keen, self-satisfied manner. I made known my wants, and he seemed dubious. "I don't know you, you know. You should ask one who is acquainted with you." I explained that I was a stranger, which seemed to be a very suspicious fact in Mr. ——'s eyes. He still hesitated, rubbing his hands like a Pecksniff. I had met this sort of man before, and having humiliated myself to ask him such a trifling favour, did not dream that he would refuse, but thought that he was only self-increasing his own importance by dallying with me. "Bring me a letter from some one I know," said he, evidently with that keen relish of the difference in our positions which is as the salt of life to some men. "How can I tell who you know?" I replied impatiently. "Well, my dear sir," said he, rubbing his hands, "I am sorry for you, but I don't see how I can do it. We have so many of our own poor, and I don't know you." "I suppose if I fell down ill in the street, I should be taken to the hospital?" I asked. "Well, I suppose so." "Did you ever read the Bible?" was my next question. "I hope, sir, that I frame my conduct in this life by its precepts," said Mr. ——, who evidently liked this conversation, his own position appearing every minute so superior to mine. "Well, then, sir," said I, "would it not be economy to have me supplied with medicine before I become so ill as to become an encumbrance inside the hospital? And, again, did you ever read that the Samaritan wanted a letter of introduction from a certain man whom he succoured? Fancy the Samaritan refusing a hospital ticket to a sick man." "You're a d——d impudent fellow," said he; "get out of my place." And I left. It was rather hard on a poor vagabond to be tramping up and down Melbourne seeking for a ticket which would open for him the door of advice and medicine. At last I found a good shopkeeper who said he would give me a ticket, but he had none; if I would get one from the hospital he would sign it.

It was too late to think of returning to the hospital that day, but early the next morning I was there, and asked the other clerk for a ticket to get signed. "We haven't any," said he, "a letter will do, it's only a form." It was a form which had cost me a good deal of tramping about. However, I got the letter and took it to the hospital. Here I saw the first clerk. "I told you to come with this yesterday; you must come on Tuesday now." I told him that I wanted some medicine badly. "Well, you may go and see the surgeon in there," said he, and I made my way to the casualty-room. Here several minor cases were being attended to by a young surgeon and a dresser. He was one of the house-surgeons I suppose, and was very pale and jaded looking—through much study and burning of the midnight oil, I presume, or else through vigils of another sort . . . "This is the last one, sir," said the dresser. "What's your name? Age? What's the matter with you?" I tell him. "Come on Tuesday," and banging together the book in which he has been registering my answers he runs across the courtyard, eager, no doubt, to get away to the Yarra for a pull, or anywhere away from the hospital. I don't blame him. Hospital surgeons are a hard-worked class—except in extreme cases they have little sympathy for suffering; they are not actually unfeeling, but are hardened . . .

I began to think that I should never obtain any benefits from the Melbourne Hospital, but on my fourth visit—one week from my first application—I was more successful. Punctually at eleven I was there, and was told to take my seat inside one of five pens into which the waiting-room is divided. These pens are provided with forms arranged so that the occupants can pass from one to the other without any obstacle. The room is not too large for its requirements. Its brick walls, innocent of plaster, are painted a sickly yellow colour. The entrance is screened by a wooden partition, which inside serves to bear a row of shelves on which the prescription books of the patients are kept. Under these is the table where the two attendants sit. Opposite there are two wooden windows in the wall, labelled, "Physicians'" and "Surgeons' Prescriptions," and a notice, "Out-patients must provide themselves with a bottle for medicine, and when they come again must bring the same bottle, and any medicine they may have left." At one end of the ward are two consulting-rooms; at the other a waiting-room leading to the casualty ward, and another consulting-room. The floor is of concrete, of a beautiful dirt colour. I wait in the pen for some time until the clerk comes and calls us, some forty, into a pen at the other end of the room. We file into it. A number of women have just finished going into one of the consulting-rooms. A little bell rings about every two seconds, and the men file in and out.

My turn comes, and I give my letter of introduction to a gentleman sitting at a table. "What's the matter with you?" I reply. He scrawls some hieroglyphics on the turned-up corner, rings the bell, and I go out and follow my predecessors, who are passing in and out of the second

The Melbourne Hospital again

MAN (with the hook)—Matter? Matter enough, I should think, to go into this 'ere 'ospital with only a mosquito bite, and be turned out in this style!
NEW RESIDENT SURGEON (with instrument case)—Ah! How thankful you ought to be to this noble institution for such a complete cure; you can hardly be sufficiently grateful, my friend!

consulting-room. Inside this is an old gentleman, who asks me, "Have you ever been here before?" "No." "You are without means of obtaining medical assistance?" "Yes." He makes another obscure mark on my paper, and I find I have "passed the committee." All the patients are now crowding round the table, where the clerks are registering their names and giving them tickets and prescription books. After much crushing and struggling I get to the front, my paper is taken, and a book and a card given to me, the latter conveying the information that my medical attendant is "Dr. ———. You are to attend him every Wednesday and Saturday at eleven o'clock. If you twice neglect to attend without his leave, you will be discharged. This card must always be brought with you, and is to be kept clean." The book contains my name, and the same number as the card. Then I follow my leaders into the first pen, the one parallel with us and opposite the door of the consulting-room, bearing the name of our doctor, being filled with women. We wait and wait, and I have ample leisure to examine my companions. They certainly none of them look as if they could pay for medical attendance. There is a mixture of nationalities—English, Irish, Scotch, and colonial; a heathen Chinee, a German, a negro, and a Hindoo from Madras, who is the most striking-looking man of the crowd, his handsome dark features and grizzled hair and moustache wanting only a turban to make him a worthy-looking rajah . . . There is a little Jew boy who is forward and disgusting in his conversation, a Yorkshire farmer's son who has fallen on evil days, and several station hands who have come to Melbourne for advice after spending pounds, as two or three informed me, with advertising doctors. There is a shabby genteel young man with an umbrella, whose whole manner implies a perpetual apology for having been born. But the majority appear to be working-men of the poorer class. However, I am surprised to see, waiting for another doctor than mine, one of my fellow passengers by the ———. Times seemed to have changed somewhat with him. On board he was the butterfly of the saloon, gorgeous in travelling suits of many colours, and wearing much jewellery. The latter appears to have vanished, and he is decidedly shabby. It appears to be often thus with "new chums". The significant announcement advertised all over the city, "Emigrants' luggage bought," seems to imply that a proportion are regularly obliged to sell their luggage . . .

To return to the hospital. The women in the out-patients' ward are much better dressed than the men. There is, of course, a great number with babies; but there is also a Dame Quickly, who wears much jewellery, and is slightly inebriated. She is in charge of a young girl, who, poor thing, blushes at her situation. She is but young in her present course of life, or she would not blush. But there are many

A MORNING AT THE HOSPITAL

Honorary help

The only physician who is regular in his attendance at the Melbourne Hospital

younger than her, the reason for whose presence here is very evident. Some are nearly children. Hospital doctors know more than the police on many social evils, and I imagine that generally their experience would be favourable to the passing of a Contagious Diseases Act—it would greatly lessen their labours. We wait a long time for the arrival of our doctor. He is often very late in arriving; seldom punctual. At last he comes, and the women commence passing into his room. Occasionally we hear loud screams from the casualty ward, where limbs are being set or wounds dressed. It is distressing to see little children hobbling along on crutches, or being borne in their parents' arms, towards this ward. The dread depicted on their youthful faces of the pain they know, by experience, will be necessarily inflicted on them is touching in the extreme. The women take much longer than the men in getting through; but, when we once begin, our progress is rapid. Certainly, the average time given to each male is not more than a minute, and one morning Dr. —— got rid of twenty-six patients in less than ten minutes. This does not allow time for any thorough diagnosis to be made of a patient's case. The treatment appears to be rough and ready. Gallons of different medicines, as prescribed in the authorities, are kept ready made up in the dispensary. What cures one will cure another, seems to be the rule, and little allowance appears to be made for different constitutions. There is not time to examine into all that . . . My case did not take fifty seconds of the doctor's time, the prescription was written out, and I took it to the window of the dispensary. "I have no bottle: can I pay for one?" I asked. "You'll get one outside;" and, at the door, I accordingly found an old Irishwoman, who makes an honest and lucrative living by begging old bottles, washing same, and retailing them here. I don't know what is the value of a brandy bottle under the present system of protection. The old lady said sixpence: I thought threepence a fair price; and we compounded for fourpence. It was by that time after two-o'clock; and, getting my medicine, I was glad to finish my morning at the hospital.

2

The Outcasts of Melbourne

A morning in the police-court is a sad study of Melbourne life. Here, for example, are two young girls—sisters—one quite a child, another a year or two older. They are charged with disorderly conduct. One girl smiles at her friends behind, and then tries to look penitent, in which endeavour she is not a success; the other's trembling lip and tearful eye show that this is her first offence. They have to go to gaol for a month, and unless some good Christian looks after them there, one girl who might have been saved will certainly now be irrevocably fixed in her downward course. Of these unfortunates—ministers to man's pleasure, who are more or less numerous in every community—the police court claims its fair share. Sometimes they are charged with theft, in which case they appear to be always instigated by some male companion, but generally their offence is drunkenness or disorderly conduct. Their apathy in the dock is striking; they recognize well that they have offended against the laws, which they think bear so hardly upon them, and hear their sentences without a murmur.

As drunkenness brings these poor women to the bar, so it does the majority of their male friends. But many others, hard-working men, also have to pay the fine and costs for indulging too freely. Intemperance seems to be the bane of the working classes in the colonies. The frightful assault cases which are sometimes heard generally have their rise in a drinking bout. "I was mad drunk, and don't know what I did," is often the excuse. Many of those who are convicted of "brutal assaults" are not criminal in their instincts, but are overpowered by the frightful lust for personal combat and for smiting their enemies, which is so prevalent in the Anglo-Saxon race . . .

And now look at these poor creatures charged with vagrancy. Homeless and houseless, they are convicted of the fearful crime of their existence. A sentence of three months is a blessing which they should

Yarra Bankers

appreciate. It is commonly reputed that a vagrant gets a heavier sentence than a minor thief; if so, it is the better for both of them. Many young larrikins are brought up "on the vag." They are known thieves and bad characters, according to the police, who attempt to rid the neighbourhood of them in this way; but, as a rule, a subscription is raised which obtains the services of a legal gentleman, who produces evidence to show that his client is a hard-working respectable youth, and the larrikin is discharged, to the triumph of his companions and discomfiture of "Mr. Detective."

In the police court father appears against son, mother against daughter, brother against brother. The prisoners in the majority of cases are, as I have said, those who may be called hereditary criminals, or made so by early association. Now and then, however, a prisoner is seen of a superior class. Look at this woman: she is haggard and worn out by dissipation, but has the remains of past beauty. She first came out to the colonies as the wife of "a gentleman," the son of a major-general in the British army. After a time, he returned to England, deserting her, but not before he had lived on the earnings of her shame. Her after-career may be imagined—drink is her only comforter now . . .

Walk along Bourke-street any night, and girls are to be seen—some merely children, "drifted, drifting, and half-anchored." The state of morality amongst the working girls in Melbourne is worse than in Paris, and they commence their downward course earlier. Work-room and shop recruit the ranks of the unfortunate. Work makes the hands black, and does not always keep the reputation white. They are led astray by a love of fine clothes and admiration, coupled with early-developed strong passions, and their fall is not purified by the ghost of love—love which is the essence of the life of a *grisette*. The Melbourne Magdalen goes her way wilfully, and of her own accord. She, as a rule, has no shame in her wrong-doing, and false sentimentality should not be wasted upon her.

"They can't be allays a workin'," said Mr. Sleary, "they must be amoothed sometimes," and the larrikin and thief, with their female companions, take their pleasure as the rest of world. Let us walk into this concert-hall, which, by the flaming advertisements which meet us at all points, should be a popular place of amusement. Let us first take a sixpenny ticket and go up into the balcony. The room is a long one, and there is scant accommodation for "the gods." We are amongst a crowd of youths and boys, with a sprinkling of girls of the very lowest class. Larrikins and thieves all of these. But there is good order amongst them, perhaps because the performances are dull and depressing, or because of the announcement prohibiting "whistling or shouting, or any sort of disorderly conduct," and containing penal clauses as to removal by the police. Downstairs, in the body of the hall, to enter which we pay one shilling, the spectators are not of a much superior class. They are better dressed, and have a little more money, but one thing appears more evident, that few people who can claim the slightest share of respectability visit this "popular resort." Here waiter-girls walk around and solicit you to "shout;" when you refuse they will give you a little gentle abuse, and return to the sweet converse of their particular larrikin lovers. The performances are of the usual low music-hall style. There are some "niggers," whose jokes are frightfully gross, and the comic songs are only conspicuous for dulness and indecency. A child of about ten dances and sings prettily, but she is being taught in the very worst school, and one of her dances is only redeemed from indecency by her youth and innocence. What will be her future? After the performance is over part of the floor is cleared away and dancing commences. The women, of course, are all of a class, and this seems to be meant for their encouragement, as we see announcements that "gentlemen will not be allowed to dance together, or the music will be stopped." Places of amusement of this kind are baiting-houses on the larrikin's high road to Pentridge . . .

Larrikins and thieves greatly resort to the cheap billiard-rooms. There are one or two in a principal thoroughfare which are daily crowded with such. They are mostly youths and boys, and those who are not thieves and sharpers are flats and pigeons, being inducted into the mysteries of the Larrikin's Progress, the stages of which may be divided into drink, gambling, rowdyism, assault, police-court, gaol, thief. The skittle-alleys claim their fair share of the patronage of this class, and in certain hotels, one of notable repute, where the votaries of chicken-hazard assemble, the thief and the fast man-about-town meet on neutral ground and call the main. With all this known to the police, it seems strange that prosecutions are not instituted against the proprietors of such houses. Is gambling only a crime when the money goes into Chinese pockets? Vice permeates through all classes of society, and the high-toned *roué*, who wishes to keep his little pleasures secret, often associates with gamblers and thieves, who desire to preserve their *incognito* for a different reason.

Where do the criminal classes of Melbourne live? Within a stone's throw of our principal thoroughfares and places of business. I do not suppose any city in the world can show such foul neighbourhoods centred in its very heart. Between Bourke-street and Lonsdale-street, there are a number of lanes, "terraces," "squares," and rights-of-way, the present condition of which is a disgrace to the city. The habitations are mostly of a kind—one-storied hovels, low, dilapidated, and dirty.

The surroundings are filth and garbage. From a sanitary point of view, the existence of such quarters is a great nuisance, if not a positive danger to public health. Go through these on a summer's afternoon. The occupants you will see are mostly women, and of what a type—low, degraded, brutal-looking, who, young and old, seem as if virtue and purity had never been known to them even by name. Young girls—there are many here—have their youth and freshness overshadowed by vice; older women, who once may have belonged to the aristocracy of the *demi-monde*, have flabby cheeks, and features now swollen by drink. The number of very young girls to be seen in these quarters is something to shock even one used to the aspects of vice in the Old World. Melbourne is remarkable for this, and, as a rule, men are not so much to blame. These women, I am told, never see innocence, but they wish to mar it, and they tempt children to their ruin—some so young that they really may be said to have never known any other state. There is little of the woman about these unsexed beings, except that occasionally they may be seen sitting in the sun, doing a little needlework or mending their clothes. The hovels, which are small, being generally tenanted by several couples, cause society in their neighbourhood to be of a very public kind, the doorsteps, the kerbstones, and the centre of the road forming convenient resting-places for the female population, who sun themselves and interchange ideas and opinions, which are generally couched in language which it is an euphuism to call merely bad . . .

The condition of things here is the fault of the owners of the property. It seems that these miserable hovels bring in rents far higher than good cottages in other localities. The worse the neighbourhood the higher the rent. This is really hard upon the occupants. Men or women who may have been a little crooked are forced to lodge here, and are swindled by the landlords, besides being condemned to associations which certainly will hasten their downward course. The proprietors of these dens of iniquity are, I am told, in many cases, men of repute, with the first seats at the synagogue; in others, they are women who have saved money in their career of shame, and now trade upon that of others who occupy their houses. But we have as yet only seen women; where are their male companions? They are mostly inside sleeping until night, or they are at the corner public-house, or loafing about looking for prey. There is one man often to be seen around here—tall, spare, with grey hair and beard, and a mild, benevolent expression of countenance. I see that most of these outcasts know him, and that he freely enters their houses. This is Mr. George Hill, the police court missionary, whose business it is to endeavour to save children and beginners in a career of vice. I don't know what sect

Larrikins of the period

The three months man   The first year man

Mr. Hill belongs to, but he is very unsectarian—indeed, secular in the good advice I have heard him give, and he is everywhere treated with respect and esteem by these unfortunates. Let us witness one of his interviews.

At the corner of one of the lanes running into Little Bourke-street stands a coloured boy, bright and smart-looking, the sort of lad who, in the old days, you would take into the house to cut your tobacco and make your sangaree. Hill is gently warning him of his mode of life, and offers to find him a place to work, but he refuses. On the opposite side of the road has been standing a young man of under-size, with bristly whiskers, scarf around his neck, and quiet, stealthy manner, which is very suggestive. He is a convicted thief. He sidles across the road, and approaches me. I doubt his intentions, but remember that I have little in my pockets. However, he only comes to listen, and, at last, turning to the boy, says, "Why don't you take Mr. Hill's offer; you'll be sorry for it in ten years' time if you don't," and then he joins his mate, and they slink off to the Eastern Market. By this time two or three have gathered around Mr. Hill, and one of them says, "Can't you get me a place, sir?" He further says that he has only just "come out," and the police threaten to run him in again, and afterwards fetches his brother out of the corner public-house, who says, "So help me God, I'll work if I can get a chance." There are three of them who have just "done" six months for assault. One—a man with a neat-set figure—has, despite a large scar, a pleasing face, which I like. I am told he is one of the most desperate ruffians in Melbourne . . . These three vow they have had nothing to eat that day, having been turned out without breakfast, but their mates had been standing beer for them at the public-house. Well, eighteen-pence will get three good meals in Melbourne, and provided with this, plenty of good advice, and a recommendation to the Prisoners' Aid Society, they leave, promising not to enter the public-house (a noted thieves' resort) again.

The sequel of these incidents is that, two days afterwards, the mulatto boy was sentenced to six months' imprisonment for theft, and that one of the three men, at least, is earning an honest livelihood, as I met him one day in Bourke-street, with black hands and face, which he was proud of, as he stopped and told me he meant to keep square in the future. As for the thief who gave the good advice to the coloured lad, he will doubtless soon be again in gaol. His style of delivery was that of one who has lost all hope for himself. But, indeed, as regards the male criminals, they do not appear so solicitous to drag youth into sin as females do. Here, outside another public-house, we meet a youth who leads by the hand a pretty little child. He, also, has just "come out." In reply to inquiries, he says he does not drink now because of his head, and he shows a frightful scalp wound not yet healed. He has several other scars on his face and head, some caused by policemen's handcuffs. (They will not let members of the force carry staffs here, but handcuffs properly used are far more dangerous.) This youth, in reply to a question if the child belongs to him, says, "He's my brother, but I hope to God he'll never grow up like me." This was said sincerely, and was evidently heartfelt, yet the speaker bears one of the worst characters in Melbourne; a policeman, whom I meet shortly afterwards, telling me that "he always ought to be in gaol, and then there'd be some peace in the neighbourhood." The police work according to their lights as suppressors of crime, and when they see a criminal return from gaol to his old haunts (and where else is he to go?) they are only too apt to take the first chance of arresting him. But even a criminal should have justice, and to arrest or threaten (and both are done) a man on the day he leaves gaol is not only unjust but absurd. The one striking difference between these thieves and those of the old world is their healthier appearance. We have seen that they have an aristocratic taste for billiards, and they are also fond of the aristocratic necessity—a bath. Whether a clean healthy criminal is less dangerous than a dirty diseased wretch is an open question.

Let us look now at another class of outcasts. In the scrub lining the banks of the Yarra, in the Government reserves, in the public gardens, and in the bush around Melbourne, during the long summer days, men and women are to be seen lying on their backs in the shade enjoying the *dolce far niente*. They are all of one class—"homeless, ragged, and tanned." They are mostly without family, without friends, without bodily strength, ignorant of any trade, of feeble health, and whose only associates are as themselves. They are vagrants, pure and simple, fear of the law and want of nerve keeping them from being actively criminal, but still ever ready to commit any petty theft, if they can do so without chance of detection. They are generally past middle age, and subsist by begging food, living during the summer in the open air. In the winter, many flock to the Immigrants' Home and Benevolent Asylum; others commit offences to be sent to gaol. The men appear mostly to have drifted into their present state through indolence and want of sufficient mental stamina to fight the battle of life. Strong drink, of course, has often been an agent in their downfall. The women are chiefly outcasts whose age and faded attractions prevent them plying their trade. In Paris, they would be ragpickers: here, they are simply vagrants. But there are a few who have seen far better days. I met one man who talked learnedly in Greek. He had been a clergyman or dissenting minister, and drink had brought him to this . . .

Melbourne larrikins

LARRIKIN (executing a step)—Is my darling true to me?
LARRIKINESS—Yes, thy darling's true to thee.
LARRIKIN—Then pay for these blooming drinks.

Now let us see what society (through the aid of religion, government, and philanthropy) is doing for the prevention of crime and the reformation of the criminal. Melbourne is well provided with religious accommodation for all sects; but the ordinary churches and chapels are entirely outside of the range of the outcast. As a rule, he will not go to look for religion; it must come and seek him. So two Gospel Halls have been erected in evil neighbourhoods—one in O'Brien-lane, the other in Little Bourke-street. These are ostensibly for services on behalf of the criminal and degraded, and are entirely supported by voluntary contributions. The management is unsectarian, although at present the conductors are mostly Baptists. I had seen the outcast at the police court, in the slums, and taking his amusement, so I thought I would see him at prayer, and one night made my way to O'Brien-lane. It is indeed a foul neighbourhood in which the Hall is situated. In the day-time it is uninviting, the dilapidated huts, reeking of filth and garbage, are pleasing to no sense; and in the night time it looks worse. An evil shadow is thrown over all—crime seems to lurk round every corner. And many crimes have been committed along these dark alleys, which seem especially made for the convenient and safe perpetration of such. The Hall is a plain brick building. Outside there is an announcement that services are held on Sunday and Wednesday evenings. During week-days it is occupied as a State School, where numbers of the juveniles of the neighbourhood are instructed.

Coming from the old country, it is strange to see the well-fed, healthy appearance of the children in such a neighbourhood as this. I have visited this school, and could hardly believe that these were children recruited from the worst quarter of Melbourne. Entering the Hall, I found that service had already commenced; a young gentleman—a bank clerk, I am told—was reading a portion of Scripture. The place was well filled with well-dressed people, every one of whom, by their appearance, might be regular chapel-goers. It is evidently a weekly gathering with them. The hymns they all know and join in. There was not a single member who, by his or her appearance, belonged to the class which this Hall should attract. It was just a weekly prayer-meeting of a few good Christians. I was told afterwards that I must not judge by appearances—that some of those present had been bad characters, and had been redeemed . . . Now, all present, I believe, could thoroughly claim to be "respectable." It was not the dress alone—although one can judge much by that; and the good, neat attire of many young women was an evidence of their inward mind—but the features of those present, which would lead to the supposition that one was a thousand miles from such a neighbourhood. Here there were none with that essentially criminal cast of countenance to be seen in the Police Court, in the slums, in the Music Hall, and low billiard-rooms. The thief and the Magdalen live within a stone's throw, but they come not to the Gospel Hall. According to the service I heard, it seems to act as the meeting-place of a Mutual Admiration Praying Society. We had prayers from about ten different individuals, besides the chairman or conductor. They were much alike—a good deal of talk about grace, which a thief would not understand. One young man, who gloried in having been "a sinner," and rejoiced, like Uriah Heep, in his 'umbleness, was, however, very confident that he was saved, and that many of us would be damned. The chairman, a very energetic and enthusiastic gentleman, gave an impassioned address, in which he referred to a young man just dead, who, having lived a sinner till within the last three months, hedged at the right moment, and was now—according to the statement—"asleep in Jesus." (How do people know these things?) The proceedings were very edifying, no doubt, to all concerned; but did not appear to be of the slightest good to O'Brien-lane. Until the last we might be in a chapel in the most respectable street in London . . .

I do not wish to run down the services at this Hall. The conductors mean well, but there is too much of the Pharisee in it, and the Publican does not stand even afar off. He protests altogether by his absence, and by a few stones banged against the door by sympathizing larrikins. Too many respectable people go to the Hall—criminals and Magdalens will not mix with such, to be stared at. One or two energetic men, like the chairman, who would go out into the slums, and bring in to the service a few real outcasts to begin with, would do more good than ten praying amateurs inside. I speak as one who has tried to gauge the thoughts of the unfortunate. This Hall does good, no doubt; but not to the class of which I write.

At the other Gospel Hall, I found the assembly even more respectable. There are one or two city missionaries and some ladies, district visitors, who do what they think best in the line of distributing tracts; but, on the whole, I think religion has totally failed to serve as an agent of prevention or reclamation from vice and crime. Mr. Hill does some good, but he very wisely seldom brings ostensibly forward the religious question. For the prevention of crime Government does little. The Industrial Schools are capital institutions for the reception of neglected children; indeed, the other day, I heard a prominent Government officer vaunting the glories of the Constitution in this wise:—"Yes, this is a splendid country, sir. If a man has an illegitimate son he may have him sent to an Industrial School, then to a Free School, and afterwards put into a Government billet . . ."

But, whilst doing great good, the schools only retain the children for a time; when they are discharged, if they go back to their criminal friends or relatives, they will soon fall into the hands of the police, and then prison or the reformatory is before them. From the reformatory they are discharged at the age of sixteen, just the time when the passions and imaginations of Australian youth are most vivid, and when they require most careful treatment. And this seems to me to be the point which has most to be considered—how to control and divert youthful vice and crime, or, in other words, how to put down larrikinism . . . It is the new generation of wickedness which we have to fear, and drunkenness and larrikinism are the two great feeders of crime in Melbourne. Day by day the ranks of the roughs are swelled by juvenile recruits; and looking at the population and the condition of our streets, the supply appears to be inexhaustible; and the manner in which they band together and defy the public and police, and the money which they seem enabled to raise to pay for lawyers and fines, is a proof how dangerous they may become when they have graduated through gaol or Pentridge. Next to the prevention of crime is the reclamation of the criminal. For this, Government has done nothing, with the exception of bestowing grants to the amount of £150 to the Prisoners' Aid Society during the past three years it has been in existence. In this time 368 male criminals have been assisted by the society, and only thirteen females. This society has done good, and is but the beginning of what should be undertaken by the State . . .

Religion and Government, then, at present have little effect on the outcasts, and private philanthropy has only done visible good through the efforts of the Prisoners' Aid Society . . . It is said that the ladies of Melbourne do not take sufficient interest in the fate of their fallen sisters, and that the reclamation of these can only be effected by them. I recognize fully the difficulties ladies will experience in attempting to deal with this class in Melbourne. It will be very disgusting work, too, for they will find the Magdalen not bathed in tears, not penitent, but probably drunk—not in the hope of finding nepenthe, but for the mere love of it. According to the testimony of Mr. Castieau,* a great number of these spend year after year in gaol, and there is little chance of their being reclaimed. I would rather suggest to charitable ladies that they should bestow their attention on the young girls who are being broken in to a career of vice. Workshop and factory supply these in numbers, like the larrikin class, quite out of proportion to the population . . .

I have not spoken of Chinese vice, that is abnormal, and is confined to that race. A few women may cohabit and smoke opium with China-

---

* John B. Castieau, governor of H.M. Gaol in Victoria Street, Melbourne.

How 'Money' is made!!

'The house which the prisoner rented, and which was used for the accommodation of the lowest class of women of the town, belongs to the HON. HENRY MILLER, who received £52 a year for the premises. A memorandum of agreement between BONAR (the negro) as a tenant for twelve months, and the HON. HENRY MILLER, was produced.'—*Argus*, August 31.

men, young girls may be sold to them, but the crime there is with the white procuress. The danger existing from the present and future race of outcasts of Melbourne is not affected by the Chinese element. *Mes amis,* these imperfect sketches of the unfortunates who are all around you, whose life is one of misery, sin, crime, but little shame, are written by one who has studied their life in the depths of which he writes. My moral is to point out to you, officials of the Government, to you ministers of the Gospel, to you who compose respectable society, that your present efforts to prevent sin and reclaim the sinner are of little avail, and that it will be well for you and your descendants if ye take heed quickly, and Government, religion, and society joining together turn away the present tide of youthful vice from the land, otherwise the future may yet see bitter fruit borne from the presence of the outcast and dangerous classes of society.

3

A Night in the Model Lodging House

It is a wet, dismal night. I consult a friendly policeman, who informs me that, at the Model Lodging-house in King-street, Melbourne, I can get a bed for sixpence. Rejoiced at the news, I wend my way through the pouring rain and biting wind. The building is a large one, of plain brick, three stories high. On the steps I find three decent-looking men smoking. Entering the hall, on my left I perceive a little window, where I deposit my sixpence, and the official in charge gives me a ticket marked 154, on the back of which he writes my name in chalk. Passing through glass doors, I mount the stairs, and, on the first landing, am received by a courteous warder, who takes my ticket and directs me to my bed. I find that, with the exception of the enclosed staircase, the whole floor is open, the landing being partitioned off by iron screens about six feet high, dividing the floor into two parts. Entering the left hand ward, I see, by the dim gaslight, two long rows of small iron beds; and, passing between these, I find my way to No. 154, each bed being labelled in large characters. The beds are placed very close together, and there is no furniture in the room but these. As I look around I see, by the beds already occupied, that it is customary for the lodgers to place their clothes under their pillows for safety's sake, or because there is nowhere else to put them. I follow the custom of the place, and am soon in bed. The mattresses and pillows are straw, the sheets coarse, but apparently clean, and the blanket and counterpane warm. There is barely room to walk between the beds. Stretching out my arm, I could easily place my hand on the forehead of the man in the next bed. Indeed, I was disturbed in the night by a stroke on the cheek from the hand of my left-hand neighbour, who lashed out wildly, killing mosquitoes in his dreams. About half of the fifty beds in the ward were occupied when I entered, and, sleepless, I watch the new comers, who troop in one by one. I find the general custom is to

Late arrivals at the Model Lodging House

strip to the buff. Night-shirts, of course, there are none; and the naked figures flitting about the room, as a rule, show a lamentable lack of physique, and would serve as examples that we have sadly degenerated since the days of the mighty men of old . . .

I see that many of the lodgers are old hands, and appear to have their regular beds, to which they make their way as to their home. There has been little talking up to this, those who have gone to bed early being evidently tired out, but now two men at the end of the room nearest me begin an argument . . . This is interrupted by the entrance of a decently-dressed youth, whom they tell not to keep them awake to-night. "I assure you, gentlemen," says the youth as he takes off his coat, "that I went to sleep last night with my finger between my teeth, and this morning it was quite sore, but I'd do anything rather than disturb you." I wonder with what strange malady he can be afflicted that involves such a curious mode of taking rest, till by the conversation I gather that before his time he has taken to gnash and grind his teeth, awaking all his neighbours . . . And now it was nearly twelve o'clock, and a natty little figure dressed in clothes of a fashionable cut, and swinging a cane, walked down to a bed nearly opposite mine. The walk was that of a gentleman, and of one accustomed to field sports, but the new comer was evidently quite at home here, as he went straight to his bed—a sure sign that he was not a new hand. At twelve o'clock the warder came along and turned the gas low down, and retired to his own dormitory, just partitioned off by the iron screen, and being between the two wards forming the two wings of the floor. One bed next to mine was vacant; it gave me breathing room, and I felt that I should hate the man who would occupy it. There is something in presentiments. After the warder had retired, a figure came down the room. If not drunk, he had had more than "enough;" there was a difficulty in getting into bed, and when once in, he perfumed the neighbourhood with a choice odour of rum. All these experiences were perfectly novel to me, and I could not sleep. I longed for a pipe which might purify the air around me . . .

Hour by hour the night passes away, the only disturbance an Irishman in the next ward fighting in his sleep, and cursing his mythical antagonist. I listen with much curiosity for any sign of the Grinder. I should have liked to have heard a specimen of his powers, but he is staunch as steel to his word; his teeth, presumably, are crushed on his finger, for he gives no sign. There is one sound, however, which continues all night, and falls gratingly on my ear. It is the continual coughing—not, as a rule, that caused by a trifling cold or bronchitis, but the dry, hacking cough which physicians know so well. The place sounded like a consumptive hospital, and as an indication of the health of the colony was anything but re-assuring. Towards daybreak I fall into a heavy sleep. I am awakened in the morning by a loud call of "Cab," some cabman is being aroused. Many of the inmates call each other and exchange morning greetings. I find that the man I christened "the swell" slipped away early; the Grinder also is gone. I am one of the last to arise, and consequently on going to the lavatory (there is one at each end of the building on each floor) I find it hard to discover a clean bit of towel. I manage to get a good wash at last and make my way down stairs and through a passage into the back yard, where I am told I can clean my boots. On one side of the yard I find a shed where there are brushes and blacking, and where lodgers are allowed to smoke. At the end of the yard is the laundry, and in the centre sheets are hanging out to dry. On the other side is the kitchen, which I enter, and find filled with lodgers, who are evidently old hands. Some are boiling water over the fire, others consuming the tea already made, together with scraps of food which they produce from the shelf or the lockers, of which there are a limited number, and which are allotted to *habitués* on payment of a trifling sum for the keys. These men appear to be generally labourers. I enter the building by another door, and find myself in a ward divided by wooden partitions about ten feet high into a number of little rooms. Rooms containing only one bed are charged 1s. a night. For a bed four in a room you pay 9d. a night. On the other side of the building is a large room furnished with tables and forms, which is used as a sitting and reading room by the lodgers. A few daily papers are taken in for their use, and draughts and dominoes also provided. Leaving this I pass through the glass doors, and over the ticket window see a framed copy of the rules of the Model Lodging-house Company (Limited), which appear fairly reasonable. Smoking in any part of the building is strictly prohibited, and no intoxicating drinks are allowed to be brought on the premises. As I am perusing these rules, the superintendent, Mr. James Watkins, comes from his office, and courteously answers my questions. On the first and second floors there are 200 sixpenny beds, and on the ground floor 96 shilling and ninepenny ones. On Tuesday night there were only two beds vacant in the establishment, and during the winter months scores are nightly turned away. The staff is composed of a superintendent, matron, and three wardsmen, with laundry girls. The institution, although not started by its proprietors with any idea of great pecuniary results, is likely to pay 10 per cent. Mr. Watkins showed me a small library which he has in his office, and from which he lends books to the lodgers . . . Mr. Watkins says that fully five-eighths of the lodgers are studious men. One-fifth he states to be men who have occupied, and may again, good positions. They are ex-army officers,

Melbourne cab driver of the 1870s and his passengers

barristers, lawyers, and doctors—men who have either been thoroughly ruined, or are under a temporary cloud. The remainder are generally tradesmen, or good, honest working-men. Altogether, after my trial of the Model Lodging-house, I left very well pleased with the courtesy of the officials and the cleanliness of the place. One or two reforms I would hint at. There are, I think, too many beds in the wards. Smoking should be allowed in the reading-room at night; on wet, cold nights men will not stay in an open shed in the yard, the only place where they are allowed to enjoy tobacco, but will certainly go to the nearest public-house. I think, too, more clean towels and sheets might be provided. In conclusion, I will mention one curious fact which may be of interest to the churches. I particularly watched at night to see if anyone knelt in prayer. Not a soul. In the morning only one boy knelt, and that after everyone else had left the room. Poor lad, I hope he was not ashamed of his devotions.

4

Sydney Common Lodging Houses

... I have never been "on the wallaby," or slept in a common lodging-house, in this country, and I don't want to try the experiment. But in Melbourne I have visited such places, and found that under the municipal regulations everything was generally fairly clean, ventilation was good, and overcrowding impossible. How different in Sydney! Here are forty to fifty dens which are a disgrace to civilization—a positive evil, breeding moral and physical pestilence . . . to members of the Council* I would recommend a personal inspection of some of the dens in Clarence and Sussex-streets. Those who dread this discomfort have no right to question my experiences of the other night . . .

In company with Dr. Cox, who is not only my physician in ordinary, but one of my best friends in the colony, we started at half-past ten on Monday night. I was very pleased to have such an eminent medical man with me, as his testimony on the sanitary arrangements would be very valuable. Clarence-street by daylight is not a very enticing locality, and although the gloom of night hides many blemishes, it cannot improve the dreary habitations. Two doors from Margaret-street we descended several steps to a boarding-house kept by one Henry Gillbody. Said Sergeant Larkins†: "This is one of the best kind of houses used by working men, but it is as well to see them all. We have no power of entry anywhere, although in the sixpenny places they hardly ever refuse us. If they won't let us see this place, we must try another." However, Mr. Gillbody, on being awoke from his sleep in the parlour, expressed his willingness to show us over the house. Well, it was not Macquarie-street, and I should object to sleep four in a room; but altogether the accommodation was very fair, and Mrs.

* The Legislative Council, which in June 1877 rejected a Bill passed by the Legislative Assembly to regulate common lodging houses.
† A Sydney police officer who had been a prominent witness before the parliamentary inquiry into lodging houses in 1876.

Gillbody, with pride, showed her kitchen, with clean-scrubbed table and crockery on the shelves. There were no unwashed things around, but everything was placed properly away for the night, and the order and cleanliness would have done credit to establishments of far greater pretensions. The charges for board here are 3s. a day, or 17s. 6d. a week.

At the next house of the same class the landlady refused to admit the police. She "wouldn't have folks poking about her house at night." Hence, I charitably conclude that her *ménage* was not equal to Mrs. Gillbody's. Then we crossed over and inspected seven or eight houses which hold out signs of "good lodgings" and "clean beds." Some of these are shilling houses, others sixpence, others have mixed prices, ranging from a shilling on the first floor to sixpence in the garret. No opposition was made to our entry at any of these. There was a difference in degree, but they were mostly abominable in the overcrowding. In some of the entrance rooms on the ground-floor there appeared an attempt at cleanliness and cheerfulness; but go to the back, ascend the dirty stairs, and the result was the same, for in five houses, containing six rooms, each about 12 by 14 feet, there were over seventy people. At least there was accommodation (?) for such, and the inference is that often these beds were occupied. The lodgers were generally stowed away in the four upstairs rooms. In some cases there were seven or eight beds, placed side by side, with not room to move between, the occupants having to crawl in from the foot. The beds were all mattresses on stretchers—the least said about the coverings the better. The ventilation in every case, although windows might be propped open, we found to be totally insufficient.

To enter these rooms and see the heaps of stifling stewing humanity was horrible. The atmosphere choked one with a fearful taste. Each man lay, sometimes almost naked, sometimes all clothed, in a feverish rest which could not fit him for work on the morrow. Those who were undressed had their garments beneath their heads for purpose of safety. The pencil of Gustave Doré would be needed to draw the different forms and positions. Some tossed about restlessly—others were evidently drunk—those awake hunted for vermin. And, considering that these were not paupers or beggars, but in many cases labouring men and sailors, it was really horrible to think that they could not have any better shelter. What diseases are not contracted in such holes? It was scarcely comforting to hear that one bed had been vacated by "a young man who has gone as cook to the —— hotel," or to have stewards of intercolonial steamers pointed out to you here. Of course, there were degrees in the abominations; but in all the ventilation was most inadequate. It seemed that in every corner where a bed could be placed a man would sleep. In the closets underneath the stairs we always

The Sydney Soup Kitchen

found sleeping-places—these were "private rooms." In outhouses in the yards members of the family or "the servant" took their rest. In one house, in a hovel at the back, I found a naked man asleep on the stones. The drunken proprietor, who was very profuse in his offers to show us everything, stood before this man, and waved the candle on the ground in front that the light might not fall on him. "You see, I'll show you everything," said he, dropping some grease on a frightened cockroach.

In the living rooms there were stretchers, which appeared to be turned into beds at night; and I think that, in a brisk time, twenty to thirty often sleep in these houses. We found in one place two lads—one fast asleep, the other nodding stupidly, waiting till the house was shut up, to take their rest on a stretcher, or where they could. These paid sixpence each for the shelter. In another house an old-timer, named "Granny," who says she is 104 years old, presides. Here I found that young Arab, Duffy, vendor of *Echos* and matches . . . Duffy makes considerable money, sometimes five or six shillings a day; he is presumed to give his savings to "Granny," but she says he spends too much on the theatre. Duffy, it appears, cannot resist the attraction of Thespian entertainments.

One of the most amusing incidents of the night was, that every "boss" insisted that his house was "beautifully clean and sweet." There was no provision made for cleanliness, except in some rooms a broken basin and jug and a tin bucket. In all the yards there was a good supply of water, but the drainage was defective in many instances, and aroused Dr. Cox's disapprobation. In every case the yards were small, often abutting on blank walls of opposite houses. Once seeing a light in a building at the rear, we found, on inspection, that it was an aperture looking into a small room, where the female servants of a neighbouring hotel slept—accommodation not at all conducive to decency. Some of the buildings we entered were substantial; others old, with worn-out rickety stairs, and plaster dropping from the walls and roofs. But, good or bad, the overcrowding was the same crying evil. In one or two places there are small single rooms for couples.

Most of the occupants of these lodging-houses are presumed to be earning an honest living; the roguery, if anything, I expect, is on the part of the proprietors. These men smoke cigars and get drunk, and generally flourish in idleness. In the "Kilkenny Boarding-house," however, young thieves are supposed sometimes to congregate; two one-storied cottages compose this establishment, and the stretchers are on a stone floor. The proprietress keeps a little chandler's shop. She is a stout, black-eyed old lady, who cursed us liberally, and expressed a desire to "lay me out" with the candlestick. I have only given general details of the disgusting enormities of common lodging-house life in Sydney. To faithfully chronicle each phase would not suit these columns. The houses we visited, too, are, I believe, not the worst. They say that in Sussex-street there is still a lower grade. And in establishments which claim respectability, great overcrowding goes on. In a noted restaurant in Pitt-street, there is a room where seven men sleep, the beds being placed on the tables which in the day are used in the dining-room. This place is crowded every night, and the weekly income from one room is forty-nine shillings. It is a wonder how men will continue to go to such places, but they have no help for it. In Sydney the supply of decent lodgings for the poorer class does not equal the demand. The trade is a brisk and good one, and model lodging-houses are urgently wanted . . . Many good people appear to have strenuously closed their eyes to the scandals around them, and have argued that "Sydney was not worse than any other large town." This is not the only evil caused by the *laissez faire* spirit of our authorities . . .

5

The Waifs and Strays of Sydney

... "Matches, sir!" "B'y box matches, sir!" One knows the cry of that worst of all nuisances, the street Arab of Sydney. But from my feet, as it were, there rises one cry, even more dismal than usual, "Maatches." I look down, and there I see the original "Ginx's Baby." It must be him! About as high as my walking-stick, thin, shrivelled, blear-eyed—with no covering on his feet, and scanty trousers and jacket, young Ginx does not seem to have improved much by his removal to Australia. He is, without doubt, the most miserable, woe-begone, comical little object it has been my lot to see for many a day. "Maatches," he cries, and on the word shuffles off, leaving me for a moment in astonishment—then I follow him.

I have just left the inside of the theatre, all light and glitter, and crowded with happy young life. The lad I am tracking is in such sad contrast to the well-fed, well-dressed youngsters there! Is it inevitable that light must always have the foil of darkness; that the highest civilization and condition of riches must have, as their contrast, abject poverty and ignorance and misery? In new countries certainly, it seems to me, it should not be so. Here, where large sums of money are devoted to bring immigrants from the old world, the street Arab and the larrikin should almost be an impossibility. Dimly turning over these things in my mind, I follow young Ginx across the road into the "Metropolitan." This is a highly respectable hotel; it possesses one private bar or saloon which may almost be said to be an adjunct of the theatre, crowded as it is every night with the occupants of the dress-circle or stalls . . .

Through this heterogeneous throng I follow young Ginx, who dives between legs, and sends up a plaintive voice from the bottom of men's waistcoats—"Maatches! W'nt 'ny maatches?" Here he seems to be well known, and is saluted by many as "Kelly." He sells a box or two of lights, and receives a threepenny or sixpenny piece. No change is tendered or asked; the people here are generous in their charities. Kelly (Ginx no longer) is on terms of familiarity with many in the saloon. He approaches young Dundreary, and whines "Maatches!" and then, in a dismal, jocose way, says—"D'ye want ter fight, 'cos I c'd lick yer." This "sporting offer" being refused, and the place being too crowded for business, Kelly slips out, and I again track him.

This little waif and stray, a flotsam and jetsam thrown up by the great waves of poverty, ignorance, and vice, toddles down King-street, and enters many places which are simply—well, *not* respectable. These are his covers, which he draws blank, except that in one case a poor girl (may her sins be forgiven her!) gives him some lollies. Kelly at last goes into a café, in which there is a company of men and women. Here he waits for a time, joining spasmodically in the conversation around. This is a favourable opportunity for me to interview him, first feeling my way with a coin, which he immediately transfers to his mouth. His name is Pat Kelly; he is six years old; his father dead—mother washes. He has got three brothers and one sister; the latter is on Cockatoo (at this answer the women around laugh heartily). One brother comes out with him to sell matches; he is dubious as to what the others do. He goes to St. Mary's school in the daytime (this answer I do not believe). Comes out at eight o'clock most nights, and goes home when he has made two shillings. Some Saturday nights makes three-and-sixpence. Has a dozen of matches given him to start with. Whilst relating this, he plays with his boxes on the table, moving them backward and forward listlessly, and counting them for pastime. "How many are there, Kelly?" says a man. "Nine!" "No; there are only eight." "There's nine! What 're yer doin' of? D'ye want ter fight?" replies the bellicose infant. I ask him how much money he has made, and he produces eighteenpence from his mouth. He has only sold three boxes of matches, so that his ostensible profession is but a blind for the real one of begging.

My questions have directed public attention to Kelly, and, for the credit of these roysterers, let it be said that the universal feeling is, that "It is a blank shame that such a child should be allowed to come to such a blank place as this." Even fallen women, with that touch of nature strong within them which keeps them from being entirely unsexed, commiserate and pity the poor child. One rough man takes the boy on his knee and nurses him. Kelly, in a half-sleepy way, plays with his boxes of matches. I wonder if he has ever really played with real toys! Suddenly he is all wide-awake, and fiercely ejaculates— "Come, we don' want 'ny more boys 'ere." This is to another peripatetic match-vendor, or beggar, of maturer years, who just enters. The feeling

The social joys of a Melbourne street arab

of the room is with baby Kelly, and the intruder is expelled. I wish to see more of this precocious infant, and, if possible, track him to his home, and test the truth of his statements; so I made an engagement to meet him at the Metropolitan on another night.

Kelly is there at the time, and first proceeds to business. "Gie me some money!" I gave him threepence. "Yer promised me sixpence last night." "No." "Yer did, now. Yer told a lie. Come!" and he playfully slaps my face and slips off my knee. I have to restore the confidence which he assumes to have lost in me, and then I make proposals to accompany him home at night. This is a task of some delicacy. Kelly is suspicious beyond his years. He, having got his "tip," disdainfully ignores my overtures, and goes through the crowd digging people in the legs and whining "Maatches!" As the saloon clears, he rests on a chair in the corner for a time, and immediately proceeds to go to sleep like a bird on its perch. Tightly clutching his boxes of matches, the poor child nods till he falls off the chair. I again open negotiations with him, but he is sceptical as to my intentions. I come to the conclusion, at last, to track him; so, at twelve o'clock, through the drizzling rain, I follow this little Arab up King-street.

He has not gone far when a woman crosses the road and takes possession of him. She seems decently clad, her most striking article of dress being a common red-and-black plaid shawl, such as is often given to female inmates of our charitable institutions. She appears to take something from the boy. I am evidently on the right track; this must be his mother. It is easy to "shadow" the possessor of so gaudy a garment; so I hang well in the rear, and keep her in sight as she passes through the people hurrying homewards. Turning the corner of Elizabeth-street, I lessen the distance between us, and find, to my chagrin, that the child is not with her. He has slipped away unnoticed. I search for him, which is a mistake; I should have followed the woman. For this night Kelly has evaded me; and, after seeking for him in some of the night-houses, I go home a sadder if not a wiser man. On the next evening I am again in King-street. About eleven o'clock I run Kelly to earth in the Metropolitan. He has come to look on me as an old friend and a certain source of income, and salutes me with the request, "Gie me some money." I effect a trade. He wants ninepence to make up two shillings, when he can consider his work done; so I take his half-dozen boxes of matches and give him a shilling. Then I tell him to run home. But Kelly lounges about the door, and suddenly discovers that he wants ninepence more. This, I inform him, is an evident perversion of the truth, and an attempt at extortion which I cannot stand. In no way abashed, the boy leans against the doorway, and appears to enjoy the moonlight night, and criticise other waifs and strays who pass up and down the street.

Women, the devoted of society, flaunt by us. Other and older *gamins* pester me with their offers of "maatches." I believe the inhabitants of Australia consume more wax vestas than any other people on the face of the earth. One of these implores me, "Gie me threepence; I've no money, and I've had nothing to eat to-day." I doubt this statement very much, and offer to buy him some food if he will accompany me. This he declines to do, and so does not get any pecuniary aid. In a few minutes afterwards, when I am in a cigar-shop round the corner buying the cheap Manilla such as the poor and humble can afford, this boy comes in and procures another dozen of matches, for which he pays sixpence. I tax him with his falsehood of a few seconds back, at which he only puts his tongue in his cheek and laughs. I keep a watchful eye on Kelly, who stands at the corner. When I return thither I find him taking great interest in a venerable waif, who is the possessor of a wooden leg, a gruff voice, and a confidential manner. He immediately bails me up. "Gie a poor old cripple something, sir." I interview him. His name is Charlie Shaw, is a *Government man*, came out in 1837, lost his leg in the quarries. I am such a new chum that I don't know what the term "Government man" means; so I ask him, if he was in the Government service, why he didn't get a pension, and why he came to this country? He winks, as if he were conscious of a good joke, and says, "Now, what did we all come out for in them days, squatters and all, many who are now rich folks, and whose sons are swells? Little bit of trouble at home, eh?" He is such a good-natured, candid old rascal, that I am quite abashed at my lack of discretion in asking painful questions; and I give him a coin, on which he implores "Gawd" to bless me, and stumps away in search of further eleemosynary contributions. Kelly has been watching this old hand with rapt attention. Doubtless among these street Arabs the man who was "lagged" is a noted character— in some sort heroic. I watch Kelly as he leans against the wall, and would give much to know what is passing in the child's brain. Suddenly a woman seizes him by the hand. "Come home, you bad boy." It is the action and utterance of a poor mother whose truant child is the cause of much distress to her. So it outwardly appears, and strangers might think, "That boy will have a spanking when he gets home; and serve him right for stopping out." But I laugh to myself at this by-play. It is the decent woman in the red-and-black shawl— Kelly's mother, as I am now assured.

They pass up King-street into Elizabeth-street. I stroll quietly after them. Then the woman wheels round sharply and suspiciously. I approach the nearest door and apparently knock thereat. As they pass under the next gas-lamp I see the child remove his money from his mouth and give it to his mother. A few steps more and she turns into a public-house at the corner of Market-street. In a minute I am at the opposite door reconnoitring. The Albion is a decent, respectable house; kept, as the name on the window informs me, by one Punch—a good jolly title for a Boniface. It is, like everything in Sydney, built after the English fashion. There is a bar, a parlour, and also a screened-off passage with a hole in it through which modest people order their drinks and sip them unobserved by the curious. I had luckily entered this, and so have a full view of the other occupants of the place, being in shadow myself . . . I watch the landlord exchange a few words with Mrs. Kelly, and then he supplies her with some dark liquor, which I conclude to be rum. When she had tossed this off, I order my drink and say to the landlord, "What was the matter with that woman who had the rum?" "Oh, nothing; but we don't serve females here, and when she asked me for some rum I would not have given it her, but she said she had been working hard all day." And Mr. Punch sighs virtuously, as if in sorrow for the proprietors of houses where females are allowed to drink promiscuously. Now it may be perfectly true that Mrs. Kelly had been "working hard" all day, yet the fact of the transfer of the boy's earnings and the immediate outlay in rum does not increase my respect for that lady. I leave the Albion, and follow the woman and boy along Elizabeth-street, keeping under the shadow of the trees on the Park side of the road. A few yards past the Synagogue, and Mrs. Kelly again stops and looks around. There is no one apparently in sight, and when she and the boy disappear the street is empty. I cross over the road, and find that they have retreated into a court, entered by a broad passage between the houses in Elizabeth-street. This passage is guarded against the inroad of carriage people by two posts, quite in the style of the London courts. The place is dark and forbidding in its gloom. I can see nothing of the surroundings; so, having run Kelly to his home at last, I determine to revisit it by daylight.

It is early on a lovely Sabbath morn when I walk through Hyde Park. Numbers are already taking the air; some poor waifs have evidently had "the key of the street" all night. These lounge about helplessly, mostly with eyes intently fixed on the ground, as if they hope to discover some trove thereon. They may have read of lucky people who have picked up purses and other treasure. Why should not fortune be kind to them? I leave these at their useless quest, and find my way to the court below the Synagogue. This is hardly the location in which one would expect to find a "back-slum," but I presume it is a relic of the days when the convict barracks were close at hand. In it there are eight small two-roomed cottages, built of bricks. In front of each there is a miniature yard, which contains the pots and pans, the tubs and buckets, and other domestic gear of the family. A handcart and barrow, with a quantity of old iron, proclaims one of these cottages to be the residence of a marine-store dealer. In the centre of the court is a water-tap, from which, luckily, there seems a plentiful supply. There is a grim appearance of squalor and poverty about the place, which, under London influences of fog and damp, would make it simply a wretched den. But the pure atmosphere, the glorious sun of Australia, make even this place light and cheerful compared with old-world slums. I am pleased to see flowers in front of one of the houses. How often have I noticed this taste amongst the very poor in city alleys in London! Two cats and a dog lie lazily basking themselves in the sun, and a neat, cleanly-dressed young woman comes and fills her kettle at the tap. I wonder where is the home of Kelly? Whilst I am speculating as to which is likely to be the place I am in search of, a little girl with frowsy hair, and a very dirty face and arms, and legs and feet, comes out of one of the cottages and runs across the road into the park. There, at least, the denizens of these crowded cottages can obtain fresh air and exercise, and so have a chance of health. I follow the child, and when she sits down under a tree and munches a piece of bread, I interview her.

Yes! she knows Mrs. Kelly, who lives in the same house; and Pat, too, he is also there. She will show me; so accordingly we recross the road together. We enter the first cottage in the court on the left. Underneath the stairs which lead into the upper room two women are breakfasting. Standing at the door, I inquire for Mrs. Kelly. The younger woman rises, and says, "She's not up yet, sir," and points towards the window. On a trestle, partly covered by an old and dirty quilt, lie Kelly and his mother. The child is quite naked, and looks more babyish than when clothed. He nestles towards the woman with that unconscious desire for protection and love which one finds in all young things, human and animal. Little Kelly has within him an affectionate strain. When I have had him seated on my knee, he has "cuddled" to me in the way highbred little boys and girls do when they say to one, "Love me." Kelly's idea of a caress, however, ended with a playful slap in my face, and a challenge, "D'ye want to fight?" I am shocked at having thus unwarrantably intruded on Mrs. Kelly's repose, and I retreat through the door, leaving the gloom, and dirt, and squalor, for the joyous rays of the sun. The woman comes out, and I extract the following:—Her name is Cawmill; the old woman inside is her mother; they and the two children sleep upstairs. (Another little girl has by this time joined us, as dirty and unkempt as her sister.)

Of course the girls go to school—they always go regularly to Saint Mary's. She goes out doing odd jobs—nursin' and the like. It's a hard thing now for a poor woman to earn a crust. And Mrs. Kelly, decent woman, she finds it hard to get work washin' and scrubbin'. And the little boy, he goes to school regularly. Does he go out at night? Well, sometimes he sells the evening papers, and makes a copper or two. Drink? Mrs. Kelly and herself never touch a drop! Thus Mrs. Cawmill; and, looking at her children, my soul is filled with pity for them. They are in as bad case as any I have seen in London, and in a few years what will be their fate? A boy or a youth may be reclaimed, but a girl once lost is, as a rule, depraved for ever. That is the unfortunate experience of the best authorities. I can only hope that these little ones are for the nonce happy in their dirt and ignorance and freedom on the dusty turf of Hyde Park.

I give the children some money, and stroll away. I hardly think it possible that Kelly, after always being in the streets till midnight, can attend school regularly; but the next day I make a trial of Saint Mary's schools. These are under the shadow of the new Cathedral and the Presbytery . . . I meet with a priest who knows me, and whom I interest in the quest for my little Arabs . . . In the boys' school we find two or three Kellys, but not the one I am looking for. They are all too clean and well dressed. The 230 youngsters here present are a fine sample of young Australia, mostly of Celtic origin . . . We ascend the steps and enter the girls' department. The building is old, and not very convenient, but it is a pleasant sight to see 140 happy smiling faces. As I say to Father Petre, they look almost too nice. I should prefer to see some of the waifs and strays of this city brought here within the influence of education and religion. I proceed to examine the girls. It is needless to say that my little Cawmills are not here. But we run Kelly to earth in the infant school opposite. Here 150 little ones are imbibing in their first rudiments. Kelly is learning A B C, and does not appear to like it. On inquiring from the teacher, we find he has only been entered a fortnight, and has not been at all regular in his attendance—which, knowing his nightly prowlings, I am not surprised at. Father Petre places him on a chair and examines him. He looks a comical little mite, but to-day has been sent out more decently dressed than usual. In presence of the priest, whose class, I daresay, he has already been taught to dread, Kelly is very quiet; but he admits that he knows me, and that he sells matches. Only made fivepence last night, sometimes makes two and three shillings; has made more than four, but never five shillings. Gives all his money to his mother. The boy is dismissed, and I inquired after the girls Cawmill, but they are not known here.

Scene in a larrikin school

SCHOOLMASTER—Your face is very dirty, and your hands worse. Do you *ever* wash yourself?

PUPIL—Onst a week, Sir, as reg'lar as clockwork. Every Sunday morning whether I needs it or not.

I persuade Father Petre to accompany me to the Kelly-Cawmill home. He is anxious as myself that something should be done to rescue this child from the degrading nocturnal life he is leading. Arrived at the court, we find Mesdames Kelly and Cawmill are out doing a day's work; but the grandmother and one of the little girls, dirty as ever, are at home. Father Petre asks the child if she goes to school, and where? Prompted by her granddame, who I am sorry to find is a most unveracious old party, she replies, "Saint Mary's." "When was she there last?" The old woman says, "She's only been away since yesterday." The child looks at her, but is not quick at picking up the ready lies which are put into her mouth, and hesitates and stammers, and lets out the truth at last that she and her sister have not been to school for about two years, at least since the time "the Sisters taught." I have now fulfilled my quest. Proceedings I trust will shortly be taken to rescue Baby Kelly from his present life, and to give him a chance for the future. The little girls Cawmill must also be taken off the streets to school and church. Mrs. Kelly no doubt will object to what is proposed, as the child must be her principal source of income; but I think she will not persevere in resisting the pressure brought to bear on her. For the present, Kelly still sells matches, and begs at night. He affects to be deeply wounded at my conduct. "Yer gied the gals a shillin' each the other mornin' when I were asleep," says he reproachfully; and in confidence he informs me that "My mother 'll break yer head wi' a brick."

Cui bono? some may say after reading this. How can we be interested to any great extent in the history of an individual waif! Wait a little, and I will show that Kelly is but one of a class—not actively or ostensibly criminal or companions of law-breakers—not apparently neglected—following a lawful occupation in selling matches and newspapers, and so not coming under the provisions of the Industrial Schools Act. Yet these are leading a life as useless as real vagrants—a life which is training them to be dangerous members of society in the future—a life to which they are brought up by their parents. For Mrs. Kelly is not the only one who appropriates and nearly lives on her child's earnings. There are many who daily turn their little ones on the streets with the order to bring so much money home at night. I have seen on a Monday, what time "the ghost walked" at the Theatre Royal, a decent woman waiting a few yards from the box-office—a very decent woman in a clean print dress, but that she was so drunk she could hardly stand. Shortly there would come out of the office her son, a smart lad who earned twelve shillings a week in the Pantomime. The mother would seize the boy's wages and turn into the first public house for liquor. There is no law as yet which touches these cases, but in these sketches I wish to point out the urgent necessity of private or public action to rescue the youthful waifs and strays of our streets from the evil influences of their homes—homes where they are only looked upon as money-makers to help keep their parents in idleness and drunkenness.

As far as Baby Kelly is concerned, I am glad to say that there is a happy sequel to the above. Through the exertions of Father Petre he has been placed in the Roman Catholic Orphanage at Parramatta, and at the present time is so fat and plump that one would hardly know him. He devotes his time principally to eating and play, and is quite reconciled to his position. Education and training during some years will, I hope, efface from his childish mind all reminiscences of the old evil life . . .

6

Sixpenny Restaurants

... Most men have to suffer a perpetual combat between their tastes and their exchequer. This is daily brought home to them in the satisfaction of their appetites. Where one has a soul for turtle and ortolans, it is hard to descend to sausages. To feel that a palate educated to appreciate *caviare* should be condemned to boiled ling in a sixpenny restaurant—what an indignity! There you feed like the beasts of the field: it is a mere question of supporting nature. In another sphere one dines, which is a fine art not thoroughly understood by the common herd, and the grossness of feeding is relieved by the poetry of companionship and association ...

Happily, I have been accustomed to rough it in many parts of the world. I glory in a good dinner, but can eat bread and cheese with an appetite; and so one morning I felt no very great repugnance at the fact of having to make a meagre breakfast, which was forced upon me by the unsatisfactory state of my finances. The day before, I had migrated from a certain hotel where I paid ten shillings a day (very cheap, too, according to London scale) to a small apartment in the suburbs, for which I paid five shillings a week. (In London it would be double.) I had sallied down town with the intention of making a cheap breakfast, and had a shilling in my pocket devoted to that purpose. Although I had been some months in Melbourne, and was aware that the necessities of life were very cheap here, I really had no thought that a breakfast could be got for sixpence. The idea seemed ridiculous, as sixpence appeared to me, up to that time, to be the lowest coin in circulation. I avoided the main thoroughfares, and at last entered a small restaurant in one of the bye streets. "Breakfast, sir," said the Irish waitress, "chops, steaks, sausages, fried fish, dry hash"——. "Stop," I cried, aghast at this list of luxuries, "I will have a cup of tea and some bread and butter." "What else, sir? there's nice steak this morning." "How much is a steak?" I asked, bent on economy. "Sixpence, sir." "And the tea, and bread and butter?" "All sixpence." "Bring me a steak, then," I said; concluding that I had fully mortgaged my shilling. I was then supplied with a small steak, a roll, and cup of tea, which breakfast I humbly ate with a good appetite. When I had finished I rose, and putting my hand in my pocket, "How much?" I asked, grandly, and preparing to fling down my shilling as if I had hundreds at the back of it. "Sixpence for breakfast, thank you, sir;" and I left amazed at the fact of having discovered the cheapest meal in the world. The dinner was even a greater surprise to me. That I could obtain soup, meat, and pastry (no matter of what quality) for the ridiculously small sum of sixpence was a revelation of inestimable value.

After the first day I gathered courage, and have since made a tour through most of the cheap restaurants. In essentials they are all much alike. The dishes appear to be stereotyped, and the cooking is much the same in all. There are generally, and especially in the summer, more flies in the dishes than refined prejudices might fancy. The sausages in all are bags of mystery, and the enormous consumption of these is a convincing proof that faith is strong in the colonies. The stews, which are mostly served at supper time, are not equal to the *pot au feu* of the French peasant, although the ingredients are as miscellaneous. Stewed lamb is a dish often on the supper bill of fare. I wondered for a long time how this was, as lamb is seldom to be had for dinner, till at last I discovered that the multiplicity of dishes consisted chiefly in the names. "Stewed lamb," with a little curry stirred on the plate, became "curried mutton;" or, with the addition of a few slices of carrot, was "haricot mutton;" or, again, with a few boiled potatoes mashed in, was "Irish stew." Thus, a smart cook will supply a dozen dishes from one base. Rabbit pie and fish are considered extra luxuries, and are generally announced by placards in the windows. What strikes an Englishman as very strange is the fact of eggs being so dear here. These, boiled or poached, are charged 9d. Fowl or chicken is absent from the *menu* of the ordinary sixpenny restaurant; but at some they are to be had for one shilling. It seems to me that one of the best speculations untouched would be a large poultry farm in the neighbourhood of Melbourne.

Sixpenny restaurants vary a good deal in style. There are some in the principal thoroughfares which shine with plate-glass, white linen, and pretty waiter girls. But all this extra display, and the cost of the handbills, which are so freely circulated, causes perceptible diminution in the quantity or quality of the viands. The places where one really feeds best are the smaller restaurants, kept by married couples, who do

Waiting for breakfast at a sixpenny restaurant

the cooking themselves. At many of these places the proprietors often work very hard, and are not by any means making rapid fortunes. These are chiefly patronized by working men, who take their dinners there. At one o'clock you will see a tremendous rush, every seat at the little tables being occupied. If one has catholic ideas on the subject of dirty hands, it is amusing to sit down with the crowd and watch the different modes of eating. The waiters are for some twenty minutes under a pressure of orders enough to tire out the intellect of most men. The *habitués* seem to strive to get done first, and he who sits nearest the door may order his "corned beef and cabbage" a dozen times, on each occasion it being captured *en route* as "my order." The great appetites of apprentice boys are something fearful to behold, the soup, steak-pudding, and piles of cabbage and potatoes being assimilated by the consumption of half a loaf of bread. After watching the performance of half a dozen of these embryo "sons of toil," you feel certain that the proprietor of the restaurant must be bankrupt on the morrow. A few quiet individuals generally dine after the one o'clock rush is over, and the same number may be seen at supper at seven o'clock, when they will have a chat together. At the restaurant I frequented there was a strange mixture. A negro gentleman from Jamaica, a noted politician in the Yankee sense of the word, who should have emigrated to the Southern States and got into office, instead of wasting his time here, where he is not believed in. A Frenchman, from the Mauritius. Several sons of the sod of various degrees of station and intellect, but mostly banded together under Holy Church in hatred of the Sassenach. A Birmingham mechanic, the best dressed man of the lot, bright, shrewd, and a liberal and freetrader of the John Bright pattern. A stray Chinaman, who is the only epicure, as he grumbles always at the quality of his "loast beef" or "cheak and lonions." A hawker, Hibernian, who orates on every subject. A young man of considerable self-assurance, who was an officer in the Southern army during the American war, and is fond of "blowing thereon." A blind beggar, often drunk, who sits near the door. A strange mixture this, truly, but really more interesting than the guests at many a first-class *table d'hôte*. The blind beggar is a character, not over cleanly certainly, but the presence of this Lazarus at the gate does not affect our appetites. The room is a long one, and he is afar off. Barring his real or simulated blindness, he reminds me of the beggar in *Tom Burke of Ours*. He seems the sort of man to sing a seditious song and humbug a jury. On one occasion he distinguished himself greatly amongst his compatriots by offering to raise a subscription to buy Signor Ricciotti Garibaldi a rope to send to his father . . . Now and then a poor vagrant creeps quietly in, and, taking the lowest seat, enjoys a good meal. All through the day miserable-looking dogs, who, according to the Pythagorean doctrine, are transformed vagrants, steal in, and, gliding underneath the tables, pick up scraps and bones. The kind-hearted proprietor often feeds them, and if the dogs fare as well at every restaurant in Melbourne, it is no wonder we see so many ownerless curs.

Restaurant waiters are not a class. They are refugees from all classes. One or two establishments employ young girls, who certainly are efficient in enticing you to order beer, when a bar-room is an adjunct of the place; but men waiters are the rule. They are of all trades and professions—new chums and old hands. Now and then you meet with a smart youth, who knows his business. Generally he has graduated at some good hotel, and drink or misfortune has condemned him to this. The cooks at these places, too, are mostly men who have begun with making damper. I know one man, however, thoroughly educated, who has passed years of his life in Parisian society, and is heir to £15,000 a-year, who is now a cook in a restaurant. Some taverns set up as rivals to the restaurants, by giving "hot lunches, with pint of ale, from twelve to two daily, for sixpence." The lunch is chiefly a plate of corned beef and potatoes, and instead of a pint of small beer you can compromise for a glass of the best. You get, altogether, about half the amount of food you would at a sixpenny dinner. Still these lunches are very cheap, and are much affected by young clerks, who may be hard up or economical, and who often steal in the back way to these places. Others, too proud, will spend sixpence in beer at an hotel bar, nibbling as much of the "free lunch" . . . as their shame will allow them. It would be far better for them if they would put their dignity on one side, and take a dinner in a sixpenny restaurant, which, up to this time, I consider to be the most wonderful example of Victorian progress and prosperity which I have met with.

7

Pauper Funerals

... It was on one of the hot-wind days that I took cab to Carlton to await the arrival of a funeral from the Alfred Hospital. The Melbourne General Cemetery is a pleasant place enough. Flowers bloom luxuriantly, and praise-worthy efforts have been made in the cultivation of trees and shrubs. In some there will be shade therefrom, but at present all vegetation is rather dwarfed. Considering that this is the chief necropolis of this great city, it is not half large enough; and even with the present system of crowding the graves together it is rapidly filling up ... A stranger, knowing the extreme youth of this city, and that another general burial-ground formerly existed, is astonished at the number of graves. I strolled around through the different compartments reserved for the various Christian sects. Even in death, it appears, these must not mingle together. The Chinese section seems strange to a European, with the curious-shaped stoves, in which paper is burnt in certain seasons of the year in honour of the dead. The Church of England department is well kept, with a profusion of flowers and shrubs around the graves. Loving care is evidently lavished upon many of them. There are many very handsome and well-known tombs and monuments in this section which I greatly admired.

I like the Burke and Wills monument. The rough mass of granite reminds me, in its conception, of the rude cairn erected to the memory of the Confederate dead in the Cemetery at Richmond, Virginia ... Close by this, I was pained to find a human bone in the path, covered with fresh mould, having apparently dropped from some soil which was being carted away. This was taken out of some "family grave" which was being opened to receive a fresh inmate. Wreaths of immortelles and withered bouquets of flowers were on many of the tombs, instancing the constant affection of survivors. All about the place grave-diggers were at work, each protected from the scorching heat by a movable canvas-frame erected above them. On such a hot day as this, when the wind was like nothing but a blast from a fiery furnace, grave-digging must, indeed, have been hard work. I wandered around through the departments of the various sects. In many there were some old and rude tombs. Rough wooden crosses were placed above where poor Irish emigrants lay. In many cases these were broken, and the graves altogether in a disorderly condition. I think the Cemetery trustees should keep all the stones or other erections, as well as the graves, in order. Everywhere I was struck with the manner in which the graves were crowded together. As I was in search of the Potter's Field, where the poor are buried, I, after a time, made my way to the lodge, and interviewed the porter or gate-keeper, a very polite Irishman. We agreed upon the weather and general topics, and then I turned the conversation on to funerals. "That's a free burial there," said he, pointing to a shabby hearse just passing out of the gate. "He's buried in the Catholic ground on a justice's order. The priest will be here by-and-by to read the service over him." I turned the conversation on to Protestant paupers, and was told they were mostly buried in the Church of England public ground in the extreme north-eastern portion of the Cemetery. "The clergyman gets 8s. for each case, that's the Government contract, and I'd like to do it for the money," said my informant. I asked if he attended every funeral, or if the bodies were taken to the chapel. "Oh, no! You can't call them funerals, they're just burials. The clergyman waits till he gets a lot, and reads the service over them" was the reply. I turned my steps towards "LL" department, where pauper and public funerals—that is, where the friends are too poor to pay for a whole grave—take place. The poor at first appear to have been scattered, impartially, among the rich—Dives and Lazarus lying side by side—the one known by his costly monument, and the other recognized only by a number, on a little iron tablet, stuck at the head of so many graves. But now each denomination has its public ground, where paupers and poor people lie heaped up—three or four adults in a single grave. There is no rule as to children and infants; they stow as many as it will hold into a grave.

I found LL section to be rather wild and rough—far different in outward appearance to the elegant reserve at the other end of the Cemetery. Hundreds of bodies are here packed in side by side, with only a foot between each grave. For the sake of economy, only every other fourth grave bears a number, and as there are three adults and many infants in each, it must be rather hard work to find out the exact resting-place of anyone. There are small tombstones erected over some, others have the names painted on the tablets, and floral offerings are plentiful. But the grave-digger there said, "I call all that foolery.

King Fever and his victims

PAUPER FUNERALS

What's the use of sticking up a monyment over three? You don't know which is the one you're after. That sort of thing ain't any use, unless you have a grave to yourself comfortable." I merely record his opinion. Hamlet-like, I entered into conversation with this man, but did not get much out of him. "The ground was blessed hard, stiff clay, and marl, and stone. It 'ud sometimes take a man all day to dig 2ft. But they never thought a man had done enough. There had been no funerals that day, but yesterday afternoon there was one. The clergyman would most likely come to-day." That was all I got out of him. Part of the old graves in this section is overgrown with moss and shrubs, and is in a very neglected condition. Many have no numbers at all; some have rude attempts at names stuck at the heads, but the majority are evidently occupied by unknown and forgotten dead. Many loving hearts across the seas are perchance praying and waiting for the return of some who lie here in a pauper's grave. *Requiescat!* I waited for the funeral, which was to have been at the Cemetery at noon; but, as the gate-keeper said, "Hancox is never punctual." As the grave-digger went on with his work he threw up two heaps of dirt, one to fill up the grave, and the other to form a mound over the grave lying parallel. According to the Act of Parliament, there must be a space of three feet from the last coffin to the original surface of the ground; and if this is fully carried out, there can only be a mere layer of soil between the three coffins put in a seven-foot grave! I suppose all this has been well considered in its day; but I cannot think it is a wise sanitary measure to crowd corpses together so near a city. There was a decidedly charnel-house smell in this quarter, which might have proceeded from the two unfilled graves, covered with wooden lids, which waited for further tenants.

Almost prostrated with the heat, I waited here amongst the dead, until at last the sound of slow wheels was heard on the gravel path. The undertaker of the Alfred Hospital is himself like the figure of Death, and his appearance, driving a hearse, is horribly grotesque. On the box with him were a man and a boy, the husband and son of the deceased woman. They drove quietly up to the side of the grave, and, dismounting, the undertaker hailed the grave-digger, and with his assistance lowered the coffin into its tenant's last resting-place. The mourners stolidly took a last look, a dozen shovels full of soil were thrown over it, and the thing was done. It was the most calm business arrangement possible. The hearse drove off, and I returned to my seat to wait for the clergyman. Broiling in the sun, I remained for more than an hour, and then I gave him up for that day and returned to the lodge. Here I found a number of cars, several private funerals having taken place in other parts of the grounds. A priest was coming towards the lodge, whom my gate-keeper friend pointed out as having been reading the service over the man buried that morning. I leave it to the Archbishop of Melbourne as to whether the directions of the Roman Catholic Church are carried out by thus performing offices three or four hours after the body was interred. My friend, too, thinking perhaps he had been too confiding in the morning, said, "The Protestant clergyman will be here at three o'clock to read over the bodies buried in the Church of England ground." I was too fatigued to stay any longer, but determined to make further visits and see how the service was performed. As I left the Cemetery, I met a man with a little coffin under his arm, covered with a napkin; it was his child's, which he had thus brought in a cab for economy's sake. A strange sight and a sad one.

On the following Tuesday I was at the Cemetery at two o'clock in the afternoon, and again made my way to the "public ground" of the Church of England. A fresh row of graves had been begun, and the grave-digger was only two ahead, and was evidently working hard, so as not to be caught up. This was a different man to the one I had seen before. Aged, but hale, with a clear Saxon face and eye, and speech as of one born of the south of the Thames. I found that he was a Hampshire man. He was merry and cheerful; not unfeeling, but custom had made his business "a property of easiness." We held improving converse together, which I worked round to the subject of funerals and the mode of performing the burial service. "There'd be no funeral to-day," he said, "but were some yesterday. The clergyman would most likely be round soon. I allays get him to read over all on 'em." "Did the clergyman come every day?" I asked. "Well, no—I can't say that he does every day; but I make him read over all when he does come."

I waited an hour, dozing away the time on a seat hard by. It was after three when a mourning coach came down the path. Rising, I went towards the graves. "This ain't a hospital case, it's a private funeral; that's one of Daley's cars," said the digger. A meek and careworn-looking woman stepped out of the coach; after her, a little child. They were clad in old rustic black garments, apparently bought from a pawn or second-hand shop. They seemed as poor as could be, yet this was no pauper's funeral, for the undertaker and Cemetery trustees had been paid. From the coach the driver produced a little coffin, and carried it towards the two open graves. The grave-digger jumped into one, and the coffin being handed to him, he stowed it away in a corner, and just covered it with a layer of soil. Standing above, the mother wept and sobbed, and the child looked down vaguely and curiously. With raised hat, "The Vagabond" completed the group.

"Will the clergyman come?" asked the woman. "Oh! yes, he'll be here to-morrow," said the grave-digger. "What is it? A boy! All right, I'll see that he reads over it." "Thank you," said the woman, "I hope he will." Then, with one yearning glance backwards, she and the child entered the coach and drove away. I have seen and handled hundreds of bodies. Military funerals and public obsequies, with all the pomp of Church and State, are familiar to me. Death, in many forms, is an old friend of mine, so I do not affect any sentiment on these subjects. But this poor woman's case touched me. The hard business-way in which everything was done. The mother's hope that her child would "be read over;" her only surety for such being the goodwill of the grave-digger. The little coffin stowed away in a corner to await the arrival of other tenants. The sense that in death, as in life, the poor have not a square show for salvation—this affected me almost to the melting mood. Then, as is my custom, I got wrath. I myself care for none of these things. I know that no priest's paid prayers can influence my present or hereafter. We, who "try, prove, reject, prefer—still struggle to effect our warfare," stand and fall by ourselves. But thousands of good Christians, of all sects, do believe in burial services for the dead; the survivors find it a consolation in their grief, and even sceptics can scarcely hear unmoved the beautiful rites of the Church of England. This poor mother would, I believe, have had her grief half-healed if she had heard the prayers of the Church read over the little one. It is a scandalous outrage that the clergyman appointed, and who receives a fee for each case (paltry enough, no doubt), should not attend and perform the services over each. In "praying over a lot," he distinctly violates the ordered rites of burial as laid down in the Prayer Book . . . The present officiator at the Cemetery evades and burlesques the rites of his Church by praying, not only over many at a time, but long after they are interred. This might be so easily avoided by having all pauper and public funerals at a certain hour, when the clergyman might attend, and in a short time get through all his cases, and earn several 8s. without putting himself to much inconvenience. The Cemetery trustees should see to this, and, if they are incompetent or unwilling, I recommend to the Church authorities that they investigate this frightful burlesque on the most solemn rite of the Church of England. It's a good thing that I did not see the clergyman on Tuesday, or I might have said something to him. I felt like it; but after waiting till four o'clock I left, determined to return again on the morrow and see if any service would be read then.

I paid my third visit to the Cemetery on the next day at two o'clock. As I neared the old spot, I saw, coming down the opposite path, two women, dressed in black, accompanied by two boys, carrying a tiny coffin. My friend, the grave-digger, was on the look-out, and directed the little procession to the grave in which I had seen the other child buried the day before. The women were evidently mother and daughter, and both manifested great grief. Scraping away some soil, the coffin was deposited side by side with several others. The digger captured a harmless lizard in the grave, and threw it out. The boys immediately chased and destroyed it before I could stop them. "Is that your little brother?" I asked, intending to give them a homily on the love of life, and the sin of destroying anything harmless. "No, it's my sister's —her by the grave," was the reply. No wedding-ring was on her finger, but her young face was quiet and modest, and I believe she mourned as truly as if her offspring was the result of a priest-blessed union. "I thought the minister would be here," said the mother. "Oh, he'll come by-and-by, and I'll get him to read the service all right; don't you be afraid of that," said the grave-digger, cheerfully. He had not finished his job before a covered waggon drove up, and a man lifted out a common wooden coffin, "blacked all over," which he informed us contained the body of the child murdered at Emerald Hill. This was wedged in by the side of the other. Directly after this a coach drove up, there being this day quite a rush of business. Another small coffin was lifted out, with father, mother, and other mourners accompanying. These people wanted "the minister." They had been told he would be there. Acting on the advice of the grave-digger, the undertaker drove back to the lodge to fetch him, as he was told, "Else you won't get him for an hour or two, and perhaps not to-day." The coffin was placed by the side of the grave, and the mourners sat waiting under a neighbouring tree. I talked to the grave-digger as he went on with his work. After a time the coach was driven rapidly down the path, and the clergyman alighted. He was a very old and infirm man. Walking towards the grave he immediately proceeded to business, the mourners standing around, and the grave-digger, bare-headed, acting as clerk. The service was commenced with the text, "Man that is born of a woman," &c., and was hurried through, being recited in a maudlin voice, most painful to hear. In a side whisper the officiator asked, "Are there any more in?" And was told, "Some boys and girls." Then he prayed for "our dear brothers and sisters," lumping, at least, half-a-dozen together. In the next grave was the body of a man which had lain there since Monday, but the clergyman did not perform any service over that, leaving it, as the grave-digger told me, "until it got full." The service was soon over, and the clergyman pocketed his 4s.— half-price for children—from the undertaker, and questioned the grave-digger as to the other interments, that he might look after his fees from the Government. It was altogether a great farce, and, as one of the men who came with the last funeral said, "I never saw anything like it in any part of the world; it's disgraceful." It is either decent or Christian-like to perform the services of the Church over "our dear brothers and sisters here departed," or it is not. If it is of any avail, the poor should have a chance as well as the rich; at present it is a mere fluke whether a pauper is prayed over, and if so, it is with others he receives that benefit, and in a manner entirely opposed to the ritual of the Church, and disgusting to decent-minded people who, like myself, care little for religious observances.

From a correspondence which took place after the first publication of this article, I find that no provision is made for any religious service being performed over the bodies of those unfortunates who die in our hospitals and benevolent asylums. They are carted away and buried like dogs, perchance receiving the benefit of being prayed over with many others as "our dear brothers and sisters here departed." This is worse than in England. There the poor man who has toiled all his life, and found in age a refuge in the workhouse, being dead, at least has Christian burial . . .

PART TWO

Life in Prison

8

Six Hours in a Dark Cell

... When we visited Brisbane Gaol and saw the dark cells, I expressed a wish to Mr. Barron* to pass some hours in one. "Certainly," said he; "I don't suppose the sheriff will object. You shall do it when you like." In pursuance of this arrangement, I received the following letter:—

"*29th November*, 1877.

"My dear Vagabond,

"'Lodgings to let.' Report yourself before noon, to-morrow, at the gaol, and you will find the apartment vacant. No indulgences nor stimulants allowed. Strictest good templarism enforced.

"Yours sincerely,
"T. H. BARRON."

I meant to do the thing thoroughly, without any indulgences or support from stimulants; but I was pleased to find that Mr. Barron entered into the spirit of the joke (?), and meant to have me treated in every respect like an ordinary prisoner. I think that, as regards physical and mental condition, the ordinary prisoner would be ahead of me. Neither in mind nor body am I at the present time at all "fit." The uneasiness and *insomnia* with which I have been suffering during the last months has rendered the slightest mental exertion painful and arduous. So I felt my pulse when I awoke in the morning, and concluded that I must eat a good breakfast and drink a couple of glasses of claret to bring myself into form, and give my experiment a fair show. Then I smoked a cigar, with a cup of black coffee, before taking cab for the gaol, where I arrived shortly before twelve. Mr. Bernard, the governor, met me, and I went into his office for a few minutes, and examined the books with the record of punishments. Twenty-four hours in the dark cell seems the ordinary punishment, although three

---

*T. H. Barron, assistant commissioner of police.

days is often given, and sometimes more. When a prisoner has a sentence of more than twenty-four hours, he is let out every day for an hour's exercise, and is—or should be—daily visited by the doctor. At Pentridge, a prisoner in the dark cell has no such privilege, but has to serve his time straight out. When I first visited Brisbane Gaol, Mr. Barron ordered the release of a man who had been in the cell since the previous day. I examined him curiously. He looked white and cowed—"penitent," Mr. Barron called it. At St. Helena we found a man in one of the dark cells there—which, however, are not quite dark, the perforated ventilators over the doors admitting rays of light. He roared lustily, "Oh, Mr. Barron! For the love of God let me out, and I'll never do it again," and on his promising to obey orders in future he was released. These were the only two cases I had met with; as, at Pentridge, under the far too lenient discipline, the dark cell is, or at least was, seldom used as a means of punishment.

Well, I was now going to test this myself, and as we walked across one of the prison yards sacred to the senseless punishment of "shot drill," I began to think that I was a very bad subject for such an experiment. I was not nervous, but I felt that my highly excitable brain might lead me into phantasies . . . I daresay the warders were rather astonished when I descended the twelve steps leading into the sunken building containing the two punishment cells. Both of these were entirely empty, save boards on stretchers which at night the prisoners lie on. I was not, however, allowed this indulgence; and the bell having been pointed out to me, and a can of water placed on the floor, the door was shut, and I found myself in for "six hours' solitary" in a dark cell 9 feet by 5 feet and 10 feet high, with massive stone walls, and cemented floor—ventilated at the top, certainly, but still very close and stifling on this hottest day of the present season.

Only 9 feet by 5 feet! There appeared to be a thousand miles of darkness around me. Or was it a solid substance? Involuntarily I placed my hands as if to save my face, and walked slowly and hesitatingly the length of my cell. Only 9 feet, certainly, and yet they seemed miles. In that darkness, which could be almost felt, there was a sense of chaos, of void, of infinity. I walked back to the corner opposite the door, and, taking off my coat and collar, sat down on the floor. The stones were cold and rather damp. I began to feel a sense of oppression on the eyeballs, which lasted for a time. Then I began to count, but that is a foolish game, at which I always get confused. Then I set to work and composed two plays, three novels, and four new series of *The Vagabond Papers*. My brain got rather tired and stupified. Then I thought it must be three o'clock. Now, I was transgressing the rules to the extent that I had my watch and some matches with me; but I took these that I might mark the effect of time. I now struck one. I had only been in *three-quarters of an hour*. This was discouraging. "I will not strike another match," I said; "but, come what will, what may, will do this thing properly, and endure like a criminal." Then a great and nameless horror came over me. There, in front of me, in the million miles of darkness, there was dreadful *something*. But an effort of the will dispelled it. Then fancy evolved two figures. One gay and sprightly, and beautiful as a Grecian goddess. "I am Fiction," she said. The other calm, sedate, grand, powerful, like an image in ruins at Thebes or Memphis. "I am Fact," she said. I laughed, and clasped her to my arms. "Come, let me reason," said I. Perhaps no man ever had such a chance of easily distinguishing himself as was now presented to me. Here I was, investigating a vexed problem. No one could deny that I passed these hours in the cell. I might write what I liked—pile a Pelion on Ossa of fiction; philanthropists and reformers would be on my side, popular feeling would be aroused, and I should be renowned as a martyr. And I could truthfully have done this. I believe I *could* have called up images of horror equalling those evolved by Mr. Charles Reade. I *could* have peopled that vast blackness before me with creatures of my imagination—fearful as those of Edgar A. Poe. I *could* have worked myself into an ecstasy of nervous delirium. Hell should not be more horrible than this dungeon, as I *could* make it. I thought of this, and laughed at how I was about to disappoint those friends who are perpetually styling me a sensational writer. In these lines fancy is put on one side, and there is nothing but real stern fact. What would a prisoner do first? I thought. Walk about, sit down, and then ——. Why, then investigate every corner, and see if he could find something to amuse himself. So, on hands and knees, greatly to the detriment of my garments, I crawled around the cell. Some dust, a very minute pebble—this is all I found, till I suddenly touched something cold.

For a moment I did feel nervous. Was it a snake? I had withdrawn my hand quickly but otherwise did not stir. An old nigger, who taught me woodcraft, said, "Nebber you git back, massa, whateber you may come on, if it's a bar, or a deer, or a rattler, or a skunk. You keep quite still always, and you won't skeer the crittur, and it won't skeer you." This was very good advice, which I always remember. So, quietly on my hands and knees I maintained for a few minutes a state of masterly inactivity. I had matches in my coat, in the corner, certainly, but I wasn't going to "git back." I listened—no sound. His snakeship asleep, perhaps. But could it be a snake? It was a cold, smooth, damp body I had touched. This was interesting; if not poisonous, a snake would be good company. I don't know what impelled me, but suddenly I darted out my hand again, and caught the thing. Then I had a hearty laugh.

It was the can of water, which I had forgotten all about. I did not have a drink, as I wished to make things as rough as possible for myself. I crawled back to my corner, which seemed like a home now. Then I investigated the walls, feeling everything cautiously and carefully. Something ran over my hands, but I was not to be "skeered" again. It must have been a spider, though where he got flies from in this dungeon I don't know.

The smooth cemented surface of the walls and floor presented no object of interest . . . I sat down in the corner again and began to sing. I yelled out every rebel song I knew, from "The Bonny Blue Flag" to "The Shan Van Voght." This was rather jolly. A prisoner in the dark cell can kick up as much row as he likes. No one can hear him. After a time I got tired of hearing my own voice echoing back to me from every corner of my cell. Then I thought again. I don't believe in prayer, or in "unseen lights," or "unseen hands," but out of one's own brain you can coin much. I thought of the murderers and villains who had occupied this cell. Crime seemed to taint the very atmosphere. Perhaps in this very spot where I lay the coward murderer may have reposed. There seemed a smell of blood in the air. Horrible suggestions and possibilities came into my mind. Again I conquered this, although I had a dull heavy pain in my head; and for a time I placed my hands over my eyes to keep out the darkness.

When I removed them I had a strange optical delusion. Far away over me in the deep darkness—thousands and thousands of miles it seemed—there was a beautiful luminous ball, of a pale yellow colour. It seemed to slowly descend. It appeared to take hours in coming down, and reminded me of the angels in Gustave Doré's picture, which are hovering over the bodies of the Christian martyrs in the Coliseum. This light was very beautiful, but, strange to say, did not get larger, although at last it seemed close to me. Now, religious or superstitious people might say this was an angel or devil; the spiritualist that it was a manifestation; but I, with ordinary scientific knowledge, knew that it was a mere delusion. "When I close my eyes again it will go," I said. I did so, and it *was* gone. I examined the circumstance. Say my name was Tom Robinson. I had been "cheeky" to the governor, and had "twenty-four hours' solitary." Some time had gone already. At six o'clock I should have my bread and water, and the board would be brought for me to sleep on. I think I could sleep for twelve hours. Then I should have an hour's exercise, and after finishing my time I should be sent to my own cell once more. Tom Robinson, this is rough on you, but not so degrading as being thrashed. My man, if you have any good in you, you can meditate now on your future, and make up your mind to mend. This is hard punishment, no doubt; but it will teach

The 'silent system' at Pentridge Gaol

you sense, and that there is no use in kicking against the pricks. Then I sang two or three more songs, and paced the cell a hundred times.

I became in time quite used to it. My pulse was steadier, I recovered my nerve, and my only sensation was that it was beastly uncomfortable to sit on a cold floor, with possibilities of rheumatism in the future. Afterwards I began to get hungry, then sleepy. I knew that night was approaching, through hearing the merry hum of a mosquito thirsting for my blood. My senses became acute, and I could just detect the distant rumbling of the trains, and occasionally a faint noise in the prison yard overhead. But during the last hour of my confinement, I say truthfully that my feelings were merely those of ordinary discomfort. I believe I could have stood eighteen more hours with far greater ease than the first five.

At last the key rattled in the lock above, then steps descended, and my cell door was unbarred. The light only dazzled my eyes for one moment. Then I walked out, and said to Mr. Bernard, "Feel my pulse." "Pretty fair," he said. "How do I look?" I asked. "You are a little pale." How did I feel? Simply hungry! Yes, after six hours in this dungeon, which according to humanitarians and novel writers should tend to produce madness, I only felt as if I wanted my dinner.

Now, as before pointed out, one man's sensations can never be a true criterion of another's. It may be right that this experiment of mine was no fair trial of the extent of the punishment to a criminal. It may be said that the uneducated, ignorant dullard will suffer a thousand times more than a man of intelligence. It may be so. I know that solitude tends to insanity, and that the records of lunacy show that ignorance produces more madmen than mental activity. Yet the man of excitable brain, of powerful imagination, will, I imagine, under many conditions, suffer as much as the fool . . .

I unhesitatingly declare that what has been written on this subject is mostly sheer nonsense. The punishment, although severe, as it is meant to be, is not calculated to produce madness; and as a punishment is far better and more efficacious than flogging. With the due precautions of a daily exercise and examination by a surgeon, there is little fear of a man's body or mind giving way. I should have little compunction in sentencing an offending prisoner to three days in the dark cell, being pretty sure that, after the first six hours, his hardest time would have passed. I am henceforth an advocate of punishment by solitary confinement in a dark cell, as well as of the separate and silent system of prison discipline. I have tried both, and know what it is. The only man who has voluntarily undergone such experiences, I give my views as being worth something, even although they only embody the ideas of one individual.

But I certainly enjoyed the glass of beer which Mr. Bernard hospitably gave me; the taste of a cigar was recovered Elysium; and, as my cab drove me to a well-earned dinner, the sky appeared brighter, the air purer, the grass greener, and the children in the streets more beautiful than ever before. All Nature and Humanity seemed smiling and happy. It was recovered Liberty which thus made everything *couleur de rose* after six hours spent in a dark cell.

9

A Month in Pentridge

I have been spending four weeks in Pentridge prison. A short sentence, most people will say, and entirely too mild a one for my deserts . . .

Having rashly admitted a knowledge of medicine, I was recommended to the Chief Secretary as a fit and proper person to fill the vacant post of dispenser at Pentridge Prison Hospital, and, the pipes being laid, I made a formal application for the place . . . Behold me, then, a vagabond no longer, but an embryo civil servant, serving the country for the magnificent salary of 6s. 6d. a day, with quarters, 1s. per diem being deducted for such . . .

For the first few days I found I had quite enough to do in mastering the details, and faithfully fulfilling the duties of my new position. At half-past five o'clock every morning the night sentry would call me, and, jumping up, I ran down stairs to the bath, the one luxury and comfort which I enjoyed whilst at Pentridge. Refreshed, I dressed myself, and at five minutes to six was ready to be let out, for not until that time was the outer door of the hospital unlocked. Then I would proceed to the gates, secure my keys, and parade at the head of the warders. Mr. Begg inspected us every morning. Always clean-shaved, with whiskers neatly curled, and general spotless attire, he was a perpetual example and a standing reproach to some of our number. Casting his eye down the line, he would pick out those with unblacked boots, and rate some unhappy warder for having on light trousers and shoes, both being "contrary to the regulations." I fell under his displeasure through my vagabond habit of coming out without collar or necktie. Having done his duty in this way, he would give the orders, "Number off!" "Twos outwards!" "Quick march!" and to the different divisions we would file off, and my irksome task of unlocking would begin. The average number of prisoners sleeping in the hospital during my stay was about thirty-four. Of these twelve were invalids, epileptics, &c.,

who, although working in the gangs, required a little more indulgence than others, and "billets" whose posts entitled them to be there. These slept in the invalid wards downstairs. Up stairs there would be some twenty-two patients in all stages of sickness, from the youth dying of consumption to the strong man temporarily lamed by an accident. Every day the patients would be changed, and, consequently, during my month of office, I had under my charge some of the most notorious criminals in Victoria . . .

My man P—— is a good representative of his county. A more faithful man in the discharge of his duties, or one more civil and obliging, I have seldom met. He acted as my "batman," and no paid free servant could have looked after my wants better . . . His little weakness is land dummying, and perjury and forgery thereanent. He certainly does not belong to the criminal class, and is a man personally I would trust. A strict Wesleyan, he is apparently a devout follower, which is the only thing suspicious about the man . . . The surgery and hall porter was a well-known character in Melbourne. A clerk in the Lands Office at a salary of £300 a year, he lived at the rate of thousands. There appears to have been absolutely no check upon him, and he took what he wanted. The lowest computation of his defalcations is £20,000. He loved horses and dogs, and freely indulged his tastes . . .

In No. 1 ward upstairs, a prisoner named Brown had the billet as wardsman. He was a remarkably unprepossessing-looking man, and the offence for which he was convicted influenced me against him. Still he did his duty thoroughly, and he was an instance of the care and judgment with which Dr. Reed selected the hospital servants. In the other ward, the "billet" was a splendid little fellow, an Irish Cockney named Sullivan, who was a source of continual amusement to me. He was good-looking, bright, and active; the man to sing a good song, do a step dance, and make love to a girl . . . Sullivan was a London "prig," who began life at home in a reformatory, afterwards graduating at Wandsworth, Brixton, Coldbath Fields, and other metropolitan prisons. He is a philosopher. "What does a man get working at home?" said he, "hardly a bellyful. In London I always had three good meals a-day, and never without a steak or ham and eggs for breakfast. D'ye think I could have got that if I had been on the square? Certainly, I was good in my line. Here it's quite different. Unless you take to the bush, which is played out now, you have to go into general business. You must be a bit of a magsman, a pincher, a picker-up, a flatcatcher, a bester. Unless you are very good, and have rare chances, you cannot devote yourself specially to one line. At home, now, it's opposite—a good magsman wouldn't sneak, or be seen with a sneaker." "Do you think this pays you now? Wouldn't it be better to go on the square?

The working man here can get three good meals a day, and steak for breakfast," said I; "I think if I was you I'd try it for a time." "Well, I did," said Sullivan; "I was doing well up the country, and I came to Melbourne to knock down a cheque. Well, I was a fool, and got picked up myself. It served me right. I ought to have known better. I hadn't got a sixpence left, and had to go on the cross again. After a bit I got a place in the country to go to, but the night before I went to a house, and there was a woman and a bloke there picking up a flat. The bloke got him out and gave it him, but instead of round his throat, he gave it him in his mouth, and the man bit his hand and cried out. The bobbies came, and the end of it was I got five years, although I wasn't in that plant at all." This graphic description of a garotting was very amusing . . .

Some may wonder at this familiar conversation between the dispenser and a prisoner, but it is an ordinary thing. The warders are all on familiar terms with favoured "billets." It takes very little to set a man's tongue going as to his former life, and the warders draw them out to relieve the monotony of their duties. Many tell great lies, no doubt; but there is always a substratum of truth. In this respect the rule prohibiting "familiar intercourse with any prisoner" is constantly broken . . .

I have now described all my "billets" with the exception of the nurse engaged on a special case. This man, Jos. Clarke, is a well-known character. Born in Leeds, he early took to crime, and was transported in 1847 for housebreaking. From Norfolk Island to Pentridge, he has had a varied experience of the penal establishments of Australia. With three others, he, so he says, escaped from Norfolk Island in an open boat, and landed in Portland Bay. Afterwards, he lived "on the square" for three years; but, meeting with old comrades, he was again led astray. In his own words, he appears to be a "natural-born thief," and, although he has often made spasmodic attempts at honesty—having kept a barber's shop, and been successful in that line of business—he soon relapses into crime. But he says now, that the thing is about played out. It isn't much punishment being at Pentridge, but Jos. doesn't want to die in gaol. When he has done his time, he intends going to California. He has an honest, good-humoured-looking face, which prepossesses one in his favour. He is a kind-hearted man, especially fond of animals, and makes an excellent nurse to his charge, convict No. 2,643, Harry Power, the renowned bushranger. It was worth while spending a month in Pentridge to make the acquaintance of this man, the last and the best of the class of criminals who made themselves feared throughout the land, but who would have been cleared out much sooner if Judge Lynch's court had been opened here.

Lying in bed, sick unto death, his life daily ebbing away, one can hardly recognize that this slight, weak, grey, mean-looking man, is the desperado who laid the whole colony under contribution . . . As fearless and daring a rider as ever lived, and one of the best bushmen in Australia, he, for years, defied the police of the colony, and would calmly ride down a public road whilst the troopers were scouring the bush. He has appeared in Geelong, and won bets that he dare not show his face there. After he broke out of Pentridge, he, one night, rode into Melbourne, and, returning, camped out in the paddock opposite the Stockade. Compared to such a dare-devil as Harry Power, Dick Turpin, of glorious memory, was a mean-spirited fraud . . . Power is now an old man, dying gradually. He is afflicted with an incurable complaint, which necessitates many painful operations, which have to be performed under chloroform. Every care and attention is shown to him in the hospital, and I calculate that he is costing the Government about £200 a year . . .

A sometime brilliant journalist was also under my nightly charge. His case is far different to that of any other man in Pentridge, and the particulars of it must be still vividly remembered by many. I will not recall the sad tale. Condemned to imprisonment for life, —— has for years led a living death. To such a man, of a lively, sanguine, impassioned nature, whose pulse beat time to the march of humanity throughout the world, who was cosmopolitan in his love for universal liberty, restraint and confinement are worse than death. But I am proud, for the honour of my present calling, to say that —— bears his sufferings like a man and a gentleman. There is nothing mean or paltry in his soul. Accepting the situation, he faces the music, and makes no complaints. To see ——, old, grey, and nearly blind, eating his frugal meal, and saying that it is good, and that there is nothing to grumble at, is a sight to command admiration. He won my respect for his manliness in bearing his lot . . . He works in the "lifers' " yard, beating cocoanut-husk to make the coir for matting, and, scorning to complain of menial employment, he says that the work is easy. But —— is not a criminal in the true sense of the word, and the forced company of the number of hardened wretches who make up the gang of "lifers" must be, to him, a punishment worse than death . . .

At various times in the hospital, or whilst in attendance on out-patients, I was brought in contact with some of the most notorious criminals in Victoria. And, in every case, the conclusion was forced upon me that the prevailing system of sentences is unjust, and not by any means equal. In No. 1 ward I had a young chemist dying of consumption, painfully coughing away his existence. It is true that everything which medical care can do is at his disposal—that he,

Gaol sentences for rich and poor
(a) Twelve months for prigging a shirt

A member of the 'Bankers' Club' at Pentridge
(b) Twelve months for prigging £16,000

like Power, receives a liberal supply of medical comforts, and is also allowed to purchase fruit with the small sums of money sent him by his friends. To obtain fresh fruit for —— I often had to scamper over Coburg. But his punishment is torture compared with that endured by others receiving the same sentence for the same offence. He dabbled in that overstocked branch of colonial industry—forgery—cleverly copying the signatures of medical men from the prescriptions he made up. Like Power, I reckon that he costs the Government £200 a year, and as regards the care and attention he receives, he may be said to be well off; but the sense of disgrace and confinement is aiding to kill him, as he feels that much more than the bushranger.

Forgers and bank defaulters meet one everywhere in the Stockade. There is what is facetiously called the Pentridge Bank Corporation, which comprises managers, accountants, cashiers, and clerks from all parts of the colony. There is the bank manager from Beechworth, who, for years, was a popular man in his district, and was considered as a general benefactor. But his benevolence cost the bank over £20,000, as he lent money on his own account, and on bad security. I am told that there are hundreds who owe a successful position in society to ——'s helping hand. He was several times in the hospital, and I could see that he was eating away his heart daily. His accomplice, the accountant of the bank, on the other hand, takes things easily. He has a billet in the office, and is a veritable Mark Tapley, looking as fat, and jolly, and good-natured as if the possessor of freedom and fortune. Now, the punishment of these two men, whose offence was the same, is certainly not equal. There is a well-known Melbourne bank clerk, once a shining light of the sect to which he belongs. He was a class-leader and local preacher, and was on the point of receiving a "call" to the church when his defalcations were discovered. In Pentridge he acts as assistant to the storekeeper, and tries to be too good. His tarnished light still shines amongst the faithful of his sect, and in choir, Bible-class, and prayer meeting, he holds forth as of yore. I sum him up as a hypocrite and scamp. Most of the members of the Bank corporation have easy billets in the office. The latest importation from Melbourne has been sent to the gaol to fill a billet there. The "bankers" generally act as henchmen to the schoolmaster and clergymen, and, with the exception of the disgrace which they must feel attaches to their position, their lot is not hard. Certainly, it cannot be said they have any "hard labour." Talking to these men, I found that the majority date their downfall to gambling in mining stocks. The haste to get rich has been their ruin. I think gambling in stocks quite as immoral as gambling in horse-racing, and in Victoria I believe more people are ruined by the former . . .

For mixing freely as the patients do there, the incipient criminal gets depraved by contact and conversation with the hardened sinners who have graduated at Norfolk Island. Nor is that the worst; at Pentridge there still remains a vestige of those offences which, in these columns, I scarcely dare hint at, but which Mr. Marcus Clarke boldly alludes to in *His Natural Life*. The discovery of this, and of a horrible "ring," was most revolting to me, and I can never sufficiently express my detestation of the damnable system which allows comparatively innocent youths to be mixed up with wretches perpetually sinning against God and man. The offences for which many prisoners are committed are those which should make them a class by themselves, never under any pretence being allowed to mingle with the rest. Yet many such repulsive brutes I had at various times in the hospital, some "lifers," others with shorter terms of sentences . . .

In my daily visits to the A Division I had, as dispenser, ample opportunity of studying the workings of the solitary system as carried out at Pentridge. All prisoners serve a probationary term here, varying from three to six months, according to the length of sentence or conduct; a term which may be extended to nine months for misbehaviour, but is never to exceed that period . . . Taken to his cell, the prisoner is generally left to his own reflections for a day, when the overseer of labour for this division will visit him. The industries carried on here are limited, being confined to picking wool for the "factory," or plaiting the materials for cabbage-tree hats, for the manufacture of which Pentridge was once renowned, and a large business done therein. But fashion has changed, and only a few bushmen or curious travellers will now purchase these expensive and elegant articles of headgear. In the A Division, however, they make all the coarse straw hats worn by the prisoners. There are generally a few workers in bone and ivory, who make paper-knives, crosses, trick match-boxes, and rings, for sale to visitors who are fond of hoarding up *souvenirs* of Pentridge . . .

The cells are not uncomfortable, and are furnished with every convenience. The sleeping arrangements, however, are primitive and quite colonial, savouring of bush life. There are no hammocks nor bedsteads allowed here, as in every other prison I have seen of this class. A cocoa-nut mat, a rug, and three blankets are rolled up in a corner during the day, and at night the prisoner makes his bed of these on the bare floor. The ventilation of the cells is as good as it can be with an iron-lined door always closed. But air is admitted through the ground glass window. As may be imagined, however, in the summer months, these cells are very stifling, and the atmosphere foul and close, choking one with a horrible taste. Besides the polished copper basin and water and gas pipes, the cells have no ornament, with the exception of the framed copies of the rules and regulations hung on the walls, from which the prisoner learns the offences—numerous and comprehensive—for which he may be punished. His duties are to rise in the morning when the first bell is rung, make up his bedding, clean the fixings, and be ready for his breakfast of hominy and brown bread. At seven o'clock he must commence work, and go on plaiting or carding wool until half-past eleven, when he has a rest of two hours and a dinner of meat and potatoes. At five o'clock he has finished work for the day. At a quarter to six there is evening inspection of the cells and muster. At six o'clock the prison is locked up, with only an armed sentry inside; and, until eight, inmates of the cells can read, or eat their suppers of bread and water, and go to rest. When the silence-bell rings at eight they must all retire for the night, but can do so at any time after evening muster. This monotonous life is broken by the day's hourly exercise in the yard, in many cases prolonged by order of the medical officer to two hours. The work done is light, almost child's play. Books are allowed—one being a Bible, the Douay or James the First's, according to creed. Another is a religious work of some sort—*Prayer Book* or *Garden of the Soul*. The third is often an interesting book of travels . . . a prisoner in the A Division can scarcely be said to be "solitary." If he has any complaint to make he can ask to see the Inspector-General or visiting justice. If he should be really ill, Dr. Reed will wait on him at any hour of the day or night, and he will be admitted to the hospital.

Certainly he has not much opportunity of breathing the fresh air of heaven, one hour being a small slice out of the twenty-four . . . When about to exercise, the traps in the cell doors are opened by a warder, and a little brass ticket, corresponding with the number of the cell, placed thereon. The prisoner has to take off his slippers, which he always wears in the cell, and put on boots. Then he disguises himself by getting inside a linen hood, and when the door is opened he walks along the corridor, a sombre object, unrecognizable except by the number on his clothes. At the door he gives the brass ticket to the warder, who places them on a hook, as an easy reference as to who has been exercised on that day. Filing into the yard, through the first division and into the tower, where a warder is on guard, each prisoner finds in his allotted portion a straw hat, hanging under the little wooden shed, which he is allowed to wear until the time is up, when he must again resume his hood. On all occasions of leaving his cell this hood has to be worn. But, even with all these annoyances, I, judging by my own feelings, am sure that the hour's exercise must to the prisoner be the brightest portion of the day. Saturdays and Sundays must be the most wearisome. Work being suspended at noon on Saturday for a day and a half the prisoner has nothing to do but read, and receive perhaps a short visit from the chaplain of his church . . .

As regards the effect of this system on the health of prisoners, a great deal has been said *pro* and *con*. It is certain that long seclusion may tend to break down both body and mind. It all depends on the subject. But for the three and six months that prisoners are confined in the "model" at Pentridge there is no perceptible increase in the ratio of disease. Dr. Reed, I believe, holds that separate confinement tends to develop consumptive tendencies, and it may be so . . .

All old hands are anxious to get through their "model" time, and be transferred to B or C Divisions, not only because they are on the road to the luxuries of tea and tobacco, but because of the association at work, and the means of communication with their old pals. Pentridge will at present accommodate about 650 prisoners—136 in A Division, 176 in B, 296 in C, and 42 in the hospital. Taking one day's muster roll whilst I was there at 435, there were in A 40, in B 150, in C 210, and in the hospital 35. So, transferred to B or C, although locked up in a cell at night, the old hand stands a good chance, amongst such a number, of meeting some former friend and associate in crime whilst mustering at labour, or at school, or church. Every bit of good effected by separate confinement will be neutralized by association with other criminals. Young and old, neophyte in vice, and hardened villain, are all mixed up together; and the consequence is an atmosphere of crime, thought, and feeling, which makes this, the second stage of our convict system, one of retrogression, at least as far as any moral influence or hope of reformation is concerned.

Transferred to B Division, the prisoner commences an entirely different mode of life. The building, like A, is erected on the "panopticon" plan, but contains three wings, and has two exercising yards, which are now useless. There are two tiers of cells in each wing, and in one an extra number are built in the basement below the surface of the ground. These, of course, are more gloomy, and not so well ventilated as those above. Here, too, are the punishment cells, or "black holes," mere caves hewn out of the solid rock, where not one single ray of light enters, and from whence the close-fitting, padded door prevents a sound being heard. Prisoners are seldom confined here, as the punishment is considered to be a hard one. "Three days' solitary," a common sentence for misdemeanour, is only seclusion in an ordinary cell, without exercising time, on a pound of bread a day and unlimited water, the trap in the door being locked to prevent any communication with warders and others. That is child's play, but the black hole is another thing. When inside, and the door shut behind you, the darkness at first seems horrible; it appears a palpable, material gloom which embraces you. Only very bad cases are sent here, and that for short periods of time, although Weechurch, who was hung for attempted murder, was, I am told, thus confined for three weeks . . .

Everything in Pentridge is regulated by strokes of the bell, rung by a warder, in the tower over the gateway. The eight hours' law is in full sway amongst the prisoners. The unfortunate warders have to work ten and a half hours for seven days a week, whilst the prisoners only make weekly $44\frac{1}{2}$ hours. Particularly *hard labour* this. When mustering, signal flags, for the guidance of warders on the different towers and at the lower station, are also used. When the muster bell rings in the morning, the yard in front of the hospital is soon filled with prisoners, who file out of B and C Divisions, and take their places in their appointed gangs. The Assistant-Superintendent is generally present at this operation, and the labour overseers are on hand. The men belonging to B Division are mustered by Chief-warder Kelly. In the yard of C Division (of which more anon) Chief-warder Maxwell musters his men. It is not a particularly lively sight. The sombre convict clothes, with the broad arrow and number thereon, and the general sameness in appearance, all at first view appearing to have one general criminal cast of countenance—this depresses the observer. Falling into squads, with good conduct men acting the part of corporals and sergeants, with warders walking up and down watching every movement, these men can yet easily communicate any item of news to each other. A whisper —and they learn to talk without moving their faces—will soon go the round of the gangs. The "underground railroad" of prison communication is really a most extraordinary one. The men appear to know many things before the warders do. In these squads the face of a celestial or a coloured man will occasionally break the monotony of outline. One or two will also come clanking along in irons. These are rivetted round their ankles, and the short chain is suspended by a strap to their waists. The irons are only seven pounds in weight, and a sentence to wear them for a year is looked upon as a joke by old hands. After a week or two the prisoners get used to them, and walk about with quite as much freedom and elasticity as English Hodge in his high-lows.

When the muster is all completed, the Assistant-Superintendent (Mr. Donaldson) will wave his handkerchief, the white flag will be hoisted, the sentries posted around the yard will close in, and the gangs under the charge of their proper officers and the overseers will file away to the scene of their labours. There are eight gangs—the quarry, the garden, the tannery, the shops, No. 2 yard, the shoemakers', and the tailors'. At half-past eleven the prisoners leave off work for an hour, and are mustered into school. Those, however, of superior education are allowed to go to the cells, where some may be seen lying on their backs indolently reading, or else, if "on tobacco," they may take a whiff in the "tobacco-yard." Muster after dinner is the same as in the morning. At night the prisoners are all counted in their cells, and just before six o'clock a return is sent to the Assistant-Superintendent from each division, certified by the officer in charge. If the total of these night reports does not agree with the office-book, if there is a man more or less, the warders will all be detained until the mistake is found out. Should an escape be discovered, all hands must remain on the ground and assist in the search. Nothing of the sort, however, happened whilst I was in Pentridge. I think it will be seen that the prisoner transferred to B division has not a particularly hard time of it. The cells are as comfortable as those in A, and they have one improvement, a board hanging on hinges from the wall, which at night may be turned up as a sleeping place. This is certainly preferable to lying on the ground . . .

The prisoners in B comprise all the "lifers," some twenty in number, and others with sentences of various periods. Some are notorious characters. Here is a young German who appears to be a lineal descendant from Baron Munchausen. My "billet" described him as being "the biggest liar from here to hell." He never tells the truth even by accident. Here is "Tommy the Nut," as amusing customer, much appreciated by the police. Here is Peter Stuart, an extraordinary character, who has attempted suicide three times, but at present seems reconciled to life. Here is an outrageous ruffian named Neville, a homicide and a "lifer." He is a dangerous character, and being strong and powerful as a bull, appears to be generally feared by the warders, and to be the terror of his fellow prisoners. I believe it is a fact that some time back he was given a "wrong dose" by a previous warder or dispenser, and either in reality or fiction he now complains of pangs in his interior, and takes advantage of his presumed poisoning to demand castor oil and peppermint *ad lib*. My experience of this man was not pleasing. Coming down-stairs one night, after mustering my flock, I found him sitting outside the dispensary door. "Now, then, give me some castor oil, quick!" he cried. Both as an individual, a warder, and a dispenser, I was rather astonished at being addressed in such a manner; but, unlocking my door, I said, "What's the matter with you?" "What's the matter, is it? You know, you murdering villain, you poisoned me, you did. Give me some castor oil and peppermint, or I'll knock your head off." "Clear out of this!" "You won't give me anything? Where's the doctor? Ugh! Ugh! I'll go to him, you villain!" "You may go to the devil," said I, annoyed at this bullying; and the man cleared out and ran across the yard to Dr. Reed's house. While doing this, one of the warders of B division came over, and explained that Neville was very violent, and they had to "humour" him, and I'd better not vex him, for half a dozen men couldn't hold him. "He's nearly mad sometimes, I think," said the man. Just then Neville came back, roaring and raging. "I'll have your life, you poisoning villain," he cried, and he threatened me for a few minutes, whilst ——, my dispenser, gave him a dose, for I would not have served him. The situation was not exactly a nice one, as I was not "heeled," and in the event of a difficulty could evidently expect little assistance from the warder present, who was decidedly frightened at Neville. However, after swearing at and threatening me for some time, Neville went away with the warder in charge of him (?) to his quarters in B division. Shortly afterwards they sent over for a dose of peppermint to help to quiet him. As the other warders put up with this man's conduct, I did not think it worth while to complain to the Superintendent, but the fact that a dangerous ruffian, no matter how ill, should be allowed to go on in such a manner is a satire on the discipline of Pentridge . . .

Let us have a look at the various "gangs" at their very *hard* labour. The shoemakers and tailors work in a new, airy, red-brick building in the main yard, previously described. In the tailors' shop we find a number of men sitting crosslegged on benches, working with far more appliances for health and comfort than many of their trade in the city of Melbourne. Here are several Chinamen, who make capital tailors. All chat merrily together, and certainly do not overwork themselves; and, as regards conditions of labour, their lot seems one to be envied by the working tailors of London. From his office and store, the overseer can survey the prisoners, but the discipline did not appear to me to be very strict. The clothes used in the prison are made here, and also those for use at the lunatic asylums. In the shoemakers' shop, things seem just the same: there does not appear to be even a semblance of hard labour. In both shops the general workmanship is of a rather inferior quality. Leaving the main yard, we pass through a gateway, under the eyes of a sentry, who is posted on a covered platform on the wall above—access to which is had by a stairway and ladder, which he draws up after him. We now find ourselves in what is known as the "stoneyard." This is supposed to be in process of levelling for the purpose of erecting a "factory" thereon. There is a confused mass of stones. Prisoners are idly shovelling away dirt, some few chipping and facing bluestone, in a contented manner. Here one old hand has a small menagerie of tiger cats, which he catches inside these walls, and handles with impunity . . . On the right of this is "No. 2 Yard," which is a large enclosure, subdivided by low brick walls into nine sections. In the first there is the overseer's office, a small carpenters' shop, and a shed where cocoanut fibre is being wound into yarn ready for matmaking. In one division there is a garden full of bushes of the Chili pepper, grown here for the purpose of flavouring the prisoners' soup. Tomatoes and melons are also grown in profusion, and flowers adorn the borders, from which I occasionally obtained a welcome bouquet for the surgery. Next to this is the "lifers' " yard. There the prisoners are breaking up "wet cocoanut." Seated under a long shed, divided by partitions, and with a quantity of wet husk before them, each man pounds this away on a stump of wood until all the refuse matter, dust and dirt, is beaten out of it, and nothing but the coir remains. These men are directly under the eye of the two sentries who are posted in the towers at the corner of the yard, but they cannot always be watching each particular prisoner. The work is light, 5 lb. a day being the regulation quantity, and the men laugh and chat together as they perform their easy tasks.

In other sections of No. 2 yard are the large clumsy-looking looms in which the cocoanut fibre is woven into mats. Most of these are ordinary door mats, but some have "Welcome," and "Peace," and ugly crowns worked in red. They are sold to the Melbourne upholsterers at a fair price. In another section some men are stone chipping. The stranger cannot help noticing that, in this yard, where the longest sentenced men and most dangerous class of prisoners are confined, there appear to be too many dangerous knives and tools scattered about the place. If one of these men wished to murder a warder, he would have every chance and a good choice of weapons here. Passing through a gate guarded by an armed sentry we are outside the walls of Pentridge prison proper, but within those of the Stockade. Immediately in front is a large space of garden ground, where some prisoners are lazily working. In this is a tannery where a few men are employed. Passing through the gardens and scaling the fence, we come into a large paddock, in which is the quarry from whence the stone was taken to build the prison and surrounding walls. The quarry is not now worked, and is the home of hundreds of rabbits, which I ostensibly stalked in the cool of the evening. My real purpose, however, was to roam about and chat with the warders on duty, and "take stock" of the surroundings. The prisoners who compose what is still known as "the quarry gang" were employed during my stay in Pentridge in making the new deodorizing works, which were badly wanted. Here as everywhere in Pentridge, the work was lazily performed. A strong able-bodied ruffian would dig up half a pound of dirt on the end of his shovel, and pitch it into the cart with as virtuous an air as if it weighed 20 lb. Then he would take a minute's breath, and go on again.

The overseer looks on, and I believe does his best to get work out of his gang, but these men are obstinate and lazy, and you can hardly blame an overseer if he does not care about taking extreme measures. Labour overseers have been grievously assaulted, and killed before now. The only immediate protection is a warder, armed with a truncheon, although all around the edge of the paddock is a line of armed sentries, sitting or walking under sheds to preserve them from the sun and rain, or sometimes perched on the numerous platforms which are raised in the paddocks. Armed warders are not allowed to approach within a certain distance of prisoners, for fear they should be rushed, and their firearms taken from them.

Crossing the paddock, and the garden of the Jika Jika Reformatory Schools, we come to the "shops"—tumble-down shanties—where the carpenters, tinsmiths, and blacksmiths labour, and do all the work in their line required on the Stockade. A great deal of attention is required in supervising these, and in adopting precautions that no tools are conveyed therefrom. Small knives and files and saws are often made here out of scraps of iron, and are concealed and passed into the cells, so that at night the owner may do a little fancy bone work "on the cross." Opposite the shops is "the factory," which adjoins the Reformatory. The door of this is locked, and a warder is on duty inside, besides the labour overseer. Here are five looms, and various machines for tearing up old rags into "shoddy," for cleaning and sorting the wool with which it is mixed, and for spinning the yarn. Here blankets, and the coarse cloth of which the prisoners' clothes are made, are manufactured. The busy hum of the looms, and the bustle of the human feeders of the machines, make this appear the most industrious portion of Pentridge. Part of this building is used as the laundry, the washing being done by the waste-steamer from the engine which works the looms. In the yard the clothes are dried, and here there is also a store, in which I found the new blankets being hemmed with the orthodox red wool by an ex-bank manager. The foregoing are the chief industries at which prisoners at Pentridge work, and nowhere is there the slightest appearance of *hard labour*. It is a misnomer. Except in the "lifers'" yard, there is no attempt at classification, and the young boy just led into crime is everywhere throughout the day's work mixed up and associated with hardened thieves, perpetual strugglers with society, or with those who have been guilty of still more revolting crimes, which should make them a branded and separate class.

After their easy day's work is over, the prisoners are mustered, and in rotation the gangs are marched back into the main yard, and to their different divisions. I have described A and B, and the hospital;

C is the only one remaining. This consists of double tiers of cells, 60 in each, built of bluestone and brick. The doors all open outwards into the yards or galleries. The furniture of the cells consists of mat, blankets, table, and stool. They are certainly not as comfortable as those in A or B divisions. The prisoners confined here are mostly those whose sentences vary from six months to five years. According to the length of sentence and behaviour of the prisoner, he is allowed tobacco, tea, and sugar, and pay for each working day, which accumulates, and on his discharge is paid to the Prisoners' Aid Society for his benefit. Daily one-sixth of a plug of tobacco is handed to each smokist. Those who do not use the weed have three farthings a-day placed to their credit instead. This is at the rate of 4s. a pound, and the tobacco is awfully vile at the price. Short clay pipes are also daily served out, but each prisoner must bring an old one, or its remains instead. The pipes and tobacco are kept in boxes, according to gangs. Smoking is allowed in, and the prisoners have the run of, one of the three yards, where they can walk about and converse . . .

In the room which is used as a chapel in B division, school is daily held at the hours appointed—half-past 11 to half-past 12 . . . There are generally about 200 prisoners here. They sit round tables, containing eight each, and there is a good deal of talking and chafing going on. It is amusement to the majority. The Chinese prisoners seem to be those who most earnestly apply themselves to learn. The education given is quite rudimentary, and many who do not require it lie on their beds and read for an hour. Like the labour system at Pentridge, the educational one is a farce. Men are neither worked enough, nor taught enough. It cannot be said that the punishment here, with the exception of the deprivation of liberty, is hard, or sufficient of itself to deter from crime. And, as regards the reformation of the criminal, I hold that the system at Pentridge—the indiscriminate association of the weak with the vilest—is not of the slightest avail; that the effect is the other way, and that the accidentally criminal leave this prison too often thoroughly debased in heart and mind, dangerous members of society ever afterwards . . .

I am glad to state that I think, on the whole, the warders at Pentridge are a very decent set of men, who do their work faithfully, and are not too well paid for the performance of dangerous and irksome duties. They are most of them men appointed by John Price or Colonel Champ, in the days when the inspector had the sole power of appointment and dismissal, and when men were liable to be discharged at a moment's notice for breach of duty. In many cases, no doubt, this was hard on the individual, but the result is that the men retained in the service are, as a body, first-class, able, and intelligent officers. Under the new civil service regulations, and system of political patronage, such men will not be obtained in the future.

According to the regulations, prisoners locked in their cells are not allowed to work, or to do anything but read and sleep. But many, with the aid of very rude tools, manufactured at "the shops," will turn out exquisite scarf rings, studs, crosses, &c., made out of pieces of bone and ivory. If they were discovered, they would be severely punished. Now, I hold this to be a great mistake. I think the quality of industry should be encouraged in these men, and that those who will work in their cells should be allowed to do so, and receive the benefit of their labour . . . At present, however, the industrious prisoner working "on the cross" has to dispose of his wares surreptitiously by the aid of friendly warders and privileged "billets." A few plugs of tobacco will buy a good deal in Pentridge . . . Trade goes on all over the prison by the mysterious "underground" communication. A plug of tobacco will be wrapped in a cabbage leaf, and dropped in a man's pannikin of soup. I saw this done once. Or it will be hidden in his hominy. There are many strange ways by which prisoners communicate with each other; confinement seems to quicken the mental activity of the most obtuse . . . I will quote the opinion of a well-known thief, who recently came out of Castlemaine gaol, as to the quality of the punishment at Pentridge. He is a graduate, and ought to know. Said he, "Melbourne gaol is an hotel, Pentridge is a boarding-house, but Castlemaine is hell." Now, I would not make a gaol a Hell, but a Purgatory, where men should do a full day's hard work to compensate the State; where solitary reflection, removal from evil associates, and religious and educational training, should have that reforming influence which would make the convict worthy to enjoy the Heaven of Liberty.

10

Gately the Hangman

(From 'A Month in Pentridge')

In less than half an hour after I landed at Pentridge I had my first "case." It happened thusly. After being shown round the wards, and receiving instructions from Dr. Reed, we returned to the surgery. There the warder addressed the doctor, "I've just come up from A Division, and there's Balleyram wants a tooth out. Will you go down there, sir?" "You can pull out teeth, I suppose?" said the doctor, turning to me. I sort of hesitated. "Who was the man?" I asked. "The hangman, Gately, but they call him Balleyram here," was the reply. I accepted the doctor's case of instruments with alacrity, and expressed my readiness to pull out every tooth in "Balleyram's" head. I have never had any practice in dentistry, and this was my maiden effort in that line. With any other subject I certainly should have hesitated, as I dislike giving needless pain; but Gately I had little sympathy for. I had seen him but once—at the execution of Bondietto—a transaction which I give him credit for despatching with much neatness. But the man's brutal appearance corresponded with his vocation, and I could well believe that he enjoyed his work, and that he was guilty of the atrocities for which he is now undergoing punishment. So I did not mind giving him a little pain. If I proved a success in this line of business, I would go on; but if not, I must renounce tooth-drawing under some pretence, and Gately alone would suffer by my inexperience. "Come along," said the warder, "I'll take you down to A Division" . . .

Entering the prison, passing the office, library, bath, and store-rooms, and through two gates of strong iron bars we find ourselves in "the model," which is unlike its sponsor at Pentonville, in that it is only designed for three wings or corridors, two as yet being built, instead of four, as in the London institution, and that it only contains two tiers of cells. Three or four warders, dressed in the simple uniform of the penal institutions, are lounging about a table over which are a number of hooks holding keys, staves, handcuffs, and other outward and visible signs of authority. To them I am introduced as the new dispenser, and we exchange polite salutations and a little badinage, after the manner of our kind. "He's come to pull out Balleyram's tooth," said my introducer, and one of the warders escorts to cell 93. The rattle of the key in the lock arouses the occupant, who springs to the position of "attention," as required by the regulations; and, entering, I find myself face to face with the last minister of Victorian law—Gately—convict and executioner.

A frightful animal—the immense head, powerful protruding jaw, narrow receding forehead, and deficient brain space, seemed fitly joined to tremendous shoulders and long strong arms, like those of a gorilla, which he resembles more than a man. All the evil passions appeared to have their home behind that repellant, revolting countenance. With an instinctive movement, which my companions would not understand, I placed my hand on my hip. As a brute and a hangman—I trust this is not a premonitory warning—the man was alike distasteful to me. But in a second I remembered that here he was but a prisoner—No. 93—and the power of authority was visible all around me. I recovered my part: "Now, then, old man, let's have a look at this tooth." He opened his foul jaws. Faugh! "Sit down." "Oh, doctor, don't hurt me," he cried, as, with a professional air, I opened the pocket-case, and spread the forceps on the little table. "Oh!" he cried, as the first pull broke off a piece of the tooth, the forceps slipping. "Just hold his head, and if he stirs bang it against the wall," said I to one of the warders. There was a laugh—the new dispenser was "a queer sort," evidently. I took out the largest and strongest pair of forceps, which would pull a tooth out of a crocodile. One grip, a roar from Gately, a twist of the wrist, and out came the tusk. With the consciousness of talent, I wiped the instruments carefully, whilst the warders looked on admiringly. "I must get you to look at my teeth," said one of them. "Have it out now," said I. "If there's one thing I can do better than another, it's this—I'm——on teeth." The warder shuddered, and said he hadn't time just then.

This little operation gave me much *éclat*, and by the mysterious underground railroad of the prison was circulated through all the divisions to such an extent that, for a time, I had quite a business in extracting old stumps, which only fell off after I broke two forceps in a man's jaw. He wouldn't try a third attempt, when I meant to put the "bull-dog" on him, and have out that stump or his jaw-bone. I left the cell fully satisfied of my capacity to pass as a dentist; and, now the thing was over, amused at my first case. Poor Gately. All the world is down on him, and when free he had not a place to lay his head. A natural brute he is as God, or the devil, made him, for it is hard to believe that any spark of aught Divine can rest in such a frame. An "old hand," he has had experience of the prisons of Tasmania, New South Wales, and Victoria, passing his whole life in and out of gaol. He goes by the several names of Gately, Balleyram, and Fagin, and was an Irishman and a Roman Catholic. But his long experience of prison life has taught him that, owing to the practice of confession, it is hard to gammon the priest, and, casting around for some other creed, by professing which he might obtain somewhat, Balleyram became a convert to Judaism. I never met a converted Jew—I believe they cost half a million each, and the article is then very inferior—but I have heard of such. A converted Christian I never heard of; and Gately, Fagin, or Balleyram should be celebrated on this account. I am afraid, however, that the respectable members of the Jewish race, who add so much to the prosperity of the colonies by their industry and public spirit, will not own Gately. However, he says he's a Jew; his intentions are good, and he ought to know. I did not examine him as to the tenets, &c., of his faith. The peculiar fact in this conversion is the cause—a longing for passover cake. Gately found out that Jews were supplied with this at the proper season, and seeing that it was a luxury compared to prison fare, has been running on the Hebrew ticket ever since. But this strange caricature of humanity is not all evil. On one occasion he saved the life of an overseer. Some years back they were working in the quarry, and a plot was made to "muckle" the overseer, who was considered a hard taskmaster. The one who was to strike the first blow knocked the overseer from the bank into the quarry. His leg was broken and a prisoner approached to finish him with an axe, when Balleyram intervened, and, by his threats and enormous strength, subdued the rioters. For this, I am told, he obtained a remission of his sentence, and was afterwards appointed executioner. The effect of such an office on the individual may be learned from the evidence of warders who have known Gately for years. These all say that his conduct now is greatly worse than when he was an ordinary criminal. Let this be recorded to his credit—he *could* be degraded and made worse by the influence of his debasing office.

PART THREE

Middle Class Morality

11

In a Fashionable Church

I certainly had no business here. A vagabond in a fashionable church is decidedly out of place, and his presence is more surprising than that of flies in amber . . . From a social stand-point it is a far cry from the Gospel-hall to the Scots Church in Collins-street. Nevertheless, on Whit Sunday, I attended a service at the latter, and now have the audacity to give my views thereon.

Although the edifice is a new one, the church (using that word to denote the body of worshippers) is one of the oldest in Victoria. The building itself is a fine specimen of architecture—worthy of a great city like Melbourne. Inside, there is no "dim religious light;" no painted windows keep out God's sun, or convey holy lessons by the representation of pre-Raphaelite figures of saints of dubious identity; there are no obscure aisles, sanctuaries, or altars which imagination may endow with an extra amount of sacredness or mystery. Everything here is cold, severe, chaste, and beautiful; there is a free light everywhere—the building is typical of the doctrines preached, which require no supernatural embellishments or material appeals to the senses, but are open to and court full light of reason. I had shed for the nonce my vagabond apparel, and being clothed in the garments of civilization and church-going, no obstacle was offered to my entry. I arrived full early, and had ample time to observe the congregation. The beauty, fashion, wealth, and talent of Melbourne is strongly represented here. The daughters of the land are in great force—could any church exist for a year without female support? For them the denizens of land, sea, and air have been slaughtered to furnish fitting attire for worship, and they wear a fortune in golden ornaments and precious stones. The civilized man, in direct opposition to the course of nature—as witnessed in the animal kingdom or savage man—wears a sober apparel, and leaves the beauties of colour to his mate; but some here present restore the balance of value by the extra size of their diamond rings . . . although a vagabond, I strive to be impartial, and I think many writers have criticised too much "the fair sinners in satins, laces, and diamonds." Outwardly and artistically, the males here may not be much to look at, but they represent a great deal. This is a truly remarkable congregation, and chiefly so for the individual and aggregate wealth of its members. Here are men whose yearly income is reckoned by the thousand, up to hundreds of thousands: squatters, whose flocks and herds are greater than those of Abraham; merchants, bankers, and lawyers, men of the first repute on the mart and in the forum. No incongruity is apparently perceived in the presence of a sporting element in the congregation. Could some modern outcast Samson pull down the pillars, I expect the amount of succession and legacy duties would free the Government from the necessity of collecting taxes for a year or two.

It is pleasant to be in such company, pleasant to look around and see fair, cultivated women, pleasant to feel the subtle perfumes which float through the air . . . So I, although my feelings and prejudices are enlisted on behalf of the poor and outcast, cannot deny to myself that this clean, well-dressed congregation is likely to be morally better than those who should fill the Gospel Halls—but don't. In the surroundings here there is everything in the favour of morality and respectability. Leaving the religious questions on one side, one feels that here everyone is likely to acknowledge an obligation to his neighbour—that received social morality which John Stuart Mill well defines as being in truth "the summary of the conduct which every one, whether he himself observes it with any strictness or not, desires that others should observe towards him." And I can readily imagine that this feeling may be increased and sustained by a superior social position, and advantages mental and physical . . . But all these advantages are dependent upon the possession of comparative wealth; and the poor man has a double ground of complaint—first, in his present state being one of disease, care, and hard work; and, secondly, in his surroundings leading him into vice and crime, and so endangering his immortal welfare. I really feel that, now-a-days (if he will), it is easy for a rich man to be moral and religious, and so become worthy of the kingdom of heaven. I have known how hard it is to feel your equals turn from your shabby coat, to fare meanly, and endeavour to keep up the feelings of an honourable man, and to resist the promptings of evil, which would lead one to do things which hereafter you might be ashamed of. If I have conquered temptations, and can feel that morally I am not much below the average church-goer, it is because years of social training and advantages in the past taught me that vice and crime are not beautiful, and

The Rev. Charles Strong

in the end don't pay; and that not only in the next world, but in this, virtue, if it can rise above the slough of poverty has its reward. But I can fully realize how, to the poor and ignorant, temptations which those more fortunately situated can throw off without effort, come with overpowering force. There is nothing in their lives, or associations, or tone of their public opinion, to aid them in resisting such—the influence, in fact, is the other way. I am obliged to admit the superior morality of this congregation, but how their position is to be reconciled by any "scheme of existence or salvation" with those of the vagabonds and outcasts from whom I hold a brief, I do not know . . .

It being the occasion of the periodical communion, the portions of Scripture which were read referred to the institution of that sacrament. The singing, in which I was glad to hear the congregation join, was good, and the organ was an excellent one. The prayer was not a long one; it was full of the ordinary appeals to the Almighty for help and protection for ourselves and others, but couched in moderate language. After the giving out of the text we carefully settled down in our seats, which were not too comfortable, and observed the minister. The Rev.

Charles Strong was selected and sent out here by Principal Caird as the best available article in that line in Scotland. He is a young man, not much over thirty, but looking his full years. There is nothing particularly striking in his personal appearance, which is not set off by the grim Geneva gown of orthodoxy. From the chaste white stone pulpit (which occupies the place of the altar in other churches) his voice was clearly heard. But his reading of the sermon could not be called eloquent, and, to my mind at least, his manner was decidedly not "inspiring." There was a harshness and dryness of delivery, which I daresay, after the first hearing, you get accustomed to. But the matter of the sermon was everything. Taking his text from the lesson, he discoursed on the communion. He showed that it was a rite of the church, one of those grafted from the Jewish on to the Christian faith. But in partaking of this sacrament we did not believe in any supernatural characteristics, or that there was anything particularly sacred or priestly in the administering of the same. We did not believe in any ritualism; and by that he meant not only the functions of the Catholic and Anglican Churches, but that worship of or veneration for forms which might and did exist in many Presbyterian country churches. We believed that there was nothing specially sacred in the form or material of any service, in the officiator, or the place in which it was held; but so long as men believed that an immaterial soul, without form or substance, would go to a very material hell, so long the belief in the efficacy of material rites and ceremonies would exist. All these, although now so thoroughly grafted into the doctrines of churches, were at first merely adopted from motives of expediency. We might look upon many of these observances as childish, but still, there was nothing particularly wrong in them; and perhaps they had in past times been necessary. We must look at, and partake of the sacrament in a spiritual light. The love of Christ, and of a Christian life, should be in our hearts, and recognizing one broad universal spirit in the other churches of the past and the present, we may see through petty forms, rites, and ceremonies the Spirit of Christ. With His love in our hearts we should strive after purity of life, and endeavour to do Christian works, helping to make a Christian city and a Christian congregation, and not leave this only a weekly "religious meeting-house or Gospel shop," where praying and preaching might be heard, but no fruit come thereof.

These were the principal heads of Mr. Strong's discourse, and fairly embody, I believe, his views on the necessity of a purity of life and good works. He is evidently no believer in the efficacy of faith, and in every idea is far in advance of the traditions of the Presbyterian Church and the majority of its ministers. The "Holy Church Universal" is to him composed of all who believe in the principles of a Christian life, no matter how they call their belief. In rites and ceremonies he sees childish aids to religion for those who have not arrived at a stage in which they can do without these. *Mirabile dictu*, he does not denounce others for believing in superstitions, but underneath these sees the Spirit of Christ, and detects love where others would only find hatred. For such a congregation as Mr. Strong possesses, I hold his views to be admirable—for myself, I desire no other; but for the majority of mankind—for the poor, the vicious, and the criminal—how will this intellectual-spiritual religion affect them? Can you appeal to their hearts through their reason, or must they not be influenced by rites and teachings which claim some sort of present super-natural authority, as in the Church of Rome, or by the emotional nervous spasms accompanying that peculiar process styled "getting belief" or "being converted?" In one case the heart is reached through the outward senses; in the other, through the nerves. Can the like process be attained through the brain? To the poor, the teaching of a kingdom not of this world which they may inherit is all-enticing. They hope to enjoy the good there they have missed on earth; and although I myself believe that very few people are rendered better by hopes of a future heaven, or fears of a possible hell, still the creed which holds out tangible rewards and punishments will always be believed in by the multitude . . .

Mr. Strong gave us a short sermon. He, I am told, generally follows Sydney Smith's advice as to the length of sermons— "twenty minutes, with a leaning to the side of mercy." Afterwards, there was the usual weekly collection. I contributed my mite; and, whilst doing so, thought of the old Scotch story of the man who inadvertently put half-a-crown in the plate instead of his regular modest donation. Discovering his mistake, he afterwards waited on the elder, and wished to rectify the same, but was told that what was given was given, and could not be changed. "Ah, weel," he said, "I winna fash mysel'—I'll get credit for the half-croon." "Na, na, mon," was the reply, "ye'll only get credit for the bawbee!" From the point of view of only getting credit for intentions, I am afraid I am not much the better for the morning thus spent in a Fashionable Church.

12

A Suburban Church

I attended Church twice last Sunday, and, in spite of my well-known vicious tastes and proclivities, I rather liked it. I went to spend the day with a friend of mine residing in the Punt-road, and in the morning we canvassed the programme. I thought it would be rather good fun to go to the Alfred Hospital in the afternoon, and be stuck-up by the hall-porter for contraband. But my friend said, "Church, it's a special collection to-day, and one ought not to miss, although there's the offertory every Sunday. I remember in my youth, in our parish church in England, if we had a collection more than twice a year, the vestryman would begin to talk about it, and want to know 'what parson was at.' Here one is always giving. But a gentleman is bound to support his Church, so let's go." I said I'd do it, though with a sort of inward idea that I was sacrificed to the collection, and we started for Christ Church.

This, the parish church of South Yarra, is pleasantly located at the corner of the Punt and Toorak roads. It is built, cross-shaped, of that useful but sombre bluestone which is ill appropriate to ornamental architecture in this climate. The inside is as dull and tasteless as the outer. The bare walls are unrelieved by any line to break the monotony. There is no severe chasteness, as in the Scots Church—simply dull ugliness. There are some stained glass windows, not of much account; and a brass plate commemorating the virtues of the late Mr. Haines, old colonist and Chief Secretary, is the only other thing to catch the eye. At the eastern end a mean wooden screen or partition forms the vestry and background for the communion-table, one of the most atrocious arrangements I have ever seen in an Episcopal Church. The organ is, I think, in the wrong place. I managed to get a seat near the pulpit, and watched the congregation coming in. The Church was crowded with, as usual, a large proportion of the fair sex. A fashionable assembly in its way, after the fashion of Bayswater or the Notting Hill Crescents. Altogether, a gathering of a pleasant local community. It is needless, however, to state that the ladies were all well dressed and handsome—in Australia *cela va sans dire*—and that it made one feel good to worship in such society. Mr. Justice Fellows, who lives opposite, is one of the great supporters of the Church—a tower of strength in himself. But even his efforts, seconded by the efforts of others, could not, some time back, prevent a great falling off in the congregation. The present incumbent, the Rev. Mr. Guinness, is old, and in the sere and yellow leaf, liked and respected by all his parishioners, who, however, except the faithful few, liked him too well to go and listen to his sermons. Sunday after Sunday there was, so to speak, a beggarly account of empty benches.

But some nine months ago Mr. Guinness received leave of absence to visit England, and the vestry was fortunate in engaging the present *locum tenens*, the Rev. W. P. Pearce, whose graphic sermons have brought back recreant pew-holders and "filled the house." His is quite a starring engagement, and has been eminently successful. An extra attraction has been lately offered in the presence of the Governor, family, and suite, who weekly attend Christ Church, Sir George Bowen being, I believe, a friend of Mr. Pearce. But the people of this colony are too sensible to besiege any public place because the Governor attends. The sight of vice-royalty is an everyday one, and I have heard theatre managers lament that "there's no money in the Governor's attendance; it don't draw an extra shilling." This being the case, I give, and am confirmed by the testimony of the oldest parishioner, all merit to Mr. Pearce for the present good congregation at Christ Church; although it is pleasant to say your prayers in the company of Her Majesty's representative.

I came out to hear Mr. Pearce, but was disappointed on Sunday morning last, for this being the twenty-first anniversary of the Church, Dr. Bromby (as a special attraction) preached in the morning, and endeavoured to draw the shillings out of our pockets. However, I always like the liturgy of the Church of England, the principal part of which was rendered by the curate, a dark, bilious, sad-looking young man, reminding me much of Mr. Ashton Dilke, brother of Sir Charles Dilke, and proprietor of the *Weekly Dispatch*, with whom I once travelled in Russia. I won't say that I was very much impressed, but even my catholic, impartial, rational, and vagabond mind cherishes a sneaking fondness for the Episcopal Church, into whose fold I was in my early and unconscious days provisionally received, and I enjoyed myself, thinking of days gone by, when, at an English public school, to which I was expatriated, I had to attend Church three times each

Dr John Edward Bromby

Sunday and every day during Lent, besides the morning prayers. I reckon that, during those four years, I put in enough time to make even now my average a very fair one.

From the ugliness of the Church I was afraid we should have a very Calvinistic service, but I was agreeably disappointed in the singing. The "Te Deum" was very well rendered, the psalms well chanted, and the only fault with the anthems was that they were a little too long. The organist and choir both deserve praise. The former is one of the masters of the Church of England Grammar School and a son of Dr. Bromby, and is a real musician. It was rather warm last Sunday morning, and one's attention wandered away from the service a good deal. The ladies I saw criticising the dresses of the Misses Bowen, their gracious mamma not being there. I admired His Excellency. Sir George is a glorious example of the healthiness of the Australian colonies, and his hale, hearty vigour is a remarkable fact, not to be overlooked in connexion therewith . . .

At last, Dr. Bromby mounted the pulpit, and gave out the text from 19th Proverbs, 21st verse—"There are many devices in a man's heart; nevertheless the counsel of the Lord, that shall stand." Dr. Bromby is

A SUBURBAN CHURCH

not an elegant-looking man, but he's good and popular. I've heard one lady say "he ought to be a bishop," which is praise indeed. He is a man of deep learning and liberal views, and his sermons are generally original: as one of his congregation said, "they are all good for something or other." On Sunday, he galloped over a considerable portion of sacred and profane history, instancing the devices of men's hearts which did not stand. Abraham and Sarah, Rebecca and Jacob, Pharaoh and Mozes, Jezebel and Ahab, Herod *re* the Massacre of the Innocents —all these, the doctor showed, had been slated in their vain desires. Then he got on to Napoleon I.—Josephine's divorce—and showed how the Lord punished the first Emperor for his abominable treatment of his wife by removing the Duke of Reichstadt, and making his nephew (and a grandson of Josephine) ruler over France. This was hard on the Second Napoleon, and a good line for the Third. If the doctor had correctly narrated the latter's parentage, it would have added an additional moral to the tale. Then O'Farrell's device in attempting to shoot the Duke of Edinburgh was instanced; and the doctor glorified in the fact that this land was saved from the disgrace of shedding royal blood. I was very much afraid that the Alfred Hospital would be alluded to, but it was not. Altogether, the doctor pointed out that we must see the finger of God in everything. The Bible record was the history of the Jews, but only such parts of their history as particularly showed the ways of Providence; and present history must be judged in the same manner, and we must draw a like moral from the events of to-day. In fact, the sequence, according to Dr. Bromby, is, that "whatever is, is right," and is directly sanctioned by Providence, and that all the devices of man's heart are of no account whatever if they fail; but if they succeed, no matter what they be, the work is God's. It was an original sermon, but a mixed-up one, which floored my theology.

As I wanted to hear Mr. Pearce, I had to attend Church again at night. Evening service is not generally fashionable in any part of the civilized world. People who feed at reasonable hours cannot bolt their dinners to be at Church at seven. In New York eight o'clock is the general time of commencement, and the service seldom exceeds an hour. I was surprised and pleased to see the large attendance at Christ Church on Sunday night, and especially the large proportion of young people of both sexes. When a clergyman can attract the rising generation, he is doing a good work. And on such a hot evening attendance at Church is decidedly a virtue, which I, for one, could not keep up through the season. The Governor's party, of course, was not there, and the only attraction was the service and sermon. The curate officiated, as in the morning, and the "Magnificat" and anthems were well sung. As regards the latter, I think some rule ought to be made, as it seems absurd to see half the congregation standing and half sitting. Mr. Pearce assisted by reading the lessons, the first of which was that celebrated chapter from Isaiah, describing how the lion will lie down with the lamb, and young children will be the playmates of dangerous reptiles. In those millennial days Professor Halford* and his remedy will be as naught, and the soul of the "Vagabond" will be no longer vexed by fears of seeing snakes doing the block on Collins-street, as one of these will be a bosom friend in every household. A very beautiful chapter, indeed; but this millennium seems as far off as ever. Even after the new era of "peace on earth and good will toward men," wars and rumours of wars, battle, murder, and sudden death are all around us, and the destructive forces of animal nature are as dangerous as ever. It was a hopeful prophecy of the grand old Hebrew writer, but one which seems little likely to be fulfilled in the present state of the world. I am afraid that, for many long years, the foolish lamb which attempts to lie down with the lion will find its confidence misplaced; and the child which plays with a venomous snake will want whisky or Halford's remedy. A gentleman remarked to me the other night that it was a wise ordination of Providence that Australia, which possesses poisonous reptiles, should also possess Professor Halford. I trust he was not chaffing me . . .

The Rev. William P. Pearce is a wandering Protestant preacher, going to and fro on the face of the earth, ably fulfilling his mission. He is a Cambridge man, and first studied and practised law at home; but I expect the chicaneries of that profession disgusted him, and he felt worthy of better things, and so took holy orders as a priest of the Church of England. He is a man of high culture, and literary tastes and acquirements, and before he became a clergyman he wrote a book. Now, many people write books and articles for magazines and newspapers; but what I respect Mr. Pearce for is, that he sold the copyright of his production and made money. That was fair and business-like; for, in my mind, if there is one detestable and for ever to be execrated individual, it is the amateur author, who, through vanity, publishes his works, often at a loss, and gluts the market with rubbish, to the prejudice of the talented men who live by their brains . . . Of course, I only refer to general literature. In the case of any great political or social principle, anyone is justified in, if he can, finding readers to study his reasons for the faith which is within him . . .

For some few years I believe Mr. Pearce has been absent from England, wandering round the world in search of rest and health, but

*Professor G. B. Halford, professor of medicine at the University of Melbourne, who believed that injections of ammonia would cure people bitten by snakes.

taking everywhere any work which came to his hand to do. I knew him in America, where at one time he officiated in New York city, and afterwards at Tarrytown, a charming retreat on the Hudson River, of which he must always treasure pleasant reminiscences. All about the States, on the West Indian steamers, Pacific mail boats, and in Californian cities, Mr. Pearce has followed his mission, and I can vouch that, as a priest and a gentleman, he was everywhere respected and admired. It's an extraordinary fact that I should find him here, but the world is a very little place now-a-days. I remember at Warwick races running across an English baronet whom I had met on the cars of the Texas Pacific Railway, he being in those parts for purposes of buffalo slaughtering. "Sir Henry, I'm pleased to have met you," said I; "at the same time I feel the fact that I can never go anywhere without being known is highly embarrassing." "The world's too small," said Sir Henry; "even in your country I felt cramped, not sufficient space or freedom. Try that dry wine" . . .

One's first impression, on looking at Mr. Pearce, is the thorough manliness of his face, and the calm judgment likely to result from the phrenologically well-developed and well-balanced head. That's about correct. In his sermons and teachings, Mr. Pearce is essentially manly and liberal. His is a broad, expansive, everyday Christianity, one which may be understood by the many without bewildering themselves amongst the mysteries of revelation, or going through the strange, nervous, hysterical process known as "conversion" . . .

Mr. Pearce deserves a metropolitan congregation, and I think it a great pity that, as I am told, he is going to India. Good preachers and brilliant scholars are rather scarce in the Episcopal Church of Victoria. His text on Sunday night was Psalm cxxii. 1—5, "I was glad when they said unto me, we will go into the house of the Lord." With a poetical description of old English Churches and Cathedrals, and a tribute to the piety and taste of many of the old monks, who built as a labour of love, Mr. Pearce artfully seized the attention of his hearers. To the natives of the colony he pointed out that, in this young country of no memories, if they had no past to look back to with love, they had at least nothing to regret. No records of bloody superstitions disgraced the Church buildings of Victoria. That's all very well as regards the Church, but I bethought me of certain memories which in New South Wales they would be glad to forget. Then Mr. Pearce expressed his surprise at the general shabby condition of the buildings of the Episcopal Church in Victoria. He humorously described how, when he first walked along Collins-street and saw "the tall white spire," he thought "of course that must be the Cathedral," and how disappointed he was when he found that that noble building had been erected by the piety and munificence, not of the members of the Church of England, but of the Scotch Presbyterians of Melbourne. He gave ample credit to the other Churches for their spirit in erecting and maintaining magnificent places of worship, and sadly contrasted the lack of zeal of the members of the Established Church in this colony. Then he, so to say, pitched into the congregation of Christ Church for their neglect of their edifice, winding up with a judicious appeal to our pockets. It was a very good sermon, very well delivered, but not one to show off the beauties of Mr. Pearce's scholarly and poetical style, as "begging sermons" must always suffer from the perceptible motive running throughout . . .

I think the collection on Sunday night was a pretty good one. "Pilgrims of the Night" was sung in such a manner, one mezzo-soprano voice rising high and clear above the rest, that I felt it alone worth double what I dropped in the plate. The only thing I have to find fault with in this Suburban Church is, that the varnish on the pews is of a quality which is easily reduced to the sticking point, and the coat which I had borrowed to attend decently was nearly ruined thereby.

13

At a Bazaar

In search of a mild dissipation, I one day took cab for Emerald Hill, and passed an hour in the Orderly-room, in Howe-crescent, where a Bazaar was being held in aid of St. Luke's Church and parsonage. I don't know exactly what is the matter with these institutions, but they evidently want money, and a bazaar is the correct mode of raising same—attraction to both sexes. In several parts of the world I have visited such pious swindles, and I know what to expect. Who can resist the charming young ladies, who, in the cause of charity, coax and wheedle the shilling and sovereigns out of your pocket? They are privileged at all these shows, and solicit your money with a delightful *abandon*. However, a bachelor's dollars are well spent, which enable him, if only for an hour, to be the object of the attentions and solicitude of such fair and enticing daughters of the land as may be seen at Emerald Hill. Their artful, pious, mercenary motives are so well concealed that one feels such attentions personally flattering to oneself, and thoughts of matrimony flit across one's brain. I have been through the whole programme before, but do not at all regret my renewed experiences.

The banners hung out on the outer walls proclaimed that there was a show at the Orderly-room. I was disguised as a young man from the country, down in Melbourne for the "Cup," and I entered without observation. Soon, however, "the first robber" was on to me for sixpence—the entrance fee. This individual informed me he had served his country at home and abroad for many years, and suggested I should give half-a-crown towards the Church. I asked what the Show was about, and on being told, said I was a Catholic, and could not give to a Protestant Church. He doubted my word, but I passed. The Orderly-room is not a very large one. It was festive with the stalls and their gay wares, and banners and floral decorations added distraction to the scene. On the platform, at the end of the room, stood a piano, at which ladies relieved each other in discoursing sweet music. The enchantment of sweet faces, figures, and voices, threw a seductive glamour over all. One could see the "put up game," the intention to lull the victim to sleep; but, as the fly and the spider, the moth and the candle, in a few minutes one's senses were dulled, and recklessly one walked around the stalls. These all bore the names of the ladies who conducted them. One was "the Sunday-school" stall, and at the end was the establishment of "the Young Ladies." I think this sign rather hard on the rest of the ladies, as bachelors are apt to flock to that attractive announced spot. But all the stalls had attached to each certain young ladies—the light cavalry, skirmishers who scoured the room for prey. I was soon secured, my innocent look and country style proclaiming me an easy victim. I was taken to a stall to be shown the chair purchased by Mr. W. J. Clarke, of Sunbury, who opened the bazaar. I presume the opening of a bazaar consists in making the first purchase, and Mr. Clarke handsomely gave £25 for a magnificent chair of blue satin, which is beautifully ornamented with oil paintings by Miss Wilkinson. The advertisement had stated that the stalls were crowded with useful and ornamental articles. The latter certainly there were, but there was little that would be useful to me. I have no use for a baby's pelisse, hood, or square (whatever that may be). Ottomans, antimacassars, workbaskets, woolwork mats, and rugs, are not of present service. All the stalls were crowded with such collections of fancy articles. I was solicited to buy some high-priced articles—a framed drawing of some deer especially taking my taste. But I soon found that selling out-and-out was a subordinate, and not sufficiently profitable, game. "Will you take a ticket for this chair? Only a shilling, you know?" I was had again for something else at the same stall, almost every article seeming to be a lottery prize. I protested that this was gambling, and that I abhorred such, but was told that the Attorney-General's permission was granted. "It is for a pious purpose, you know?" I said, "Yes, that covered a multitude of sins." The connection between religion and raffles has always been a mystery to me.

I went the round of the stalls, at each being "stuck up," not for one, but for many raffles. I stood to win chairs, music stools, china services, and cakes, smoking caps and slippers, toilette ornaments and babies' apparel, and possessed a lot of "scrip," one ticket being numbered 1,235. The Show did well. For ordinary raffles, however, I was requested to write my name on the list, and was informed each was sure to come off on "Saturday night." I suggest to the young ladies that they had better have a bonfire and begin afresh, giving the money to the Church. I was being ruined rapidly, and bankruptcy stared me in the face.

Fancy Fair at the Town Hall

But how could anyone resist such temptation. "I know you'll take a ticket for this smoking cap"—a killing glance—"I worked it." Or, "I know you want a bottle of scent, only half-a-crown"—cost price ninepence. Or, "You must buy a book!"

Lotos Leaves, which contains sketches by many old friends, was the only work present which I fancied, so I asked for "Ouida's" novels. The effect was striking—daughters laughed, and one mamma rebuked me severely. "You don't expect to find 'Ouida's' works at a young ladies' bazaar, do you?" I said, "Madame, I have never read them myself, but whenever I do see those works they are in the hands of ladies. I thought they were instructive tales." There were not many visitors present, it being early afternoon, so I was exposed to the attacks of all the light cavalry. One friend—Dr. Molloy, late of Kew Asylum, which he has deserted for a private practice at Emerald Hill—was there. I hope his practice is a lucrative one, for I saw that he was being severely punished. One young lady (shall I ever forget her?) was particularly anxious that I should buy the framed photograph of Mr. Dickinson, the incumbent of St. Luke's. I said I was a heathen, and would prefer *her* portrait, and suggested that they would sell well at half-a-crown each. This reminded me of one of the fancy fairs at the Crystal Palace in aid of the Dramatic Society. These are always highly successful, as the prettiest and most talented actresses have stalls. Ladies flock thither to see how these dress and look off the stage, and men go to admire and flirt if they can get the chance. At this particular fair, Miss Lydia Thompson, now married to Mr. Alexander Henderson, late of Victoria, had several boxes of cigars, and sold them at one guinea each, first biting off the end with her pretty teeth. It was a novel idea, *chic,* and she did a splendid trade. I should have liked to have suggested this to my young lady at Emerald Hill, but only advised sale of her *carte.* "I'll buy one," I said. "What will you give?" (Ah! mercenary sex.) "Whatever you ask in reason." "Come to-morrow night and you shall have it then." I am sorry to think that I could not keep my promise then made; but if the young lady will send me her *carte,* on the word of a Vagabond, I will keep my contract, and the transaction shall be buried in oblivion.

It was really pleasant for a poor, homeless, and friendless Vagabond to spend a short time amongst the beauties of Emerald Hill, married and single. It was pleasant for once to be free from the shackles of conventional society—put aside for this occasion only. It was pleasant to have unrestrained converse under pretence of barter and sale. It was pleasant to look into lovely eyes and see poetic suggestions—possibilities of depths of pure maidenly love. *Ay di mi.* I believe I left something else behind me besides my shillings. Well, I enjoyed myself for a time, feeling young once more, aroused from my aged lethargy by the artless prattle of the young ladies. Seeing the piano, I hinted that a dance was the correct thing. "You see they don't allow dancing, but between six and seven, when the place is closed, so that we may get some tea, we generally have a dance." I begged that I might stop, said I would be very good and that dancing without a male partner must be slow. All this was admitted, and in the States might have been got over; but here, as I well knew, laws regulating introduction and such are immutable. However, my "aged and venerable appearance" induced some young ladies to confide to me that they were afraid that they would not go to "the Cup." "Pa and ma" went every year, and they were left at home. The same authorities also in several cases objected to dancing, and "would not allow me to go to the Governor's ball." I suggested an organized rebellion; such conduct on behalf of the old folks at home was simply shameful . . . Having run the gauntlet of all the stalls, I was leaving, but was again stuck up by a lady at the door. I must take a ticket in her lottery. After that I went to the refreshment bar, and asked for whisky. They didn't sell it, and ginger-beer is no use to me, so I left.

I trust the ladies, old and young, who have worked so hard to make this Bazaar a success, will pardon my few jokes. Not for the world would I hurt their feelings. Seriously, I enjoyed myself very much. If anyone has a few shillings to spare, and wishes to dispose of them pleasantly, and in a good cause (which is quite a side inducement with many), he cannot do better than pay a visit to a Bazaar.

14

"Sabbath-Breaking" in Sydney

Sydney prides itself upon its "respectability." People here widen the edge of their phylacteries, and keep well chalked that outer shell which they present to the world. Church-going is considered equivalent to godliness, and, judging from their talk, many would inaugurate here the Puritan Sabbath, and have acts of Parliament passed for its regulation as absurd and arbitrary as the "Blue Laws" of Massachusetts and Connecticut. But alas, the natural man is strong in the multitude; within them is the spirit of the old Adam of the Garden of Eden, where all the days passed as one continual Sabbath of happiness and praise. It has been an undeniable fact, which has much vexed the souls of the godly in this city, that thousands of people here will not spend all the hours in church, chapel, or Sunday-school; but on their one weekly day of rest will go in for healthful recreation.

The steamers which ply to Manly-beach and the other beautiful waterside resorts in the harbour are always crowded on fine Sundays, and the roads to Botany and Coogee are thronged with omnibuses, and private vehicles. The beautiful Domain, too, is filled with Sabbath-breakers. Here on summer mornings one finds hundreds walking around or lying on the grass, inhaling the pure air and shaking off the rust of the week's hard toil. Working men, clerks, shop girls—even John Chinamen—all enjoy their cessation from labour. Bill and Emily perchance may do a little quiet flirting, having met here for that purpose; but there is no harm in it. The majority simply enjoy the *dolce far niente*, and idly watch Woolloomooloo and the harbour, with scarcely a thought of envy for the denizens of the aristocratic mansions on Potts and Darling Points . . .

On the waters of the harbour there are moving objects of interest—passing steamers, a few yachts, and sailing and rowing boats; but all about the Domain there is the real Sabbath calm of perfect laziness,

Returning from Botany

broken now and then by the sweet notes of the English song-birds which have been released, and found a home in the Botanic Gardens hard by. To Mr. Walter Bradley, the gentleman who, at his own cost, has imported and released many hundreds of feathered songsters, the colony owes many thanks, which, of course, are never likely to be paid.

It is not only "the people" who thus break the Sabbath in the Domain. "Respectability" in England was held to consist in keeping a gig. On that theory many very respectable persons offend by riding and driving to Mrs. Macquarie's Chair on a Sunday. In the mornings, too, aristocratic conveyances are quietly walked around whilst their owners are in church, the coachmen smoking their pipes and enjoying themselves after their own manner. Of course, in this employment of man and beast there is no sin! At one o'clock, on Sundays, the people in the Domain thin off, and in some parts it is nearly deserted, except that in nooks some sad ones sit disconsolately—there is no doubt that they are dinnerless. But in an hour the crowds again come trooping in, and make their way to the Botanic Gardens, which are open from two till four in the afternoon. Thus, in fine weather, those who have not money to spend in Sunday excursions by water or road, can rationally seek health and strength in the Domain and Gardens. But how in wet weather or in winter? In real truth, all over the world there are different social laws for the rich and the poor. Dives can sit in his mansion or club, and, listening to the rain beating against the window-panes, find that the knowledge of the discomfort outside only increases his enjoyment of his easy chair, magazine, and cigar. But the poor man, who only occupies scanty lodgings, has no resource but to go to the public-house. In that he breaks the law; but such laws will always be broken, for you can never make people moral by act of Parliament. But a truly democratic Government should be essentially paternal; and although people cannot be made moral by legislation, still much can be done in encouraging them in higher tastes than those engrafted in the pot-house. The present Parliament of New South Wales has immortalized itself by an act, the example of which should be followed in all the colonies, and throughout the world, wherever the true welfare of the masses is held of any account. It was done suddenly and quietly, and we have hardly yet got over our astonishment thereat. Mr. Hurley, the member for Hartley, is about the last man one would have picked out as the instrument in carrying through this great reform, with which his name will be for ever connected . . . Mr. Hurley carried his motion, "that the Public Library and Museum be opened for certain hours on a Sunday," through the Legislative Chamber, and he deserves every credit for his action therein.

When the news was published, the Sabbatarian party was aghast. No one had thought it possible! Meetings were at once held, and resolutions carried showing that the opening of these institutions on the Sabbath was an outrage to liberty, religion, and morality; and that the welfare of the world in general, and the British constitution in particular, was threatened thereby. Representatives of all creeds and sects were unanimous in the one opinion that Mr. Hurley must be a direct missary of Beelzebub, and that the result of his machinations would be unutterable ruin to the colony. In the House a motion was brought forward to rescind the resolution, which, it was stated, had been passed "secretly and against the wishes of the majority of the members and the people of the colony." I am happy to say that this was not successful. Then the Sabbatarian party changed their tactics, and urged that the opening of the Library and Museum on Sunday was a work of supererogation, that no one would go there, that the working classes especially did not want them opened, and would not attend. It was to test the truth of this that, last Sunday, May 12, I spent the afternoon in these institutions, and now give the readers of *The Argus* a plain unvarnished statement of what I saw.

The Sydney Public Library is a gloomy building at the corner of Macquarie and Bent streets. The style of architecture I should describe as the "Early Convict." It is totally inadequate to the requirements of the times, but I am glad to say that it is proposed shortly to erect another and worthier building. Mounting a long flight of steps, one passes by a lavatory, and through a recording turnstile, into the one room of which the library is composed. This is gloomy and dismal, about a quarter the size of that in Melbourne. The roof is high enough, and there is a narrow gallery round the sides. There are five tables in the room, with fourteen seats at each. Other chairs are scattered about in the recesses between the shelves. One of these said recesses is sacred to ladies. On ordinary days there are never very many people in the library; I do not think I have seen more than forty at a time. At night, however, there are more, and in winter-time I presume it is better patronized.

It was a lovely day, one on which all the world should be taking the air out-of-doors. As I went up the steps, shortly after two o'clock, I thought that this would not be a favourable opportunity to judge of the success of the new departure. Only the third Sunday of opening, when the fact would not be known to many people, and such charming weather. Certainly many would not attend! I was the fourth person in the room, and, selecting a book, seated myself and awaited events. At a quarter-past two there were sixteen people present, at half-past two over forty, at three o'clock *ninety-nine, with the room more crowded than I have ever seen it before.* Amongst this number there were some ladies and children, but the majority were of the class unable to attend on week-days—artizans, mechanics, and labourers. There was no mistaking them. Under pretence of searching the shelves—which are not nearly so well supplied as at Melbourne—I prowled around the room, and "took stock" of everybody. The two attendant librarians, who were on duty, and looked decidedly as if they thought this very wicked, eyed me suspiciously. I think they imagined I meant to free-select a volume or two. There is always a decided difference between the *habitués* of the Library here at day and night-time. By day there are students and loafers; at night young clerks and working men. But many of those present last Sunday were not regular attendants. You could see that they were strangers by the manner in which they hunted for books. One man told me afterwards that, living up at Surry-hills, when he went home at night, and had "a clean up" and a bit of supper, he wanted a pipe and a rest, and he hadn't any time to come into town again and back. "I'm fond o' readin'," said he, "I'm a workin' man now, but I've saved a bit o' money, and I may be a master some day. I don't want to be ignorant of everything then. I can come here quiet of a Sunday afternoon, and learn a lot that'll be useful to me. But I think, mate, they ought to have it opened in the morning as well as i' the afternoon." I dare say there were many cases like the above. Most present were respectably, even well dressed, as is the privilege of the working-man in this country of high wages, but the marks of their vocations were plainly to be seen. Some had the peculiar colour of the skin which appertains to blacksmiths and those who work amongst great heat. Others had their hands engrained by working in metal, or had cuts and scars which showed the carpenter or joiner. There was a merchant sailor with gold rings in his ears; and two jack tars from the *Sappho* came in just before three o'clock, and buried themselves in some nautical works.

Pleased as I was to see that this new privilege was so soon taken advantage of by the class it was intended to benefit, I was even better pleased on noticing the character of the books which were read. I have written fiction myself, and thoroughly believe in healthy novels as a means of amusement and relaxation. Still, there is a higher type of literature from which true knowledge is gained. On Sunday last at the Sydney Public Library fiction was at a discount. Technical works, historical works, books of travel, geography, politics—even on religion, these were principally in vogue. Almost everyone present must have learned something, and have left with an improved mind after his Sunday afternoon's reading. It is true some boys were reading Captain Marryat's works, and one or two of the *genus* loafer didn't appear to be reading anything in particular, but only just "putting in the time." However, I don't think there was much harm in this.

After spending an hour in the Library, I was so thoroughly satisfied of the success of this "godless experiment," that I left, and wended my way towards the Museum. This is situated about a mile from the Library, opposite Hyde Park, erstwhile a racecourse, and beforetime site of the convict barracks. The building is not remarkable for beauty. Crowds of people were thronging up the steps, and, inside, locomotion was almost impeded by the numbers trooping around. This difficulty was much increased by the fact that, instead of passing along in a regular cue from right to left, the visitors formed two solid and opposing bodies, which were always coming into contact from different quarters. At the door was a visitors' book, where each name was supposed to be recorded, but the crush was so great that the attendant was content in most cases to register the numbers as they came in. On interviewing him, I found that on the second Sunday of opening it was calculated that *two thousand eight hundred visitors attended.* There were more last Sunday, I was informed, and in the three hours, from two to five, that it was opened, *at least three thousand must have visited the Museum.* This is a striking sign of the popularity of the new movement.

I do not think very much of the "Australian" Museum, as it is ambitiously termed. It is very like that at the University in Melbourne, with the exception that there seems too much of everything, and the specimens are not so well mounted. There are skeletons of whales and casts of pre-Adamite monsters. There are cases of stuffed animals and birds, and quite a plethora of minerals and shells. There are thousands of other birds, which, cured and ticketed, lie on their backs under the glass, looking remarkably like the pictures of the dead cockrobin in the story-books. There appear to be bones of every living thing—including three entire skeletons of the human form divine. Art is only represented by some plaster casts of celebrated statues, which are at the southern end of the building, and a cartoon depicting Chaucer reading his lays to an admiring crowd comprised of king, queen, nobles, ladies, and priests, dressed in the costume of the period. This was, I understand, painted for the competition for the frescoes of the House of Commons at Westminster. Not being successful, it was some time back bought by Mr. Coombes, an ex-Minister. It was a source of great wonder to the throng on Sunday last, and, as the only bit of colour in the Museum, I think deserves a better place.

But the human show was what I came out to see, and with this I was wonderfully pleased. It was a representative Sunday throng of the people. Mechanics with their wives and families, small tradespeople with their belongings, clerks, shop girls and shop boys—almost everyone present belonged to the classes which work hard on the six days, and depend on the seventh for health and recreation. There were certainly present a few gentlemen, who, like myself, had gone thither out of curiosity; and Mr. Hurley looked in for a time, and appeared proud of his work, as well he might be. The one fault was, that perhaps there were too many children and babies knocking around. Still, though these got in your way, they doubtless imbibe some valuable object lessons. On every side one heard remarks from working men—"This is the best thing they ever done in Sydney. It ought to have been opened before."

At five o'clock the Museum closed, and then I returned to the Library. The reading-room was still crowded, but little by little the numbers decreased, people adjourning for their meals. At six o'clock, when the lights were turned down, I went with an attendant and examined the register at the door. In the four hours *two hundred and fifty-four persons* had visited the Library, a number, I believe, far exceeding anything known previously on week-days. The Sabbatarians are evidently defeated all along the line, and henceforth the opening of the public institutions on Sunday must remain a fixed law. Sydney, for once, has emerged from its Sleepy Hollow, and set an example to Melbourne, which I trust will soon be followed.

15

Sydney Theatres and Bars

(From 'The Waifs and Strays of Sydney')

I stand in the vestibule of the Theatre Royal, gloomily looking at the photographs of celebrated *artistes*, with which the walls are decorated. I have been upstairs, but the humours of the pantomime delight me not. The notes of the imported and gifted "star" fall flat on my ear. The People's favourite—Everybody's Maggie—for as is the custom with our pets, we speak of her familiarly by her Christian name—life and soul of the piece though she is—cannot please me tonight. Even Signora Pasta, the personification of graceful motion, about whom we raved when she was in Melbourne, but who is not appreciated here, for once fails to arouse my admiration . . . I am more than "out of sorts;" I am ill at ease, for I have taken a new departure. I have, as it were, sold my soul to another printer's devil, who is howling for "copy." I have arranged to become, for a time, the servant of the Sydney public, and I have grave doubts in my own mind as to the sort of master the said public will prove . . .

The likenesses on the walls are mostly those of old acquaintances, for "poor players" and "mummers," being vagrants by Act of Parliament, are the natural companions of a "Vagabond." And now I get a brilliant idea. His Lordship the Bishop of Melbourne has lately been upholding the drama, and the works of my ancestors' friend, William Shakespeare, as moral agents. I believe he is quite right. But would it not be a good stroke of business if I were to take up the opposite side, dispute every one of the Bishop's propositions, and prove that theatrical entertainments in general and in the colonies in particular, are instruments of the Evil One, to be discouraged by all right-minded citizens? I should have a great advantage over the Bishop, in that I know all about my subject, and he does not. His Lordship does not go to the theatre, and, with the exception of my friend, Mr. Creswick, has no acquaintances on the stage; whereas I have all my life been an inveterate playgoer, have had a company of my own (by which I lost considerable money), and know the public and private characters of most of the prominent *artistes* in the world. I think I could dish up a fair indictment against the stage, and earn the everlasting gratitude of many good people who disapprove of this form of amusement. But then, unfortunately, I am "indifferently honest," which has been a great drawback to me in the many political careers I have started on in different parts of the earth. I believe all that his Lordship of Melbourne has written, and I would sooner cut off my hand than write one word which should asperse the characters of the very large proportion of good men and women who earn a poor and hard living on the boards ministering to the pleasures of the public. There are black sheep in all flocks; and the fierce light which beats upon a throne is nothing to that cast on the stage and its players, which too often makes the dusky ones far blacker than they are.

So, giving up the idea of contradicting the Bishop, I again look at the pictures. The portrait of the young lady who rejoices in the *sobriquet* of "the Kicker," and who has praiseworthily kicked her way into a handsome competency calls to mind the naïve remark of a Scotch friend of mine, who was a *compagnon de voyage* of Mdlle. Sara. Said he, "She's a very gude and decent lassie, yon. She's got a whole row of houses in London." I think cause and effect were rather mixed in his mind . . . Then I gaze at one of Bradley and Rulofson's masterpieces of natural beauties, and in the corner I see printed "Muybridge, Photo." This calls to mind my travels with this said eccentric artist; of the number of times I have been dragged out of bed or hammock by him to pose on a rocky foreground, or against tree or ruined temple, or on cathedral steps, to bring the "human interest" into the picture. Disguised in a sombrero and poncho, or Panama hat, loose shirt, with pistol stuck in sash, I figure in photographs in half the albums in America. Ah! those were happy days then—succeeded by dark troublous times; for, when my companion returned to San Francisco he found the proof of his wife's infidelity: he shot his wronger dead, and, standing his trial, was honourably acquitted by a Californian jury. The pistol there is a great conservator of good morals.

These reminiscences, however, do not assist me. Of course, in Sydney they are all "chaste wives, pure lives;" and if otherwise, the injured husband seeks redress in the Divorce Court. Should he take the law into his own hands, I am told that he would be hanged. I think this is hard on husbands. Whilst musing on this, and on the lamentable decline of the *duello*, considered as a moral agent, in Great Britain and its colonies, I am disturbed by a throng of men descending the stairs.

The first act is just over, and these pleasure-seekers are going outside to drink. In America, when one leaves the present or future partner of your joys whom you have escorted to the theatre, it is an euphumism to say, "My dear, I am just stepping out to see a man I know, who is at the back." But in the colonies there is no pretence of apology made. The heat, perhaps, excuses it; but, anyhow, male theatregoers flock out *en masse* for drinks between the acts, and the ladies appear to recognize it as a necessity. And, standing at the door of the theatre, one sees enormous preparations for satisfying the cravings of this thirsty crowd.

In Castlereagh-street to King-street there are, in the immediate vicinity of the theatre, no less than fourteen public-houses. There are bars on each side of the theatre, over its entrance porch, down the passage to the pit and gallery entrances, on the opposite side of the road—everywhere is held out the temptation to smile. Within a stone's throw of the Royal there are no fewer than thirty-two licensed houses. Some of these are decidedly *not* respectable, but I do not intend to sicken the Sydney public with salacious details of the proceedings therein. The character of their business is so outwardly and flagrantly proclaimed that, as I have before stated, it is a mere question for licensing magistrates and the police to consider as to whether the law is outraged. It is, however, a great marvel to me how the proprietors of all these drinking houses manage to make a living. Adulteration, wholesale and artistic, seems the only solution of the problem (?). Why, too, should formerly eminently-respectable and dull Castlereagh-street be selected as the site for these night-houses? But I remember the history of the foundation of the Theatre Royal, and I am sorry that the temple of the drama should attract to its neighbourhood the lowest votaries of Venus and Bacchus. The thirsty crowd surges past me, the individual members hurrying into one or other of the bars. On the opposite side of the way there is a row of men seated on the pavement, with their feet in the gutter. This is a novel sight to the stranger from Melbourne, in which city swift-flowing water, more or less clean, running by the side of all the footpaths, prevents this eccentric indulgence. Shall I go over and interview them and get their opinion on Mr Farnell's policy, and the present crisis in Victoria? It might be worth while, but then I don't like sitting with my feet in the gutter.

I look to the left and see a gathering round the box-office door. A strange assembly always collects there. At almost any hour of the day until midnight one may see a number of individuals who have taken up free-selections under the verandah of the theatre. Actors out of work, or whose turn is over; theatrical agents, unsatisfactory stage parasites of recent growth—wonderful beings, who in their full-blown glory are much akin to betting-men, their sole stock-in-trade consisting in

Sydney at night, after the close of the theatres

unlimited cheek and a display of diamonds. What do these men do to enable them to flourish thus? Like the prosperity of the ring men in Australia, this was at first a deep mystery to me, until I discovered that their chief occupation consisted in endeavouring to circumvent managers on behalf of the "stars" for whom they are engaged, or in circumventing both manager and "star" on their own account. I think they generally "collar" both ways, hence diamonds. A crowd of these are now talking to the "spirited *entrepreneur*" and a mild young man who looks too good to be connected with a wicked theatre. Can I get an idea out of these? I am afraid they have not one amongst them; and, should I approach, I may be asked "to shout"—a proceeding obnoxious to every well-regulated journalist . . .

The saloon bar of the Metropolitan hotel is, of course, presided over by a young lady. In America we think it a degrading thing for a woman to dispense drinks, but in England and its colonies the sex is not so highly respected. I reckon a barmaid has much harder lines than a domestic servant. The former works about sixteen hours a day, and certainly does not get the number of evenings and Sundays "out" which the poor "slavey" claims as her rightful due. But the amount of flattery and admiration accorded to a popular barmaid by all classes of her customers, I suppose, compensates for hard work and bad pay. I have no doubt many girls consider her position an envied one. In American cities it would be thought quite other than so. In New York the attempt was once made to introduce the English barmaid system. Mr. Alexander Henderson, of Australian theatrical reputation, imported several of Messrs. Spiers and Pond's prize maidens and started them in a saloon in the best business location near Wall-street. It was a total failure. All New York set its face against the innovation, and would not encourage the sacrifice of respectable womanhood to the service of Bourbon or lager. I decline to believe that the break-up of this adventure was due to the fact that no female ever yet knew how to "sling" a cocktail or julep properly.

It is very different in New South Wales. Woman is here everywhere devoted to the ministry of Bacchus. The young lady who officiates in the saloon in which I now stand is, I am informed by a leading professional man, "one of the institutions of Sydney." Her bar is like that of Justice, in that all sorts and conditions of men may be seen there, and they are all served alike. Here may be seen naval officers, members of Parliament, civil servants, lawyers, doctors, merchants, actors, journalists, squatters, betting men, and millionaires, mixed up with far more humble individuals. Occasionally there is a stray peer or baronet, or foreign nobleman or adventurer, such as Sydney society takes such pride in capturing. Here is the dreaded Colorado beetle, the bookmaker's terror, taking a drink with a smart young man who is described to me as a "mystery"—that is, he is supposed to spend two thousand a year on an income of two hundred. Several such "mysteries" have been pointed out to me here. Why, London is full of them, only there one generally commences with no fixed income at all. Here is the dark-eyed steward of a leading hotel, who much laments his native Venice. Next to him is a popular yachtsman, listening to the words of wisdom which fall from the lips of a jolly Yankee captain. Here is another smart young American, who is enlightening all the colonies as to the geography of North America, through the medium of useful maps, price one dollar. It is to be hoped that the study of these, and especially of the railroad lines, which like a spider's web encircle the United States, will educate Australians to imitate, in some things, the great nation of the Western World . . .

PART FOUR

Cold Charity

16

A Day in the Immigrants' Home

... I walked down Swanston-street the other day, *en route* for the Immigrants' Home, with my "fondest hopes," built not on the affections, but a stronger passion, desire for food and shelter . . . If a Southern gentleman could have been shown the Viceregal palace as it now stands, he would have said, "Elegant! Yes; almost as good as our Governor's house at Columbia; and these, I reckon, are the niggers' quarters." For, planted just at his gates, the iron and wooden sheds which form the Immigrants' Home seem to a stranger to be an appanage of the Governor's establishment. I believe it was proposed a short time back to remove the home, but I suppose it is left in its present situation that it may serve as a useful warning to succeeding Governors of the vanity of human endeavours as exemplified in its inmates, and the reward of merit as shown in their own cases. But a pistol-shot from the ragged tramp sleeps the governor, arbiter of life and death. I don't know that I should like this establishment so near me if I held an exalted position . . .

Passing through the gateway on one side there is a high fence separating the establishment from the grounds around the Government-house. On the other, the first thing which strikes the eye is a closed sentry-box. Behind this is an iron building, supplemented by a verandah. Ascending some steps towards this, I am met by an ancient porter, who, in reply to my inquiry as to the whereabouts of the office, informs me gruffly that "There aint anyone there, and won't be till two o'clock." I fling myself down on the bench under the verandah, and eye my informant. He looks as if he was going to order me off—I shall contest the point. However, he contents himself with informing me that "the clerk will be in the office at two. It's no use anyone coming 'ere as won't abide wi' rules. Folks can't do as they like 'ere." A wondrous old man is this ancient warder. Charles Dickens, I am sure, would have been delighted with him. His trousers are of many colours, but not of one seam, as the substances are as various as the shades. The neatness with which those pieces (one cannot call them patches, for who can say which is a patch?) are sewn together is wonderful. He is, altogether, a very neat-looking old man, apparently over fifty, the model of a workhouse warder, his spare frame and sharp features giving him a cantankerous appearance, which must be very useful to him in his position, and which his conduct fully bears out. He returns to the room in the shed, of which I take advantage to stroll around the place.

On one side of the drive leading to a house situated in a pleasant garden, and which I presume to be the superintendent's, is a row of little wooden huts, all joined together. A few flowers are about, and they look cheerful and homelike. This is a deception. These huts are the habitations of the female inmates, who are kept together, wives separated from their husbands, the managers of this institution being wisely of John Stuart Mill's opinion regarding "hereditary paupers." Before you arrive at these there is the office, and parallel with the iron house first mentioned there are several more iron erections, one marked "Dormitory," another "Bath." The door of a third is open, and I see it crowded with men and women picking oakum. Evidently you must work for your food here. The old warder follows me, and tells me, "You'd better come and sit over there; you can't go about like this. It's agin the rule, and fellows as come 'ere must abide by rules." So I return to my first post under the verandah, where I cannot see any of the other buildings. A sleek, well-fed cat comes and rubs herself against my legs. Strange that cats always appear to make a good living where the nobler animal, the dog, would starve. By and bye some old men walk down the path, and go out into the road. One old man brings out a plate of scraps from the house; the cat immediately deserts me for him. Two old women creep in. Next come two boys with a kite, which they have been making round the corner. They have to put this up hurriedly, and join a procession of about 30 boys and girls, which start for the schoolhouse. This, with the hospital, is situated on the other side of the St. Kilda Road. Then, with a wheelbarrow, there enters a most wonderful dwarf, wanting but the hump to be a splendid Quasimodo. He rests opposite to where I sit, and eyes me steadily. I dare say he is wondering what is my history. I wonder as to his. He passes, and it is getting dull, when an old lady enters, and immediately makes things lively with the porter. She has evidently suffered with grievances all her life, and she sympathizes with herself. She relates her present grievance to the porter. "Those who come 'ere must abide by rules" is his unvarying dictum. "You must sit down there and wait for the clerk," and so she sits by me. "Folks 'as come 'ere 'as to 'umble themselves," she remarks, to which I cheerfully assent. "They 'as to abide by rules," says the porter. "I little thought I should ever 'ave come to this, when I might 'ave gone to New Zealand and done well," says the woman. "Pity you didn't," says the porter, and retires to view the St. Kilda road. She confides to me that he is a "disagreeable old brute," and afterwards that "If I 'ad money I would never go 'ungry," a statement which I on my own part heartily endorse. The clerk comes at last, and, following him into the office, which also appears to serve as a store, as a pile of loaves of bread is stacked in one corner, I ask to be admitted to the Home. "You want to come in for a night or two? Well, come again at half-past five" is the reply.

Before returning to the Home that night, I read in *The Argus* that the weekly report of the Immigrants' Aid Society gives the number of the inmates as 460, of whom 140 are sick, 128 oakum-picking, four stonebreaking, &c. I also read that "no fresh cases of scarlet fever have appeared in the institution," which is encouraging. At half-past five punctually I am at the gate. The old porter is on the watch, sharp as a terrier, ready to pounce on all comers. "There's no one in the office; sit there," says he, "and remember them as comes 'ere 'as to abide by rules." Several men are already sitting on the bench under the verandah. Next to me is a decent-looking man, fairly clad, who has his swag with him, and looks like a station hand. On the other side is a poor, ragged, disreputable, diseased old man, who clings to a large basket affectionately. Shortly there enters a blonde-bearded, spectacled individual who, barring his shabby-genteel clothes, would make a capital model for "our artist," as he is generally depicted in the London illustrated papers. Others troop in; amongst them, one woman. We all wait patiently under the verandah, the porter prowling around, having a sharp word for all, and seemingly looking on every casual as his natural enemy. He knows many of the crowd, who have been there before. One man explains to him how he had got rid of his money. "That shows what plenty does. It makes a man make a fool of himself—that's plenty," says our Diogenes. To another who creeps in, "Well, you have got the cheek of the devil to come 'ere after bein' turned out this morning." "What can a man do?" says the unfortunate. "Do! why, do as you've done afore!" which, as by his appearance he's been going to the dogs, is not charitable advice. A desultory conversation is kept up, some relating their bad luck in looking for work. "There's one thing as is no use; it's no good a-looking at advertisements," says a youthful disbeliever in the power of the press. I am thinking of investigating the grounds for this extraordinary statement when the clerk arrives and we troop round to the office. Several of the regular inmates are before us, and are supplied with loaves of bread. Two or three who apply for re-admission are refused, one of them for being drunk on his last visit.

The clerk is courteous, but firm, to all. My turn comes. "Your name?" "Age?" "Religion?" "Occupation?" "Ship in which you landed?" "How long since?" "You have no money?" All these questions being answered, I am told to stand on one side for a minute. Four others go through the same formula, and then a paper, with our names written thereon, is handed to one of our number, who, familiar with the place, leads the way up the road, past huts and sheds, until we arrive at a large wooden building. Entering this we pass to the end, where there is a little room, in which sits a warder, reading by the light of a lamp, surrounded by cut hunks of bread. A large can of tea is on a stand, and a shelf above is piled with tins. The paper being given to him, he calls over the names. "Fitzgerald?" "Here." "Take some bread, and help yourself to tea." As I take my hunk, which weighs about two ounces, he tells me I can have more bread if I want it. We sit down on the forms in the large room, and wolf our meal. The bread is good—the tea will not affect our nerves. One man has a plate of meat given to him by one of the inmates who is working out, and pays a shilling a day for his board.

Our supper finished, we have time to look around. The room is bare, with the exception of the benches and forms and some Scripture texts and religious sentiments nailed on the walls. In large letters it is set forth, "I have learned, in whatsoever state I am, therewith to be content," a motto which seems to me to be singularly inapplicable in this connexion. Surely we are not to be content with this. It is the contentment of the masses in their ignorance and dirt which causes most of the disease and vice in this world. We are allowed to smoke in the room, and there is a shed outside, also, for that purpose. I light my pipe and wander around. The inmates appeared to be allowed a deal of liberty, as I walk all over the place. Lights are in some of the buildings. Peeping through the windows, I see the dining-hall of the habitual inmates who are sitting comfortably taking their supper. A brick building opposite this is a dormitory. It is furnished with neat iron beds, mattresses, and blankets. "This is not so bad, after all, I think;" but on asking Blonde Beard if we sleep there, he says, "Oh no, we have to sleep on the floor; you'll find it anything but a paradise." The trees, low buildings, and general outline of the place, still remind me forcibly of the negro quarters on a large plantation as seen at night. There is one exception—instead of the happy laugh of the African, everything here is very quiet. Men walk to and fro, mere shadowy outlines, with the head defined by the glow of the pipe. It is a cold, dark night. The lights of the city gleam out brilliantly. It is eight o'clock, and Saturday. Bourke-street will now be crowded, and hundreds are hasting to spend their surplus in pleasure and dissipation. Whilst here?—well, we have this consolation, that we cannot "make fools of ourselves," for want of "plenty."

At half-past eight a bell rings; it is our signal for retiring. We cluster around the door of another wooden building. Our names are called out, and one by one we enter. Thou had'st reason, my friend; this is not a paradise! It is a rickety old shed, lighted by six barred windows. A number of mattresses are rolled up on the floor. I am lucky enough to secure one. There are about forty of these, which are soon all appropriated, and spread out on both sides, and in the centre of the floor. Inside each mattress are two rugs of the shoddiest of shoddy material. We soon prepare for rest. Some strip to the buff, and roll themselves in the rugs. Others merely take off their coats to act as pillows, and lay down with their clothes on. I hang up my coat, waistcoat, and hat, and drop on to my mattress. It is straw, of course, but my thoughts are not as to its softness—for that I care little—but as to its cleanliness. It is old, torn, and dirty. Faugh! I must rest content for one night at least. The wardsman remains in the room, talking to several whom he knows. He is an Irishman, and the best type of official I have seen, as his rough humour has a greater influence with the men than the crabbedness of the porter at the gate. There is a good deal of jesting of a Rabelaisian nature, in which the warder takes his due share. He leaves after a few minutes, enjoining us not to smoke on penalty of immediate expulsion, and retires to his room, which is partitioned off next to the door. A brisk conversation is being carried on, chiefly on the side opposite to where I lie, as my neighbours are silent. The great theme is the conduct of one of the men who applied to be admitted, and being refused, immediately went and broke the lamp at the gate in order to be locked up. The sentiment of the ward is altogether healthy, and against this act. Everyone considers the man was wrong to injure the property of an institution from which he had previously received benefits. "He was a blackguard. Shure, why didn't he go and hit the policeman on Prince's-bridge if he wanted to be locked up; there'd be something noble in that," says an Irishman. "Ah, but maybe the perliss would give him a —— good hammering afore they run him in," says another. This remark impresses itself on the ward as a profound truth, which no one disputes. "Then, why didn't he go and smash one of them big windows in Bourke-street," says a third. The general opinion is that he should have smashed anything or anybody sooner than the lamp at the gate. "If he wanted to be locked up—but liberty's sweet—I wouldn't like to part with my liberty," is the expression of an individual who, by the pathos of his voice, has at some time or another felt the deprivation of that sweetness. "Who was he?" asks one "Why, the man with the broken nose—the one Tip M'Grath hit two years ago," is the reply.

Picking oakum at the Immigrants' Home, Melbourne

"What, Tip M'Grath, the preacher?" "Yes." Then ensues a long discussion on the merits of the *soi-disant* Rev. Tip M'Grath. His fighting capacities are duly appreciated by many of the crowd, but as a "preacher" I cannot hear much of him, except that "he had turned" that way. A man with a larger swag, and well clothed and booted, who says he has just come from Launceston, is asked his opinion of Tasmania. He "——'s the —— country to ——," swearing he has spent £20 since leaving Melbourne, and could get no work.

The wardsman re-enters with two new arrivals. The beds all being taken, they have to lie wrapped in their rugs on the floor. We are now very close together, and a complaint is made of the basket belonging to the wretched old man. "What hev' yer got in that, now?" asks the wardsman. "Only a few oysters," is the reply. There is a general laugh at this, and a request to hand them around, but the old man is forced to take them outside. I remembered what particular care he had taken of this basket, but never dreamt that his whole swag consisted of a few oysters. I look around the room. The figures crouching, rather than lying, on the floor deserve the pencil of a Cruikshank properly to delineate them. In one thing most of them seem alike—they have their right hands in their bosoms. I wonder at this for a moment, until the horrible truth strikes me that they are vermin-hunting. At nine the warder brings in a tin bucket and lowers the gas. I do not know if the door is locked, but am told that a few nights back a madman was locked up with the rest of the inmates for two or three hours. He had suddenly commenced his pranks after retiring to rest, and the wardsman and night watchman being both powerless or frightened, they quietly locked the door and sent for the police. He did not do much harm, but frightened the other inmates a good deal. Conversation still goes on. Several are talking about Ballarat and Sebastopol, which they appear to know well. An Irishman, naturally, is great on the affairs of Scotland, explains all its laws, and describes Berwick-on-Tweed, Edinburgh, and Gretna Green, "where me grandfather was married." There is a better tone in the conversation than could be expected—for a time. In this age a truthful account of the conversation and scenes in such a place as this could not be printed. It might have been possible in the reign of Elizabeth. Life in the bush and on the diggings is not conducive to decency either of speech or conduct. At last one says to the Irishman, "You'd better shut up and let us go to sleep now, or you'll be reported in *The Argus*." This causes a general laugh. I am slightly amused to think that they have read my experiences in the Model Lodging-house, and that, unwittingly, one has spoken truth.

One by one my companions all drop off to sleep. Until they do so, and even afterwards, there is one horrible sound—a continued scratching. One would imagine that this crowd would be more unhealthy than the inmates of the Model Lodging-house, but here there is none of that consumptive coughing which struck me so painfully at the King-street establishment. Mosquitoes, which in the upper parts of Melbourne are now things of the past, torment me frightfully, also other insects; but even without this annoyance I could not sleep. The smell is sickening; everything is foul—rugs, mattress, floor, and walls. Unwashed humanity—and there are some good specimens of it here—is abominable to every sense. And as I lay awake here the moral atmosphere seems heavy. May not moral contagion hang about certain buildings the same as physical? . . . Yes, to-night I feel that foul thoughts and ideas hang about this place. Strange suggestions of possible crimes come into my mind. Horrible surmisings seem attached to the dirt of the walls. I am haunted by the ghosts of evil sayings and aspirations, if not of deeds. I would give anything for sleep, but it comes not. Hour after hour passes throughout the night. In the earlier part several more arrivals are ushered in, and have to lie on the bare boards. But later on everything is quiet. I hear the clocks strike, and the sound of the goods trains. Inside there is the snoring and scratching of my companions. About three o'clock it becomes very cold; the wind whistles through the many crevices in the building. Lying on the floor as we do, we are exposed to every draught. The air becomes a little purer, but the cold is very great, and the thin rugs not sufficient protection from such. Sleepless I lie. One; two; three; four; five. There seems a glimmer of light, and I rise, blistered and benumbed, from my sleepless couch.

Underneath the gas lamp I stand naked, my first care being the examination of all my clothing. I capture a curious entomological collection:—Item, two ants; item, fleas; item, what the Yankees call "chintzes;" item, strange little specimens of an insect described by some one as "man's nearest friend" . . . Clothing myself, I am the first to leave the dormitory. The morning air, though cold, is clear, and after holding my head under the water tap, I find myself considerably refreshed. I walk around the place. Very few people are yet astir. The settlement is such a rambling collection of incongruous erections that it would require a guide book and plan to thoroughly describe it. Of three new brick buildings, one is a women's ward, separated from the men's by a high fence; the others diningroom and dormitory of the regular inmates, who fare much better than the "casuals," of which I am one. To become an inmate one has, I believe, to obtain a recommendation from a subscriber and satisfy the committee of disability or inability to obtain work. The inmates are mostly old men. They are engaged in picking oakum, breaking stones, &c., but I do not think their labour is very arduous. Many of them appear to have been here many years. I

Casuals in the Immigrants' Home

interview a good many of them, but cannot discover that there is any regular system of selection. It appears all a fluke as to whether a man gets in or not, and once in, if he behaves himself, he is likely to stop. The casuals are only admitted for a night's lodging and a meal of bread and tea, for which they have to pay by picking oakum or breaking stones for an hour in the morning. With the exception of the clerk, all the officials I have seen seem to be inmates. They wear no uniform, but walk around in shabby garments, and are generally to be distinguished by carrying a stick. They are mostly old men, and seem to me very unfitted for their positions, to which they are I suppose appointed from motives of economy, receiving perhaps some little extra luxuries or privileges. The good order prevailing seems to me to reflect greater credit on the inmates than on the system of management.

At six o'clock the bell rings, and the inmates of the casual ward are told to turn out. Two men are selected to go to the kitchen to fetch the tea. I follow them and get a warm in front of the large boiler fires. Breakfast is served out in the same manner as supper. Afterwards, certain "casuals" are selected by name to clean and sweep out the different wards, including those of the regular inmates, who—aristocrats of the place—do not wait upon themselves. Then we break up into groups, smoke and talk. The children, I see, are sent off to the Sunday School. Later on some religious service is held in the dining-hall, but it is not very well attended. I am having a long and interesting conversation with an old bushman. At twelve we have dinner—a great feed in honour of Sunday, soup, meat, and plum "duff." Again in the afternoon there is church, but before this I have slipped out of a gate into the cow paddock, over the rails on the other side, and into the Domain. I could not endure another night in the dormitory, and am informed that no one is allowed to leave on Sunday. If the committee of the Immigrants' Aid Society think I wished to shirk the oakum-picking or stone-breaking, it is a mistake. I am willing to return and give my share of work, or its equivalent—not that I consider I shall be a success in either line of business, but I do not wish to evade any obligation. Simply, I was craving for a bath and change of raiment, which, happily, I was soon able to obtain . . .

17

Three Days in the Benevolent Asylum

... To obtain admission into the Melbourne Benevolent Asylum it is first necessary to get a recommendation from a subscriber or life governor, one who has given £20. He fills up a form recommending you for admission to the committee . . . This form contains blanks to be filled up by your sponsor in answer to questions as to age, occupation, infirmity, family, &c., and two very important ones—"Has the applicant any relatives or particular friends in the country; if so, what is the relationship, and what are their names, employments, and places of abode?" and—"Has the applicant any means of subsistence, and to what amount?" It is stated that "without satisfactory answers to these queries no application will be received," and your introducer has also to vouch for you as follows:—"Having *minutely inquired into the circumstances* of the bearer, and satisfied myself that he is a fit object for reception into the asylum, I beg to recommend him for admission." Armed with this you march up to the asylum at three o'clock on Thursday, and are brought before the committee. If you have any influence perhaps some member thereof will be friendly, and after a formal inspection by the doctor you will receive an order to enter at a certain date. You may undergo a searching examination by the committee, and be remanded for a time, or there may not be room in the institution, but if you are well recommended, and the answers to the queries are judiciously worded there is little chance of the committee, as things are at present managed, picking a hole in the application, and sooner or later you will become an inmate. I myself had little difficulty in so doing. When you have obtained the order of admission on presenting yourself at the asylum you will again be taken before the doctor, who, according to your age and infirmity, will classify and appoint you to the proper ward. It may be that you will be requested to then make your will, although this is sometimes deferred for a day or two. A printed form is filled up with your name, by which you "devise and bequeath all the real and personal property, &c., &c., to which I shall be entitled at the time of my death unto James M'Cutcheon, the superintendent and secretary of the said Benevolent Asylum . . .

Having passed the doctor and executed the necessary documents, you are committed to the guidance of a nurse, who introduces you to your ward and bed. The young person who took charge of me was a fresh, pleasing-looking girl, with her hair worn in the fashion of an English dairymaid. She was a good, kind girl. Having got it into her head that I was blind, she seized me by the arm and carefully led me up and down the steps, instructing me how to walk. I was rather staggered at this proceeding; but as I never feel any repugnance to being linked with a pretty girl, I did not protest. The asylum originally fronted the south, with a cross wing at each end, and the offices in the rear. But, like many institutions and politicians, it has now changed its face, and the addition of two new wings at the eastern end makes that the front, the place now being that of a peculiar-shaped capital T. All the wings are three stories high; access to which is had by many staircases, which divide each ward. As, however, the female inmates were on the first and second stories of the ward to which I was assigned, I had to enter by a staircase at the southern end; and, after getting to the top floor, walk the whole length of the front till I reached No. 1 ward on the north-eastern side . . .

I examined the room. It is long and lofty, lighted by many windows, and well ventilated. At one end is the wardsman's room, on one side of which are the lavatories, and on the other a small room containing only two beds. The ward itself contains thirty iron bedsteads, each provided with horsehair mattress, clean sheets, and (to my great joy) a clean towel at the head of each. There is ample space between the beds, and the room is broad enough to allow tables to be placed down the centre, if necessary. At the head of each bed is hung a card, stating the occupant's age and complaint (if any), and the doctor who attends him. There is also a dietary scale. The majority, I see, have "No. 3 diet," and take their meals in the dining hall . . . The bye-laws contain regulations for the conduct of the attendants and inmates. The day-nurses have long hours, being on duty from six o'clock in the morning till nine at night. The night-nurses are only on duty the remaining portion of the 24 hours. The regulations for the proper care of the wards and patients are thorough and explicit. The inmates have to rise at 6 o'clock in the morning during summer and 7 o'clock in winter. They must make their own beds in a proper manner, and on leaving the wards must not return to the same until 7 o'clock in the evening without permission of one of the resident officers. The lights in the wards are ordered to be put out at 8 o'clock p.m. Breakfast at 8, dinner at 1, and supper at 5.30 are served in the dining-hall. All inmates considered capable of work are required to do so, commencing their employment at 9 o'clock a.m., and continuing till noon; to resume at 2, and leave off at 4 o'clock. These hours are certainly light enough.

I see that, true to my vagabond tendencies, I have already contrived to break one of the most important rules—"Any inmate introducing or having in his possession victuals, drink, or tobacco, not furnished by the institution, shall be forthwith reported to the committee." Now, I have in my pocket several plugs of very good tobacco, which I hope to enjoy in defiance of the rule aforesaid. It is forbidden to enter any ward but your own, or to play cards or dice, smoke in the house, or be guilty of improper behaviour, &c. Any inmate is required to hand over any money or other property in his or her control—another rule which I have broken. After perusing these rules and calculating how I could break some without incurring the wrath of Mr. M'Cutcheon, I made my way downstairs, transgressing again by making excursions along the different wings and examining the wards. They are all much alike, with the exception that the rooms in the new wings at the north and south-eastern corner are higher and perhaps better ventilated. The centre wing of the old building is divided into small rooms, each containing a few beds. Some have cupboards in the wall for the inmate's clothes. A portrait is hung at the head of one or two beds; and there is an occasional scroll of religious texts. I wandered about mostly unheeded, as this time of the afternoon the inmates are all working or walking in the grounds. Returning towards the south wing, I find myself in the hospital wards. These are mostly occupied by very old and infirm men, sufferers from chronic rheumatism or paralysis, or that incurable complaint, "old age and debility." There are many in the asylum in the last stage of all "second childishness and mere oblivion, *sans* eyes, *sans* taste, *sans* everything" but a vegetable desire to live. There are fires and easy chairs in these wards for those who can sit up, and they look clean and comfortable. I will give hereafter the opinions of the inmates as to their treatment.

At last I made my way into the open air, and skirting the buildings, find myself at the dining-hall. It is now four o'clock, and about two hundred inmates are assembled there waiting for the "muster." There are those who have been out on leave, and who have to report their return at this hour. In a few minutes the superintendent appears. Mr. Mc'Cutcheon is on the right side of fifty, a young man for his years, tall and stout, with a fair flowing beard, a pleasant face and good-humoured eye, but with the look of a man who would "stand no nonsense." He brings with him a book containing the list of those who have been out, and calls over the names, to which the owners respond, showing themselves at the same time. One man does not answer, and the result we shall see hereafter. The men then troop into the yard and mingle with the rest. Saturday and Sunday, it appears, are the two days in the week on which leave of absence is granted, between nine in the morning and four in the afternoon, and this privilege is liberally taken advantage of, there being an average of more than two hundred absent on these two days. The others, too infirm to go out, or who have no friends, and find their only sources of interest in the asylum grounds, still welcome back the holiday-makers, and manifest a languid curiosity as to where they have been and how passed the time. This was my first introduction to the inmates in general. The first glance would divide them into two classes. Old men crippled by paralysis or rheumatism, and younger and hardier men who are blind. There seems hardly a man in the asylum who does not walk by the aid of one stick, and the majority seem to require two. Nearly all are clad in white moleskin trousers, which are supplied by the institution.

I am soon "spotted" as a new chum, and many are the looks cast and inquiries made about me. Taking a seat in the garden, by the side of a strong-looking man with a green shade over his eyes, I light my pipe and look as if I was used to this sort of thing. Says my companion shortly, "Yer'll not be here long?" "Only come in to-day," I replied. "And what hev yer had the matter with yer?" I can truthfully reply that I have suffered from rheumatism. "Hev yer been in the hospital?" Again I do not violate the truth when I say that I have been in there, though not perhaps in the sense which my questioner means. "And did they give yer any butter with yer bread?" Jesuitically I answer that I had none there, and ask if there is any butter allowed here. "Sorrow a bit, there's nothing but dry bread; it's a miserable place entirely for a man to be in," is the answer. I learn that this man has been in the asylum eight years suffering from ophthalmia, and with no chance of getting better. With him and some others who join us I sit conversing until it is near the supper time, when the men flock round the doors of the men's dining-hall, which is a separate building (the women dine in the ground floor of their ward). Between one of the doors and the kitchen there is a verandah in which a few privileged inmates congregated; and there is a little joking with the young and good-looking servant girls who pass to and fro with the provisions. At half-past five the bell rings, the four doors of the hall are opened, and we all file in. I am shown to a place about the centre of the hall, which is large and vaulted, and built in two wings in the shape of a T. About three hundred are present. Each man has his place according to his ward, and they all take their seats quietly and without confusion.

A pannikin of tea and a slice of bread are before each man, and the maids who wait on us walk up and down with trays of bread, supplying those who want more. Many men, presumably those who have been out and may have feasted with their friends, have little appetite; others will eat two slices of bread, and some three. The old men all break up their bread into the tins, and eat the "sop" with a spoon. The bread is good, the tea hardly as good as that supplied at the Immigrants' Home. However, I ate my meal humbly, and with an appetite sharpened by a purposed fast. During supper the superintendent walks up and down the centre of the hall, seeing that every one is supplied, and that order is kept. The meal is far from a sumptuous one, and not equal to what I expected, but at all events you can have enough, and have no need to go to bed hungry. Such as there is, it is wholesome, and the servants are attentive. In about ten minutes after we all get settled down and served, the bell rings again, the superintendent and servants leave the room, and many of the inmates, who have not overcome their early habit of food-bolting, follow. The rest finish their meal quietly, and then march out.

It is a beautiful starlight night, the moon shines on the waters of the marsh, and the lights of Melbourne are a pleasant prospect. Very many of the old men go off to bed at once, a few walk round the grounds, or sit on the benches under the walls and smoke and talk. I join a group, and offer little courtesies in the shape of tobacco and lights. One man is talking very loudly and excitedly, and as he moves under the lights of a window I examine him. He is a stout man, with a head phrenologically well developed, a quantity of grey hair, and a grey beard. He must have been a Nazarene for many years, and have a deadly hatred to knives and scissors, as his finger nails would do credit to a Chinese; they are long as a tiger's claw. This gentleman is evidently superior to a petty regard for appearances; his shoes are unlaced, his waistcoat unbuttoned, his shirt torn across the front, and he is sufficiently unclean in every respect to be a man of genius—his finger-nails alone should have made his fortune as a German professor. After a little conversation he speaketh me flatteringly. "Sir," said he, "I imagine by your talk that you have been used to something better than being in a place like this, where men feed and sleep like the brute which perisheth." I admit that I may have seen better days. "Ah!" said he, "I am a gentleman myself. I am a professional man, a doctor, and I had a large practice in Melbourne, but was unfortunate." Strange though it may appear, the fact of his having been "a doctor" in Victoria did not *per se* impress me much, but later on the conversation of my friend showed me that whatever his failings may have been, or are, he is a man of education and talent, which it is sad to see brought to

The Benevolent Asylum, Melbourne

such an end. The doctor, it appears, was the man who did not reply to his name at muster, not having been back in time. Talking with his cronies he expressed a fear of being "jammed." I was curious as to the meaning of this phrase, and at last heard that it meant to have one's leave stopped. Thus one might be only "jammed for a day," or for a week or six months, whilst some even have "life." These latter are hardened offenders, who never go out but they return drunk, and so their leave is perpetually stopped, unless they like to take up their swag and walk out of the asylum, which any inmate can do at a moment's notice. It appears that the doctor had received, after being in the asylum 20 months, "a walking ticket," that is, 14 days was allowed him to find employment, and at the end of that time he must clear out. It certainly seemed absurd to think that anyone attired like the doctor would obtain a professional situation. He said that he had no chance in Melbourne, but if the committee would pay his fare up the country and give him a shilling or two he would leave. "I'll ask them next Thursday," said he, "and they can but refuse.". . .

During the time I had remained with the group round the doctor I saw enough to convince me that the inmates did not waste their time on Saturdays. One man counted out 4s., which he had got whilst out (how, he did not say). One or two others perceptibly smelt of spirituous liquors, and evidently had money or friends to procure them enjoyment every Saturday. They seemed acquainted with all the public-houses in Melbourne. I had been endeavouring to obtain an insight into the place, and make friends of some of the inmates, and in doing so had missed a prayer meeting or service of some kind in the dining-hall. Every night there is a religious meeting. "A d——d lot of church-going, but little religion," said the doctor. "All you can do here, sir, is to live, and eat and drink; there's no society at all, nothing to pass away the time, so some go to church every night." I am afraid the doctor's idea of society means a glass and a game of forty-fives. As I pass through the wards on the way to my bed I see men in all stages of undressing. One or two were at prayer. Their clothes, whether their own or supplied by the institution, all seemed warm and sufficient. When I get to my room I have a little talk with the wardsman. He is an inmate, an active little man, but has one hand crippled by rheumatism. For the appointment of wardsman he receives the magnificent salary of 12s. a month, and does not even obtain better rations, as he takes his meals in the hall with the rest. There is only one wardsman not an inmate, and he is the attendant in the hospital ward. I undress and get into bed. The mattress is soft and comfortable, the sheets clean, the blankets warm, and the air much purer than I expected. But what is this apparition which steals noiselessly along the ward, feeling its way with a stick? The Heathen Chinee, as I live! Yes, a nearly blind Mongolian sleeps four beds distance from me. Many would say it is a judgment, and from an aesthetic point of view I certainly do feel that this is a most frightful experience; but practically I do not suffer any ill effects from the presence of "John," who is a harmless, quiet fellow, and, to their credit be it said, appears to be generally liked by his companions, who have not yet imbibed the prejudice against his colour . . .

Eight o'clock is certainly very early to go to bed, and quite foreign to my habits. I lie awake looking at the whitewashed walls and the lights of Melbourne to be seen through the curtainless windows. The gas has been turned down, but the white walls reflect the faint light from outside, and the dim shadowy forms of the inmates can be seen lying on their beds. Some, evidently old bushmen and used to camping out, have cunningly rolled the clothes around them to obtain and preserve the greatest warmth . . . Their talk dies off, but the inmates do not rest peacefully—balmy sleep is not for them. Many sit up in their beds, and cough and groan; others painfully turn and toss, moaning a prayer for rest, or for the morrow. The majority of these men are old, and their suffering—brought then most vividly home to my feelings—is a sad lesson. However, our instincts are essentially selfish, and being warm and comfortable myself, I in time drop off to sleep . . . I awoke about six, after an excellent night's rest. I am rejoiced to say that, like a disappointed fisherman, I did not get a single bite . . . Taking my towel, I went to the lavatory, which is well supplied with hot and cold water. There is also a capital bath, as good as any in Melbourne, with a splendid shower. The discovery of this I hailed as a blessing, and after paying my devotions to the spirit of cleanliness, I felt like a giant refreshed with wine. These lavatories and baths are the best things in the asylum . . .

When I arrive outside I find it a glorious morning. Many of the inmates are promenading, and I take the morning air with the additional purpose of viewing the surroundings. Proceeding towards the front gate—outside the lodge of which sits the gnarled old Cerberus, who, despite his rough exterior, is very polite—I turn to the left, and, walking along the outside path, find that I am skirting the drying-ground of the institution. In this a few sheep are nibbling the grass; and there is also a croquet lawn marked off, presumably for the use of the superintendent's family, as few of the inmates are young or supple enough to play that game. Keeping to the left, I come upon a small smoking shed, in which perhaps fifty people might be crowded. A little further on are the offices lying at the back of the building as originally erected, but now being at the side. Just past this—down by the fence and near a gate—is a cow-shed and poultry-yard. There are three cows in this shed, which have a history. They, I am told, belonged to an inmate, who, on entering, made the usual assignment of his property; and the committee finding out that he possessed these, attached them; the late owner has, at all events, the satisfaction of seeing them. There are some geese and fowls in the poultry-yard. I am now at the back of the asylum. This is devoted to a garden, in which vegetables of all sorts are grown, potatoes only being bought. Arrived at the end of the walk in this direction—at a corner where the iron fence connects with a brick wall—I see a strange sight. Underneath the wall—side by side for some fifty yards—are a quantity of old boxes, cases, tubs, tin pails, &c.—anything which serves as a receptacle. One or two of these have locks, but the majority are merely covered with boards, bags, old pieces of sacking, cloth, or tarpaulin, kept in their places by bricks and stones. These contain the *lares et penates* of the inmates, who are only allowed to keep a small bag at their bedside, with a comb, brush, and razor. In the extreme corner one man had, Robinson-Crusoe-like, erected a little shed composed of some old boards, bags, and pieces of zinc. It was not as large as a good sized umbrella; but, sitting on his box underneath this, he no doubt felt as happy as a king. Old coats and hats were hung on the wall over some of the boxes. Many of the proprietors of these rich stores were already at their treasures. The sight was a ridiculous, and yet painful, one. To see these poor old men hoarding up a lot of rubbish reminded one of the acquisitiveness of schoolboys, and was a proof how strong that passion is in the human breast. Completing the circuit, I arrive, at last, at the cottage of the superintendent, which is pleasantly situated in a nice garden, railed off from the other grounds. Spying through the bushes, I see an aviary and small conservatory, which denote the presence of a refined female taste . . .

At eight o'clock the bell rang for breakfast, and, following the rest, I easily found my place. We have a small plate of oatmeal porridge, a pannikin of tea, and dry bread, the same as at supper, and the service is in every respect the same—the superintendent being there, and keeping a watchful eye on our wants, and on the girls who wait on us. After breakfast I again walk round. This is Sunday, and many men are reading Bibles, some aloud, others are hobbling about sunning themselves. Two men are carried out, and placed in Bath chairs. One of these, from his ponderous manner, has been christened "the Bishop;" he is quite a character. There is a great consumption of tobacco. I early run against "the doctor," and find that he is "jammed" for the day for not being in at muster last night. From him and from others I obtain some information as to the *status* of some of the inmates. Some would interview the first old man on crutches, and seeing that the majority were outwardly like him, would immediately put him down as a type; but the study of faces during meal-times assured me that all were not of one class.

Amongst those who now help to fill the Benevolent Asylum there are some who were known years ago by their friends as men of repute, shining prominently in the social circle. Clothed in broadcloth and fine linen, they were the respected heads of families. It is not fair to expatiate on the manner of their decline—in some cases it was their own fault, in others they were victims. Now their friends have forgotten them, hope is dead, energy and effort long since paralysed, body and mind alike blighted, they are helpless and worthless in the struggle for existence, and are only fit to drag on their few remaining years in this asylum. There is one clergyman of the Church of England (an Oxford man), two surgeons, a lawyer or two, merchants, officers of the Royal Navy (in the female ward there is a lady, widow of a R.N. captain) another Oxford man belonging to Christchurch, a Hungarian who held at one time a high legal office in his own country, a Swede an ex-army officer, a London tradesman from Oxford-street, a War Office clerk, a sailor who fought with Nelson at Trafalgar, and many of the class of *employés*. A short time back there was the son of an Indian general in the asylum, but he has left. These are mixed up with a number of old Tasmanians, some of whom have been great ruffians, and can spin yarns to which the graphic horrors of *His Natural Life* appear milk-and-water stories. There is an old Irishman who was in the rebellion of '98. He has lived long, and has witnessed many struggles of his countrymen, all with the same object, whatever name they may give the particular outbreak, and still the red is above the green. A sailor, ex-master of a merchant ship, admits having been a slaver, but says the only thing which troubles his conscience was the fact of having, whilst first mate of a vessel trading to Charlestown, South Carolina, enticed the free negro cook on shore, whom the captain sold, and he pocketed twenty dollars for his share. Men there are here who have been in many of England's wars. Some draw a small pension, which, however, is always appropriated by the committee. There is a Staffordshire miner, who, upon my rashly admitting that I had heard of Dudley, launches into praises of its castle, and the prowess of the late "Tipton Slasher," champion of England. There is nearly every class of mechanics and labourers here, but they are all crippled, or so old as to be past work. One old woman known as "Granny," and who for many years kept an apple store on the beach at St. Kilda, is popularly supposed to be much over 100 years of age, and is the female patriarch . . .

I have no prejudice against the church, and was glad to hear that its services would be held morning and afternoon in the dining-hall. At half-past 10 the bell rang for a few minutes, and I made my way to the hall. I found that a temporary pulpit or desk had been placed at one end of the longest wing; by its side was a small harmonium, behind which sat a young lady of pleasing appearance—a volunteer worker, evidently, in the good cause of administering religious consolation to the inmates of the Benevolent Asylum. About 100 were present, half of them women. The majority of both sexes were old and infirm. They paid little apparent attention to the service, but with closed eyes dosed away the time. I believe that most of them come merely for the sake of shelter, and to pass away the tedium of Sunday, which is a particularly long day in the asylum. If it be true that many of them attend all the services of the different denominations held throughout the week, shelter and distraction must certainly be their motive in so doing. Their religious opinions, to say the least, must be rather mixed. Most of the women wore the stuff or alpaca dresses and the cotton bonnets provided by the institution, but a few retained the remnants of faded prosperity and gentility. One old lady sported a respectable moustache, and her size and general appearance reminded me much of Falstaff in the character of the Fat Woman of Brentford. The blind Chinaman, my ward mate, was also in church. It appears that he and his companion, who left the asylum a short time back, have both been baptized and received into the fold by the truly Eastern and poetically appropriate names of Barnabas and Ebenezer. This was Ebenezer. I would have given a little money to have known his thoughts on the service. I noticed that he had not cut off his pigtail, the sacrifice of which I believe fully denotes that a Chinese has abandoned the faith of his fathers. I hope Barnabas and Ebenezer will not backslide. The service was read by a layman, a little man, who may be a Scripture-reader or a volunteer. He read well, but the singing was execrable, being a series of breakdowns . . . It was altogether a dismal, dreary service, only enlivened by the flights of two swallows, which may have their nests inside . . .

At one o'clock the bell rang, and proceeding to the hall I ate my first dinner in the asylum. This, being Sunday, consisted of roast meat and potatoes, with a small portion of boiled rice afterwards. The meat was good, and there was a sufficiency to satisfy appetite. The superintendent every morning goes to the meat market and purchases the day's supply, and the asylum is supplied with as good meat as there is in Melbourne. Of course, in the process of cutting up portions for some hundreds of people there is a good deal of hacking about, and it does not present the most tempting appearance upon your plate, but this is not likely to prejudice many of the inmates. The superintendent is present at dinner, as at every meal, and everything goes quietly and with clock-like regularity.

After dinner I again walk round the grounds and interview the inmates. Many of these appear to always select the same spots, where they congregate and sit and smoke. As I approached each coterie I was at first viewed with suspicion, but little by little I managed to pick up many scraps of information, which will be found in this article. The nicknames which the prominent members of the community have had conferred upon them are most amusing. There are "The Pirate," "The Smuggler," "Badger" (the slaving sailor before mentioned), "Quicksilver Jack," "Garibaldi," "The Bodysnatcher," "Jacky-all-to-Pieces," "The Nurses," "Pet," "Billy Buttons," "Nipper," &c. Many, I am told, are "Whitechapel birdcatchers," whatever that may mean. But the man whose name is often heard, and who appears most popular, is "Scandalous Jack." I have a great desire to see this worthy, but he is out on leave.

The feeling everywhere met with, which I afterwards found to be general, is one of discontent with their lot. "It's a miserable place," "A place for a dog to live in," are the expressions heard on all sides. As a rule, the inmates appear to be thoroughly ungrateful for the shelter and food they gratuitously receive. Each man has his own pet troubles and wants which he cannot get supplied, and it is natural that he should grumble. Every man is essentially selfish, and thinks only of his own case. This is natural, especially with old people. Leading the talk on to the officers, I was pleased to hear the favourable opinions expressed about the superintendent's management of the institution. Some few had complaints, if they thought they had been harshly dealt with in the matter of being "jammed;" but the prevalent feeling was, as expressed by one man—"Mr. M'Cutcheon is the best man we could get. We'll never get a kinder man over us." From a three days' experience in the institution I agree with this remark, and the cleanliness, order, and discipline maintained reflect great credit on his organisation. Mrs. M'Cutcheon, the matron, I only saw once in the building. She carries with her an atmosphere of good looks, good humour, and kindly sympathy, which must be refreshing to whoever is brought in contact with her. I am quite inclined to believe the "Doctor's" statement, that "she is one of the best women in the colonies," and can understand that she is a general favourite, and has great influence over both the male and female inmates. Twice during long years of service the superintendent has had a holiday, and during his absence Mrs. M'Cutcheon managed the institution, and it is said that during that time the inmates did everything in their power to avoid giving trouble, and many volunteered assistance, and did work which they would not have done if the superintendent had been at home. This speaks well for the feelings engendered by years of supervision, and for the manner in which that must have been conducted.

If there be any truth as to the benefit which is said to exist in "seeing ourselves as others see us," Dr. Heath ought to be very much obliged to me, and will derive much good from the perusal of the following opinion of the inmates. According to their statement, Dr. Heath is a man after Brough Smyth's own heart. He is harsh, brusque, and unsympathetic, and is a regular terror to the inmates. The general statement is that he is so much disliked that none will go to him, unless they are very ill. They say that he does not properly attend to his patients, and the inmates of the hospital wards complain that he is very loathe to increase their diet or give them any extra comforts. As far as I could judge, the dietary scale and allowances to patients at the Melbourne Hospital are far better than at the Benevolent Asylum. I am only giving the opinions of the inmates as to the doctor's character. He may be a very estimable gentleman, but when the unanimous voice is against him I think there must be some ground of complaint. In institutions of this kind we generally find that the doctor is the popular man and the superintendent disliked. Here it is the exact reverse, and there must be some cause for it. The *vox populi* states that his predecessor was kind and attentive. I have been told that the doctor detected some cases of malingering in the hospital, and had them turned out, but that would scarcely affect the popular voice; people here are too much occupied with their own troubles and too purely selfish to care much about the misfortunes of others. Each man here speaks for himself, and from his own point of view, as to his treatment. Dr. Heath has his lines in a pleasant and easy place. The average number of patients in the hospital wards is between 150 and 200. The majority of these are old men and women, chronic invalids, who require little medicine or attendance, but just sufficient extra nourishment or comforts to enable their lamp of life to flicker out peacefully ... A number of other patients are seen in the dispensary, the days of attendance at which are only Mondays and Thursdays, and I am told a man must be very ill indeed who dares to risk a snubbing by troubling the doctor on any other day. This seems a great farce. A resident medical officer is kept, yet inmates are only allowed to consult him (unless seriously ill) on two days a week.

There is great talk amongst the inmates about the proposed removal of the asylum to Sunbury. The feeling is generally against it. They consider that it will be a great hardship in depriving them of the opportunity of seeing their friends on their weekly leave of absence.

"We'll have no enjoyment at all then," says one man; "It'll be just the same as a prison then," says another; "I won't stop in if it is moved," says a third. From their point of view, it will be a hardship being shut off from the world in the country and removed from all chance of seeing their friends . . . However much they grumble at the asylum, many inmates who have been in Sydney compare it most favourably to the institution there. According to their account, that has not much improved since 1862, when, at an inquiry by a committee of the Legislative Assembly, much of the evidence was said to be too shocking for publication. One inmate said it was impossible to keep clean, as they never had clean clothes. Once a new pair of trousers was given to him on a visit from the bishop, but afterwards they were taken away. In her charitable institutions, Victoria seems far ahead of New South Wales. Later on in the afternoon there is the church service in the dining-hall. A clergyman officiates, and the attendance is about the same, and composed of the same individuals, as in the morning. After church there is the muster of those who have been out on leave, and then tea-time soon comes round. One meal here is the *facsimile* of another. After tea many go off to bed, and some remain to a service—Wesleyan, I believe—which is held in the hall at night. I, however, prefer to stroll round the gardens, and, failing to capture any inmate of ordinary intelligence, I join two of the maid-servants who, arm-in-arm, are walking in the cool of the evening. The committee need not hold an investigation on this case. Our conversation was as dull as in the politest society; and whilst I—remembering certain instructions given to me by a gentleman who understands this sort of thing—tried to make myself agreeable, I also acquired a little information. I trust, however, that my companions will always think that it was the charms of their society that attracted me. I was amused to hear from them that my character and person were being actively canvassed. Some said I was a detective, because I "looked at everything so sharp," but the prevailing opinion was that I came out by the *Durham* on her last trip, fell amongst thieves *à la* New Chum, and so my friends put me in the Benevolent Asylum.

To bed again before eight; seldom or never have I been so virtuous . . . On Monday morning we are most of us out by seven o'clock. One can easily see that a fresh week has begun; there is life and bustle everywhere. In the laundry, which is between the dining-hall and the kitchen, girls are already working. The washing and cooking here is all done by steam power, and there is a capital boiler and small engine, which, amongst other things, turns a washing-machine. Clothes are being hung out to dry. The horse and cart are being taken out of the stable, and the carpenter's, tinsmith's, and cobbler's shops are open. In the carpenter's shop they do all the necessary repairs, and make the coffins; and I have been consoled with the assurance that, if I die in the asylum, I shall have "as good a coffin as there is in Melbourne." I reply, I "donate" my carcase to the "body-snatcher," to be sold to the Melbourne Hospital at the current rate. The stores and one or two of the shops are situated on the ground-floor of a long building called "Barracouta;" on the floor above are a few single rooms, which are occupied by old married couples. Sloping from one side of this building is a low shed devoted to the interesting pursuit of oakum-picking. I make a tour of all these sites of industry before breakfast, and also explore the linen-room, which is in charge of one of the inmates, a very polite little gentleman, formerly in the Royal Navy, now doubled up from wounds and rheumatism. Here all the sheets, &c., belonging to the different wards are kept. Every week a clean sheet is issued to each bed; and to each inmate a clean pair of moleskin trousers, a shirt, and a pair of socks. Clean underclothing is issued fortnightly. This attention to cleanliness is one of the greatest features in the asylum, and is the only approach to that luxury which many people outside are under the impression the inmates riot in.

After breakfast, every one, except the chronic invalids, starts to some employment: some assist the gardener, others are employed in the various shops, stuffing mattresses, tinkering pannikins, cobbling boots, patching trousers, hammering coffins, or picking oakum. Others are engaged about the house; some specially detailed to examine the bedsteads and extirpate vermin; a few assist the cook by peeling vegetables, and three or four are employed in the office or stores. About half of the women inmates do very little. They are chiefly old and very infirm, and attending upon themselves is as much as they are equal to. The rest, some ninety in number, are engaged in their dining-room knitting socks, making men's shirts and their own dresses and underclothing. Everything of this sort is done on the premises. A forewoman is appointed over them, under the supervision of the matron. They work the same hours as the men. In the dining-hall there is also a separate library for women, the books, however, very much worn and dilapidated.

There is an overseer of work, who walks round seeing that no man is skulking. The superintendent sets every new chum to a job the most fitting for him; but not waiting for orders I entered, and took my seat in the oakum-shed. I should think about one hundred and fifty men were here; a dozen or so were working at tailoring, and the remainder oakum-picking . . . Of this I certainly did very little, as it was my first attempt, and I do not consider that I should ever be a success in that line of business. I picked enough, however, to make my fingers very sore, and render writing this a painful operation . . .

Men go in and out when they like, and appear to be under little restraint. They are required to pick about 38 lb. of oakum a month. If they do this, they are given five plugs of tobacco; if less, three or four; those who do no work being allowed two. I am afraid it would be a long time before I should earn more than two plugs at oakum picking. The shed is very low and close, and thick with oakum dust. In the summer it must be anything but a desirable working-place. I am told it is as hot as Hades. At twelve o'clock most of the crowd give over work, but a few still picked away, and the tailors were working merrily at their benches. I had been sitting next to the "Body-snatcher," who was, so he says, formerly a schoolmaster in the Royal Navy . . . He is a nice, pleasant old gentleman, and politely takes and introduces me to "Scandalous Jack." This celebrated individual is a cripple, a comparatively young man, now engaged in tailoring, which he has picked up since he has been here. He is a fellow of infinite jest and most excellent fancy, and I am not surprised at his popularity. By his side is an old man, who is carefully working a piece of embroidery, one of those long strips of linen-work which ladies pass their time in cutting holes in and sewing them up again. The Body-snatcher, and Scandalous Jack, with myself, have some rare jokes, and I solemnly bind myself apprentice to the latter, to learn the art and mystery of tailoring, for a premium of two plugs of tobacco, and find my own "tucker."

By one o'clock I have a good appetite for dinner. To-day we have soup and boiled mutton, potatoes and bread, all good and plentiful. This is the dinner for four days of the week. Sunday's dinner we have seen; on Thursday there is also roast meat, and Wednesday is *un jour maigre*, on which the bill of fare consists of soup, potatoes, and boiled rice. On Fridays, members of the Roman Catholic faith may have fish. The one great evil in the dietary scale is the want of fresh vegetables. Potatoes only are bought, and the present garden does not appear to afford more than sufficient of cabbage, carrots, onions, &c., to supply the soup. Now, fresh green vegetables and salads are in this country, and in the hot months especially, nearly a necessity, and I hope, when the Asylum is moved, enough garden ground will be secured to produce an ample supply for the inmates. I shirk the oakum-shed during the afternoon, and acquire information elsewhere. The night comes on wet and misty, and now I find out the greatest evil connected with the asylum. There is no place of shelter for the inmates during the bad weather. According to the rules you must, unless in the hospital ward, leave your room at seven in the morning, and not return till seven at night. You may be working under cover during the daytime, but at five the shops and oakum shed are closed, and after tea time there is abso-

Free concert at the Benevolent Asylum

lutely nowhere for the inmates to go except the small smoking shed, or the religious services in the dining-hall. A wet Sunday must be a frightfully miserable day here. There really should be some place where the inmates could be under cover, and read or play a game of draughts, until bedtime. It certainly is anything but in keeping with the name of the institution to make the poor inmates herd together under a small shed or on the lee side of the building, trying to obtain shelter from the winter's storm and rain. The books in the present library are nearly all worn out, but there is little use in replacing them if no place is provided for reading during the winter months. This wet weather disgusted me with the institution, and on the morrow I left, perfectly satisfied with my experience.

Is this charity seriously imposed upon? is a question of the day. After seeing all the patients, mingling amongst them, and listening to their talk for three days, I think I, as far as my judgment goes, must decide in the negative. That there are men here who have small amounts of money, or whose friends might keep them, if so inclined, seems perfectly true. But none of these men are able to earn a living, and their means will not keep them outside. The maintenance and attendance, which the committee calculate to cost £25 a-head inside, could not be obtained privately in the case of a confirmed cripple or invalid for £100 . . . Hundreds have been yearly refused admission to the institution for want of room, and, according to the superintendent's report, "numbers of these can only be regarded as deserving cases, some of them indeed in a state of pitiable destitution and chronic disease." It is just these people who are not likely to know any influential subscribers, or have interest with the committee. It is to be hoped that the new asylum, wherever it may be, will be large enough for all, and that cases such as mentioned, and those who can contribute something, may all be accommodated there . . . Inmates who are in receipt of pensions have the same appropriated by the committee; and, since some three years back, when an inmate was found in the possession of a large sum of money, and acknowledged regularly receiving same by post, letters are opened by the superintendent, in the presence of the owner, and any money found therein is handed to the committee . . . many of the inmates get money from their friends when they go outside—not much, perhaps, but enough to enable them to enjoy themselves once a week. One man said, "I've got a pound or two yet, but nobody knows where it is." Another man was pointed out to me as the reputed owner of a house, but its situation was equally vague. If there are many who have money they keep it to themselves, as the frequent raids have taught them caution, and it is said by some that there is a "secret police" in the asylum. On the whole, however, I think that only a few of the inmates can from any source obtain even a few shillings a week. The temptation, except in the chronic cases of disease, to impose on the committee is very slight; the food, if good and plentiful, is very plain, and the fare is monotonous; there is certainly no luxury, although an amount of cleanliness and decency which, compared with the Immigrants' Home, is striking. The many restrictions imposed upon an inmate would soon disgust any man who was enabled to live outside . . .

In conclusion, I must apologise to "Scandalous Jack" for not fulfilling the terms of my indentures; but although an absconding apprentice, I am willing to pay the premium at any time, and to him, the "Bodysnatcher," and other gentlemanly inmates, I return my thanks for courtesies received during a stay of three days in the Benevolent Asylum.

18

At the Sailors' Home

. . . Sailors, it is claimed, are now treated as rational beings, floggings on board men-of-war are of rare occurrence, good food for the body is served out as well as for the mind, and a large amount is annually saved by Her Majesty's Government through the falling-off in the consumption of rum, owing to the establishment of Good Templar lodges on board many of the ships. The merchant seaman is equally well treated at sea; and ashore—instead of, as formerly, being at the mercy of the low boarding-house keeper and crimp, who, when he landed, kindly took care of his money, provided him with unlimited rum and tobacco, and in a week showed him a bill and kicked him "outward bound"—he goes to a Sailors' Home, attends a Bethel, temperance lodge, and Sunday-school, puts money in the savings' bank, and sings Moody and Sankey instead of Dibdin. The old idea of the British sailor is now thought to have been a disreputable one; I question if the new one is more real. It is certain, however, that the British sailor has now far better aids provided to keep him straight and protect him from landsharks; and of these, Sailors' Homes are claimed to be the chief . . .

The Melbourne Home was opened in 1865, being erected on a piece of land—granted, I believe, by the Government—opposite the Spencer-street railway station, and the cost of the building defrayed by Government grants and public subscriptions, the English shipowners and their agents giving largely. The Home rapidly became very popular, and has been largely patronized by seamen visiting this port, no less than 16,405 having passed through the Home as boarders during the ten years it has been in existence.

The other day I thought I would go to sea—at least, as far as the Sailors' Home; so one afternoon a ragged, disreputable vagabond, in semi-nautical attire, was to be seen entering the gates of the institution.

Spencer-street is not a lively locality, and the entire absence of nautical surroundings would lead one to imagine the building to be anything but what it is. The iron palings and shrubs in the front garden are not suggestive of the briny. On the right hand side of the hall is the superintendent's office, and, knocking humbly at the door, I was told to "come in," and found myself in the presence of the chief boss John George Allbeury, ex-master mariner, and therefore always accosted with the brevet title of "Captain." This gentleman is a native of one of the Channel Islands, and looks like a Breton farmer. Cap in hand, I respectfully answered his queries as to whence I came, my last ship, why I left it, if I wanted another, and could I pay 19s. for a week's board? That sum being handed over, and my answers registered in a book, I was asked if I had any money to deposit. I had none, so was confided to the care of a young man, a Swede, the "runner" of the establishment. Taking a key, he ushered me upstairs to the fourth story, and into a little room on the wing facing Little Collins-street. The rooms are 100 in number, and are situated on both sides of the passages on the different floors, from which and from each other they are separated by partitions of corrugated iron, thus saving space and providing cleanliness. There are low windows in each, looking into the streets or the inner yard, and over the door glass transoms admitting light at night from the gas-lit passages, no lights being allowed in the rooms. My room was perhaps 10 feet square, the only furniture being a low iron bedstead. The floor and walls were not very clean, dust and cobwebs being plentiful. I immediately examined my bed, and, finding dirty sheets, struck for and obtained clean ones, and was promised a chair. Leaving my room, first locking the door, and pocketing the key, I went below and examined my "home." The shipping office was formerly located here, but has recently been removed to new quarters near the Custom-house. The front facing Spencer-street is now occupied by the office, store-room for luggage, and a day-room for inmates. This is furnished with tables and forms, and is a particularly dirty and dingy place. It is adorned with coloured prints of biblical events, such as David slaying a gigantic lion. Over the fireplace is a notice that advance notes will be cashed "at the usual rate of 2s. in the pound," which to me seems rather extortionate. In this room inmates congregate and smoke, play cards and draughts; "no gambling, however, being allowed." There is a spacious yard at the back, at the end of which is a good room devoted to skittles. Quoits are provided outside, and under the verandah there is a board containing a number of hooks, on which, from a certain distance, you pitch rings, or endeavour to do so. Altogether quite a fund of amusement. In this yard a number of inmates are always to be seen taking short quarter-deck walks to and fro.

The force of habit is here strangely exemplified. Confined at sea, like beasts in cages, sailor constitutionals never exceed a certain number of paces each way, and on shore they cannot get rid of the habit.

The dining-room is in the wing facing towards Little Collins-street, and is a large room, capable of accommodating 200 ... Breakfast consists of mutton chops, beefsteaks, and sausages (component parts unknown), tea or coffee, bread and butter ... But, alas! I have not acquired a taste for the *cuisine* of the fok-sle. The meat and sausages are all fried together, with a liberal allowance of onions, and served up on great dishes, without any pretence of distinction of viand. The consequence is, everything tastes of grease and onions. I object to both. Dinner consists alternately of soup and meat, or meat and "plum duff." The soup is not A1; the meat is pretty fair, but the cookery, as I have suggested, decidedly of the fok'sle. Beef, mutton, sea-pie, and curry are brought in haphazard, and one generally seizes the first to hand. There are plenty of vegetables, and everything is served without stint. At dinner each man is allowed a glass of ale—colonial of course, but good of the class. The Good Templars of the crew hand their beer to their mates, and are consquently much respected for their temperance. For tea there is hash, stew, and cold meat, with coffee, tea, bread, butter, and salad. This was the meal I relished most. Supper consists of cold corned beef, bread, and cold water. I went in to look at this meal once, and shuddered to see men devouring piles of this indigestible food, washing it down with pure Yan Yean. I think the committee might allow tea and coffee, or a glass of ale, to each man at night ...

I suppose the beds at the Sailors' Home would be luxurious to a "weary sea-boy;" for myself, I thought mine rather hard, and could not sleep well. I was glad that it was winter, or I might have had companions. The lights in the day-room and passages are turned out at eleven o'clock, but when I retired at that hour I had little chance of rest. Boarders would come home at all hours, clattering along the passages—every sound reverberating along the iron walls. I found it very cold, too. I always opened the ventilator above the window, and the transom over the door; and, the bed-clothing being rather scanty, I often awoke shivering in the night ... On each landing there are two open spaces in the passages acting as lavatories. A great blessing at all the public institutions of Melbourne is the bountiful supply of water. Soap here was procured from the steward who looked after the floor, each man having a piece given him for private use. I do wish they would also give them a towel each. The Benevolent Asylum is the only institution I have seen here where this great aid of cleanliness is understood. Here the towels are only changed once a week, and they are considerably, as may be imagined, soiled by use during that time. But, in any case, I object to have the chance of drying myself after a Chinaman or a negro; and I had to supply myself with relays of pocket-handkerchiefs for that purpose, being afraid to introduce a towel, as it might be thought too high-toned for a Vagabond. There is an attendant to each floor, the chief being a German named Joe, who spends many sixpences in the Chinese lotteries, being on quite intimate terms with Little Bourke-street. The other two are quite boys. These, besides making the beds on their respective floors, are supposed to do all the cleaning, both up and down stairs, have to set the tables, and wait at meals. When the Home is full, these men have hard work, but are sometimes assisted by an inmate who may give a hand, getting in return some slight reduction in his board money. The whole establishment is worked economically; besides the three stewards there being only two cooks, night watchman, runner, clerk, and superintendent on the staff. There is enough work for everybody—more than enough, perchance, and consequently a want of general cleanliness and attention to the comfort of the boarders...

English, Irish, Scotch, Welsh, and colonials from all parts of Australasia, were mixed up with one Yankee, Frenchmen, Germans, Italians, Greeks, a Malay, an American citizen of African descent, a pure negro, and the Chinaman who appears to be always with me. A black man sat next to me at table, greatly to the disgust of my Yankee friend, who said, "By ——, sir, this is the first time I ever boarded with a nigger"...

The idea of the British tar on the wallaby seems a heresy, yet many of the men at the Home appeared, by their talk, experienced bushmen... According to them, Melbourne, as a port, was getting nearly played out, and the number of sailors unemployed was instanced as a proof. When the wool season comes on some might get a ship, but so many of the English liners ship their crews out and home, that there would not be a chance for all. If, too, they shipped to London at good wages, they would have to, in many cases, work their way back at the nominal pay of one shilling a month. "Adelaide's the place," said one man to me: "Melbourne's going to the dogs." "How do you make that out?" I asked. "Well, you see, they get no cargoes coming out here. What they do get they carry at such low rates that it don't pay 'em. Ships only come now for the wool. The customs is so high that it stops goods being sent out. Now, at Adelaide, they get good cargoes both ways. Every year you see more ships come in, and if they don't alter the customs here, Adelaide will get all the Riverina trade. When I once get away from here, I'll never come to this port again. Adelaide is the place for me." All the sailors I talked with were free-traders to a man.

The present seems, indeed, very hard times with the sailors in this port. The wages offered are very low, and it is only the existence of a Sailors' Union which keeps them at a minimum of £5 monthly for able-bodied seamen. I was myself offered £6 monthly for a nine months' cruise, but I wanted £7. Every day the majority of the inmates of the Home go down to the shipping-office, around which they loaf, waiting for captains short of hands, who come out. Then they return to their meals; and on wet days lounge about the passages, play cards in the dayroom, or read in the library. This is a room on the first floor looking into Spencer-street—it is small and dirty. At one end are locked bookshelves, containing a good selection of popular works. On the tables are the daily papers and a fair supply of English illustrated and other periodicals. Books are given out from the shelves every morning. In this room a certain number of inmates always congregate—they are generally of a superior grade. Here one or two daily bring their books and slates and work out problems in navigation, by those mysterious processes which enable nautical mathematicians to take a reckoning. They are studying to pass for first mates. There is an evening school at the institution, at which boarders are given instruction to enable them to pass either as second and first mates, or masters. It is a good thing that a man at sea should understand navigation, no matter what position he holds; but from Melbourne these students stand little chance of obtaining positions as officers, as the number of mates ashore is quite out of proportion to the seamen, or the demand for such . . .

The managers of the Sailors' Home have, during the present winter, caused a series of popular entertainments to be given for the pleasure not only of their boarders, but of all seamen in the port. I was present at the fourth of these. It was a very fair show on the whole, although some of the amateurs were a great infliction. I do not know if all the performers were volunteers. Some of them I have seen before at that refuge for the destitute and school for rising talent, the Temperance Hall. The tables in the dining-room were cleared away directly after supper, and forms placed fronting a portable platform some six inches high. The Trades band, discoursing the music of "Madame Angôt," played in the company. The tables, piled at the end of the room, were favourite seats, those on the highest tier being equivalent to the seats of the gods of a theatre . . .

The first gentleman attempted to give a song of the present degraded music-hall stamp. He had no voice and could not sing, his only qualification for the part being his looks, which were suggestive of the "Great Scamp," "Jolly Dod," or other professional *comiques* of renown. A comic song is always dreary, but when given by an amateur it is worse. We didn't care much about this, and the gentleman in question was such a muff, that a seaman next to me threatened to throw something

The Sailors' Home

at him if he came out again. Another said, truly, "It's a —— insult that chap getting up, and can't sing a bit. I suppose he thinks anything good enough for sailors." The next performer was introduced as "having left his work, and his books, and his papers, and come all the way from Sandridge to sing here to-night." "What the —— does he do working at night?" growled one. However, this gentleman gave us the "White Squall" in a style which brought down the house. We sailors appreciate good music, and especially nautical ballads. Mr. —— is a young gentleman with histrionic proclivities. He gave us the dialogue between Bumble and Mrs. Corney, from *Oliver Twist*, in a manner which agreeably surprised me. The sailors enjoyed this hugely, and encored Mr. ——, who was not quite so successful in his rendering of "Fagin's Dream," which is not a pleasing subject, and which Charles Dickens himself had great difficulty in rendering to an audience. The success of the evening was Mr. W. S. Gilbert's amusing "Bab" ballad, "The Nancy Belle," which Mr. —— gave with great unction. One of our number, who had been communing with spirits, was particularly noisy in his repetition of the chorus "Brave Boys." Another, however, suddenly left us when the song arrived at the stage where the crew cast lots as to who shall be killed. I met this man next day, and said, "Mate, what was the matter with you, last night, that you went off in that way?" "It's all —— fine to make a joke of it, but if you had been in that fix yourself you wouldn't care 'bout hearing the like made a song of," was his reply. I whistled, and felt inclined to ask him what it was like, but he stalked off moodily, not inviting interrogation. A man who has eaten his fellow-man is an object of interest to me. He doubtless has feelings and sensations which I do not understand. Messrs. —— were very successful in the gendarmes' duet, from "Genevieve de Brabant;" but the crowning joy was "The Death of Nelson," by Mr. —— the gentleman who had "come all the way from Sandridge." "God save the Queen," and cheers for Captain Allbeury and others, finished the show, and we retired quietly and without disturbance . . .

I was sitting one night in the library, hearkening to some harrowing tales of the sea, when the sound of music and singing arose from below. A rich strong soprano voice was delivering "Hold the fort, for I am coming," one of the gems of the collection of Messrs. Moody and Sankey. I don't know that I bet my bottom dollar on these gentlemen. Mr. Moody I knew before he went to England, and remember the time when he could not draw a house . . . Going down to the dining-hall, I found that it was doing duty as a chapel. The congregation, however, was a small one, not twenty sailors being present. At a harmonium a lady was seated, playing and singing in a style which, after my experiences of the religious entertainments provided at the Benevolent

Asylum and at Kew, was most gratifying and pleasing. The service was conducted by the Rev. Mr. Johnston, of the Seamen's Bethel at Sandridge ... The lady musician was his daughter. The small congregation was a very attentive one, and was composed of some of the best men in the Home, the presence of Captain Allbeury not being needed to keep them in order. Mr. Johnston did not bore us; after two hymns, he gave a short prayer, then a portion of Scripture, then a short homely address, a prayer and hymn concluding the service. But the sailors wanted another tune, and they had two. As with Messrs. Moody and Sankey, the singing here is the great attraction ...

In spite of Good Templar Lodges, Rechabite and Total Abstinence Societies, and Sailors' Homes, strong drink is the rock on which many a seaman is still wrecked. Certainly, the majority of the inmates of the Sailors' Homes were sober men, and the amount of drinking done at the neighbouring public-houses was small. Still a few made good time, and one man lost his ship through over-indulgence in colonial poison. He had been in the Home some time, and left one morning for his new ship at Sandridge pier, wishing us all good-bye in an elated manner, and envied by many. Two days afterwards we were surprised to see him walk in, looking ill, and with scars of combat on his face. It was the old story of folly and bad drink. He had obtained an advance, and, meeting a friend at Sandridge, felt bound to treat him. Queensland rum soon did its work, and Jack was shortly staggering on to the pier, where he met his captain, who told him that he didn't want any drunken men on board. Jack retorted, and struck at the captain, who knocked him down, and gave him in charge of the police. After being locked up all night, he luckily escaped with twenty-four hours' imprisonment ...

Three men, who left a well-known liner because, as they assured me, she leaked so much they did not care about going round the Horn in her, were, however, lucky in obtaining berths in the Lincolnshire, but I expect they shipped home at low wages. Four men had their passages paid to Launceston to fill up the crew of a vessel there; in fact, from what I could glean, every port in the colonies seemed at this time better than Melbourne for a sailor. Whether the evil of centralization of labour, which is apparent in the trades here, also applies to sailors, I cannot say; but the supply of seamen, anyhow at present, far exceeds the demand, and the wages offered are, as a rule, very low. The foreigners of our crew generally shipped at these low wages; the only instance which came under my notice of a fair rate being given was on a ship bound for an indefinite time to Malden Island for guano. This is a cheerful spot, near the equator. If Dante had ever been there, he would certainly have added an extra circle—a guano one—to his list of torments. A man who knew the place, said he would not go there for £50 a month. Owing to having been so long ashore, we were mostly impecunious, which may have accounted, in a degree, for our general quietness. Many were stopping on credit, and would repay what they owed out of their advance, or when they returned from their cruise. This is one great advantage of the Sailors' Home, that when "all Jack's money is gone and spent," he is not kicked out, as he would be at a common boarding-house. Men who trade along the coast, and are regular *habitués*, are freely trusted, and, to Jack's honour be it said that he generally pays. In the last report £304 is stated to be owing by seamen, of which £96 is returned as bad and doubtful—a very small percentage on the business done by the Home since its establishment; but during the year an amount of £357 was received, previously owing by seamen, of which £42 had been considered bad. This speaks very well for Jack's honesty and for Captain Allbeury's vigilance in looking up debtors to the institution . . .

A gentleman who knows as much about seamen as anyone in Victoria assures me that "five years in the fok'sle will take all the good out of a man, if he ever had any in him, and will make a brute and ruffian of him." Officers, too, have not a good word for the ordinary A.B. I was once walking in front of the Home when a young mate asked me to drink. "When a man says wine, straight I drain the flagon;" so I made a move towards the corner "pub." "Not there," said my friend, "don't you see those sailors there? I'm surprised at you, who seem to be a pretty decent man, talking or having anything to do with them. You know they'd sell either of our lives on board ship." I was very sorry to hear this; with such a feeling between officers and crew, no wonder that sometimes anger and malice are engendered, and mutiny and murders occur. But Captain Allbeury, at least, has not such a bad opinion of the sailor. His children play around with the inmates, and are a source of great joy and amusement to them. A sailor, who so seldom has a home and family of his own, loves children with a womanly fondness. The whole connexion between Captain Allbeury and the inmates is that of a kind-hearted skipper and his crew, and I do not think anyone could be more popular with them than he is. I believe that he has the good of the institution and of the inmates at heart. For myself, I can say I was well treated, and the captain and Mr. Barras, the clerk, kindly took an interest in getting me a ship . . .

This article was in type when the news arrived of the wreck of the ill-fated Dandenong and the sad loss of life. But we also heard of the gallant conduct of the captain of the Albert William, which rescued the survivors, and of the heroism of the "boat's crew of the Dandenong." May they be for ever famous! Amongst the lost was, alas! an old chum of mine at the Sailors' Home . . . He was *en voyage* to Newcastle, to become chief officer of a ship there, when he met his doom, bravely sticking to the vessel, although only a passenger. May he and all other gallant sailors who thus perish rest in peace beneath the waves!

19

Ragged Schools

THE SECULAR

... although the extreme poor are not with us, as in overcrowded cities of the Old and New Worlds, still daily the youthful criminal and dangerous class is increasing, and every effort should be made to stop its further progress. Education, I believe, will do much, and the establishment of a State School in O'Brien-lane, off Little Bourke-street, was a step in the right direction—an invasion of the headquarters of Melbourne vice and crime. This more than any other of the kind in Melbourne bears resemblance to the popular idea of a "Ragged School," although conducted thoroughly on the State system, and without the religious element present in London and New York . . .

There has been so much talk lately about Ragged Schools and education, "godless" and otherwise, that, the other day, I thought I would go and thoroughly inspect the workings of this institution, where endeavour is being made to reclaim, without the aid of the Churches, the little waifs of this city; so I solicited the services of my friend Mr. Hill, the police court missionary, to introduce me without my object being known. I find that I am getting a very unenviable reputation amongst civil servants, and to obtain the truth I have to travel under the disguise of mediocre respectability, and not as a vagabond. Nature has aided me in this endeavour, and no one could be more unconscious of my identity than Mr. Ellis, the teacher, who kindly showed us everything, and volunteered the remark that "if the 'Vagabond' was to come round here he'd get a fine study of character." We arrived at the school at two o'clock, and found all voices joining in the chorus of "Silver Threads," the accompaniment being played by the young lady assistant, Miss Hutton, on the harmonium . . . There were about 100 girls and boys present, of all ages, from three to fifteen years. The average attendance is over 120, but on this day (Wednesday) many children were absent, selling in the market. Friday is another day on which many children are kept away from school, sent gathering wood, &c., by their guardians; and every afternoon a number of boys leave at half-past two, to obtain the first instalment of the *Herald*, which they sell in the streets. Partly for their sake the school is opened in the afternoon half-an-hour earlier than the usual time. The room is rather dingy and dirty, the only ornaments a few maps; but the children, seated on forms, sang heartily and merrily, and appeared to thoroughly relish the music. After "Silver Threads" was finished, a boy of about twelve was called out to sing the solo of the "Little Crossing Sweep." His name was John Stanley. He had only one hand, but a magnificent voice, and would have made a good chorister. The other children joined in the chorus with a will. Then some girls sang "Little Sister's Gone to Sleep" in a very affecting manner. The music and singing were altogether good, and the children seemed to enjoy them and to appreciate the sentiments of the songs, and I cannot but think that they did them some good . . . The conclusion of the musical performance was the singing of a verse in very "pigeon" English by a little half-caste Chinese boy, five years of age. He was well clothed in a knickerbocker suit, and when Mr. Ellis perched him on the desk he laughed and crowed with joy, and no one would have thought that he was the Ginx's baby of the establishment.

This is the history of Master William Ah Sing. His father is a Celestial, his mother from the Emerald Isle. It is uncertain as to whether their union was blessed by priest or bonze, but the result is the merry little chap before us. He took his father's name, Ah Sing, to which his mother added William, or Billy, for the sake of distinction. The father, at one time a wealthy man, lost money in gambling, and took to evil courses and opium; his mother took to drink. The downward career of Ah Sing was rapid, and in time the boy's mother abandoned him and her child. All his life the boy had been sadly neglected, varied by occasional active ill-treatment, and now he seemed in danger of perishing outright from cold and hunger. But even in the foul alleys and rights-of-way out of Little Bourke-street human nature is not quite dead, and little Billy Ah Sing received kindnesses of a precarious nature from many who would not be considered highly respectable by church-goers.

The other day the teacher, Mr. Ellis, prowling around in search of prey—young children whom he might snatch up and carry away to be devoured by the "godless" monster, State instruction—came on the child, half-starved, dirty, and miserable, clad only in a shirt. He ascertained that the father would be glad to be relieved of the nominal control of his child, and then took little Billy off to Mr. Ah Goon.

This gentleman appears to be a sort of Chinese Jack Hamlin. By profession he is a gambler, great in lottery shops and the fantan game. He is reputed to be a wealthy man, is generally considered a good fellow, and is the legal owner of a gorgeous Caucasian wife. He, however, is childless, and has a love for male children, so Mr. Ellis soon persuaded him to adopt Billy Ah Sing; and that young gentleman's lines have now fallen into comparatively pleasant places. Billy is one of sixteen Chinese half-caste children now at the school. These are scattered all about in the classes—amongst Anglo-Saxons and Celts. The Chinese children are, as a rule, the best dressed and cared for, and are decidedly the smartest. Their heathen parents appear to take pleasure in availing themselves of the Education Act, and send the children to school at a very early age. Here, *par exemple*, are the two Masters Hang Hai, aged four and six years respectively. The youngest has one of the finest heads I have seen for a long time, and is very precocious. When Miss Hutton takes charge of the junior class, containing about thirty children, and, giving a slate to each scholar, makes a series of figures on the blackboard, which they have to copy, Master Hang Hai commences displaying his skill by filling up his slate with a quantity of hieroglyphics, which he triumphantly shows to me. In return, he wishes to see what I have got in my note-book. Before I left I was on quite intimate terms with this young gentleman; when I returned to his class he saluted me with a friendly nod of recognition, and playfully shook Miss Hutton's cane at me. He had possessed himself of this instrument of tuition, and was banging the blackboard with it, evidently, in his own mind, "bossing" the class—altogether a most humorous young customer.

The children are rather of mixed appearance. They are mostly cleanly; some of the girls are very pretty. Here is a beautiful Irish child side by side with a young Australian, who has disfigured herself by "banging" her hair in imitation of some frail sister residing in these perlieus. The majority are of poor but dishonest parents, although some are respectable in their connections. Many of these infants are not untainted with crime. Here is Master "Mouchy" who has been twice before Mr. Sturt, on clear charges of larceny; and the last time, for stealing a meerschaum pipe, was begged off by Mr. Ellis; and I was witness of an inquiry into the conduct of a boy charged by another with fowl-stealing. He had been away from school in the morning, passing the time in chicken larceny, and when asked by Mr. Ellis where he had been, he shamelessly replied, "Please, sir, having my hair cut." Now, as his matted locks hung down his back, this was a strong assertion. Then the inquiry commenced, and it seemed to me would terminate in a case of not proven. "A man gie me the fowl to sell," said the boy, "I was goin' down the street, and he see me——" "He saw me," corrected Mr. Ellis, evidently determined that, whatever this boy's moral turpitude, he should be grammatically correct. "He told me to sell it for eighteen-pence, and I did, and gied 'im the money." The other boys evidently thought this story rather "thin," and laughed at it, and all the children seemed to take this charge as a very common one, and not particularly interesting.

If the young St. Giles of Melbourne here present bears little resemblance to his brother in London, it is, at first, because he is better fed, and secondly, better clothed. But in many cases the latter is due to the exertions of the teacher, Mr. Ellis. Many parents made an excuse that their children could not attend school on account of want of sufficient clothing, and Mr. Ellis has accordingly appealed in every possible way to the charitably disposed for left-off children's clothing. To a certain extent his appeal has been responded to, and he has been enabled to make his scholars both decent and respectable. I only saw one boy with bare feet. Still, supplies of clothing are always wanted, and on behalf of these little ones I appeal to the wealthy to spare them a little of their abundance. Parcels of clothes, and second-hand talebooks, and toys discarded from the nursery, may be addressed to Mr. Ellis, Gospel-hall State School. It is my own thought to beg for toys, which I am sure would be a great joy to these poor waifs. A few books have already been sent to Mr. Ellis, but they are mostly of a class entirely unsuited for these children . . .

I am glad to say that many Catholic children are present here. Mr. John Duffy may be surprised to learn that these formed 60 per cent. of the scholars. Lately, many have been removed by the priests, who appear to have had a sudden fit of energy in looking up the stray sheep of their flock. Some of these will drift back here again, their parents being satisfied that no attempt to tamper with their religious faith will be made. The conductors of the Gospel-hall Mission, however, are about to start a religious meeting, after school hours each day, for such children as they can secure. This being a private building, only rented by the State, after or before school-time it may be used for any purpose compatible with its object. I think myself it would be much better if a school-house was built in this neighbourhood. There is plenty of ground about there, if it could be procured, and it is highly desirable to have the schoolhouse, baths, and playground altogether. The latter is a great desideratum, as at present the children have to play in the rights-of-way, and get scattered about during recess. The master, young lady assistant, and one pupil teacher have quite enough to do to look after the children at this school. The duties are heavy, and the mode of instruction is necessarily sometimes rough. The ordinary State School

Inside a Hornbrook Ragged School

curriculum is carried out, which, for these children, I think might be greatly improved by the Pestalozzian system of object lessons. The three Rs, with grammar, geography, needlework for the girls, and singing, form the course of instruction, and these youngsters appeared to me to have quite as good a chance of learning these thoroughly as I had . . .

Mr. Ellis is a young man, smart-looking, in appearance not at all like the popular idea of a school teacher, but I think he is in the right place. To the children he is kind and familiar, yet firm. The cane is not brought into request too often, but I suppose it is sometimes needed here, although I strongly object to any flogging in schools. But I am very pleased to say that I heard no harsh word pass the teacher's lips. He was severe in tone sometimes, but gave utterance to no expression unbecoming a gentleman, or which might not in reproof be applied to any gentleman's son. Mr. Ellis performs the duties both of master and "truant officer." In the byeways, brothels, and opium dens of this quarter he daily searches for children, and every afternoon looks up truants at their homes. His energy has been rewarded, and he is now trusted both by the children and their parents. After school hours I went round with him to see the houses of some of his scholars. Everywhere he was received on familiar and friendly terms, and the Chinese parents of children seemed particularly pleased to see him. He has quite an extensive knowledge of the inhabitants of this unsavoury neighbourhood, and introduced me to some queer cribs. William Ah Sing's father lives in a broken down shed built over a closet, for which he pays 5s. a week. It was without furniture, all the money he can get being spent in opium. Afterwards we went to see Mr. Ah Goon, who had adopted little Billy. This celebrated gambler lives in a brick house, comparatively well furnished, and generally ornamented by the presence of his splendid possession, Mrs. Ah Goon, seated on the step. This young lady is a good-looking Australian, clothed in gorgeous robes and much jewellery. Her husband is a spare, pleasing-looking Celestial, who, when he smiles, seems very intelligent. Has any one noticed the difference a smile makes in a Chinaman's face? I was glad to shake hands with him, and he was much pleased when I talked about the boy. I don't think, however, that little Billy will have the best of times with his adopted stepmother. We visited several other places inhabited by Chinamen and their European wives and offspring. This mixture of the races appears to be looked upon with great charity by Little Bourke-street, and the children resulting from such unions are generally strong, healthy, and intelligent-looking; and, as a rule, the Chinese are very good to their Caucasian wives and children.

Altogether, I was very pleased with my visit to the Gospel-hall State School, which I have taken as an example—the only one in Victoria—of a "Ragged School" conducted without any religious teaching. I trust I have said nothing against such teaching, but I have been endeavouring to show that, in spite of its absence, education has some sort of moral effect upon children, and that knowledge does decrease crime. I believe these children are rendered morally better by attendance at, and the discipline of, the school. The music cultivates their tastes, and the course of tuition expands their minds, evidently rendering them more fit to receive any religious instruction which the city missionaries, ministers, or priests may give them. That is the affair of their guardians —the said instructors—and not of the State, which has plainly said that it will look after the minds, while the Churches must attend to the souls of the rising generation. If we admit—and I think few reasonable people will deny it—that in this country of democratic institutions and manhood suffrage it is even more important that our rulers should be educated than the governed masses of the old world, it is certain that the only way to properly do so is through the State Schools—secular and compulsory. The admission of religious teaching on the part of any one sect or creed into these institutions is an affront and insult to the others. All contribute alike for their support through taxation, and all—Heathen Chinee, Catholic, Presbyterian, or Atheist—have a right to an equal amount of mental education for their children. In such a neighbourhood as that surrounding the Gospel-hall School, where so many conflicting social elements reside, the religious question must be very jealously excluded from the State Schools. I imagine, too, that modification of the mode of tuition, hours, &c., might in such neighbourhoods be usefully left to the discretion of the teacher or the board of advice. One thing is certain—the teachers at such schools have hard, unthankful, unrecognized work to perform, for which they require special qualities, and should receive special remuneration. In the United States teachers of the primary classes receive higher salaries than those of the superior grade, it being wisely considered that it requires a far higher order of intelligence and command of temper to break in a child's intellect than to merely direct the same afterwards. This theory applies with double force to Ragged Schools. I am always in favour of retrenchment by economy of administration, but in some cases—of which this is one—niggardliness to *employés* proves destructive to the permanent interests of the community.

THE RELIGIOUS

"The primary object of these schools shall be the gathering in and instructing in the Word of God destitute children, for whom no other means of instruction are available." This is the first rule and key-note of the Hornbrook Ragged School Association—the religious method, as opposed to the "godless system of State instruction" for "gutter children." This Association was founded in 1862 on the death of Mrs. Hornbrook, a venerable lady who held neither her time nor her comfort dear unto her in the good work she first started, of gathering together children from the lowest class of the population, who but for these schools, had *then* no other future but a career of ignorance and vice. At the end of the first year of the operations of the Association ten schools were opened—five situated in Collingwood, two in Little Bourke-street, one in Little Lonsdale-street, and two in Prahran,— being planted in what were supposed to be the most populous and destitute localities. In a few years' time the number of these schools increased to twelve, with a total of 1,000 children on the roll. Each school was worked independently by a small committee of ladies, who provided the funds necessary for its maintenance, visited the school periodically, and exercised a general superintendence over the teacher. The central committee kept a watchful eye on each school; prevented the local committees from infringing the articles of association; and collected funds, which were distributed according to need, or devoted to the opening of new schools, or the acquirement of school buildings. It was generally admitted that the secular instruction was necessarily and *"designedly"* (I quote from one of the reports) very elementary, attention being principally directed to having the children thoroughly instructed in the Word of God (the translation of James I., and not the Douay one), and trained to habits of cleanliness, order, and industry. There was, however, no sectarianism allowed in the administration of the Hornbrook Schools, and on the different committees ladies, members of the Church of England, Presbyterians, Baptists, Wesleyans, Independents, and Plymouth Sisters—all worked together amicably.

From the first Miss Fraser, a noble-hearted lady, who worthily bears the mantle of Mrs. Hornbrook, has been the honorary secretary of the association, and Lady M'Culloch has long been president, and efficiently helped in the good cause. For some years the local committees worked energetically, and in every report the association claimed to be performing a great work amongst the juvenile criminal and vagrant classes. I have no doubt of this; every species of education I believe to be good, although perchance much training may be thrown away or misapplied. It is certain that the "designedly" small modicum of secular instruction was not thrown away in every case: indeed, I am told that a successful dentist in town received his only education in a Hornbrook School; and the amount of Bible knowledge imparted, which must have been rather staggering to an ordinary mortal, was, perchance, effective. Looking at the number of larrikins of both sexes who now haunt the streets of Melbourne, I cannot help wishing that, ten years ago, the Hornbrook Association had been enabled to extend its sphere of operation a hundredfold, and that the present rising generation of vice might have felt the effects of its teachings. A mocking spirit within me suggests that perhaps some of these juveniles did. *Retro Sathanas!*

The last report of the Association, however, dismally laments that they have now only five schools in operation—two in Little Lonsdale-street, two in Collingwood, and one in Prahran. This the committee attempt to account for, and attack the present State School system in the following paragraph of their report.—

"The committee trust that they may be able to keep up these their five remaining schools, for they feel that they are being driven out of the field by a system which practically ignores the class for whose benefit, it might be supposed, free education was mainly intended. It is well known that, in our present costly system of State education, the 'arabs' have neither part nor lot, nor does there seem to be room in our State Schools for the children of a numerous class of even tolerably respectable parents who are either too poor or too careless to seek for their children the blessings of education. Of this class the Hornbrook Ragged School Association had, at one time, in their schools, nearly a thousand children—gathered mainly from the streets and lanes of the city. These have, to a large extent, drifted away from them; but they are not to be found in the State Schools, and never will be, until they are compelled to come in. The alarming increase of juvenile crime, lawlessness, and insubordination in our community attests the urgent necessity existing for some measure which will make such children sharers in the bountiful provision made by the State for secular education, to which there should surely be added, in their case, the further benefit of moral and religious training. To combine the two has been the great aim of the Hornbrook Ragged School Association; and it is with a feeling of extreme regret that they see the work taken out of their hands and practically left undone."

I can understand that, in many cases, the State School is now doing what the Hornbrook Schools did before; but I cannot see that, in ignoring the class of "street arabs" or "gutter children," the State School system is driving the religious one out of the field. If the State takes no heed of these, all the more reason that an association, founded expressly for that purpose, should be able to reach them. An interview with Miss Fraser—to whom I am indebted for information kindly given me on this subject—did not help to solve the mystery of the fact of children drifting away from the Hornbrook Schools, and still not attending State Schools. I found out, however, that the great falling-off in the amount of subscriptions had much to do with this. People who formerly subscribed to the Hornbrook Schools now say, "There is a State School a hundred yards from yours—why should we maintain both?" and they are right; every child should attend the State School. But, as the report says, until they are compelled, all will not do so. Still I cannot think that, through the extension of the State School system, many children are now left uneducated who would have been formerly reached by the Hornbrook Association. In many cases, where their schools have been given up, it appears to me that the policy of State education has been vindicated—the religious school could not exist side by side with the secular one. If the latter has not as yet gathered in all that it should, the work of the Hornbrook Association is to glean what is left, according to its programme—attacking vice and crime in their strongholds, and not lament that a certain amount of work is being taken out of its hands.

Is this now being done? To answer this thoroughly I have paid visits to all the schools now owned by the Association, and have endeavoured to arrive at the truth according to my lights. I would bless if I could, for I recognize and sympathize with the spirit which animates the officers and the ladies of the committees. Many of these, I am afraid, will think I deal harshly with their Association; but the truth must be told. From visits and enquiries made, not only in the neighbourhood of the present schools, but of those which have lapsed, it appears to me that the objects of the Association have been defeated, or at least that any great result is *now* being frustrated through the prominence given to the religious part of the programme. The Hornbrook Schools have been Bible Schools, not Ragged Schools in the true sense of the word: many of them, it seems to me, never had the slightest claim to that title. The Association, instead of concentrating its forces in the plague spots of the city, encouraged the formation of a network of daily Sunday Schools around Melbourne; and, consequently, when a State Schoolhouse was built, the higher education given there caused parents to remove their children from institutions where the boys, at least, learnt little else but texts. A Sunday School once a week, I believe, is sufficient for most children; a daily Sunday School, when any other educational establishment is available, is decidedly behind the age. "The designedly" small amount of secular education given at their schools accounts, I believe, for the present state of the Association, at least as regards the attendance of children. With respect to the closing of many of the schools, it seems to me that the interest displayed by many ladies of the different committees was spasmodic and uncertain. Animated by a sudden glow of religious charity, many rushed into the scheme, eager to gather to the fold of Bible instruction every child in their districts. Committees would be formed, presidents, and secretaries, and treasurers appointed, and for a time the management of the schools afforded a new amusement. But by-and-by it began to grow stale, and the interest flagged. The counter-attractions of the world and the flesh —milliners and matrimony—prevailed. Many of the schools, too, being governed by ladies living in an entirely different district, there was a want of local interest in them, and they were only taken up as the charitable amusement of the moment. This, I understand, to be one cause of the failure of some of them. Of those which have survived, the ladies composing the local as well as the general committee are to be praised for their long persevering efforts in the cause which they think just.

I paid my first visit to the School in Little Lonsdale-street west. This is held in a building belonging to the adjacent Independent Church, for which a rental of £39 a year is paid. All the other school buildings are owned by the Association. I found thirty-two children present, the number on the roll being fifty-one, their ages ranging from four to twelve. They seemed of a little superior class to those at the Gospel-hall State School. There were no Chinese half-castes, no young thieves, or newspaper hawkers. Their clothes were mostly comfortable, only two being barefooted, James and Peter Ramsay. These two lads had been, according to the statement of the teacher, Mrs. Rishton, turned out of St. John's State School on account of their lack of clothing. This is a scandalous shame, and in this case at least the Hornbrook School did good work. From inquiries as to the parentage of the children, I found that some of these at least might perchance be held to be members of the class for which the Association was founded, although none of them were of the low grade of Little Bourke-street. The little girls were sewing, the boys doing sums. Needlework and patchwork appear to be the most useful things taught at these schools; as the boys don't learn such, their attention is concentrated on texts. Hung round the walls there are many pious devices, which, like the religious teaching, are supposed to be entirely unsectarian. Bible instruction and hymns form a large portion of the *curriculum*. From a Protestant point of view, the Scriptures cannot be converted into anything sectarian; but how as to hymns? I have two such specimens before me now. One, Calvinistic, gloats over the torments of lost souls, and describes how "Justice has built a dismal hell." The other, one of the most beautiful lyrical confessions of faith ever penned, ends with "Hold thou the cross before my closing eyes." These don't fit in together. I can foresee that difficulties may have arisen amongst the ladies of the different committees on the religious question. The teachers, also, sometimes display too much zeal in their religious instruction. I have heard of the introduction of

The 'Erald Angels

CUSTOMER—Here you are, but why don't you give us an aitch with 'em?
BOY—Can't afford it, sir; keeps 'em all for the *Hages* in the morning.

the Church of England Catechism, but any such vagaries are promptly suppressed by the hon. secretary. The idea of the Association is to leave the child in a state as well adapted for one Christian creed as another. Does not a secular State School also do this? Several of the children present were of Roman Catholic parentage, although they often come with instructions not to read "the Book," which, after all, I must admit, is not quite milk for babes.

A teacher's life amongst such a lot of juvenile larrikins is not quite a bed of roses, and Mrs. Rishton complained much of the annoyances she experienced by the stone-throwing propensities of the outside barbarians. Even as she spoke to me several stones were banged against the door—the protest of Little Lonsdale-street against Bible-teaching. I was wrath, and said to myself, "I will stop this for a time;" so, suddenly opening the door, I marched out, stick in hand, prepared to administer condign punishment to the offenders. Behold, there was only one small boy, about six years of age, a well-dressed little urchin, decidedly not of the larrikin breed. He burst out into a frightful howl when he saw me, and attempted to escape; but I caught him, and gave him a good lecture, telling him a truthful story of a little boy who threw stones at the school-house door, and ended in being a member of the Legislative Assembly. That frightened him.

I next took train for the pleasant suburb of Prahran. Walking around this township, it seemed the last place in the world where one would meet with "street Arabs." The cottage gardens were pleasant with the bloom of fruits and flowers. I could see no indications of squalor or vice. Eastbourne-street is a pleasant locality, where I would not mind living. I had asked many people where the "Ragged School" was, but could obtain no information; but at last I struck it myself, in the shape of a red brick building, bearing the inscription "Scripture Reading School." Mrs. Brown, the teacher, was unfortunately away, but I was shown around the place by an intelligent young person, who was very enthusiastic about the good done by Scripture reading. This is the best building owned by the association, and in every respect the best school, which arises from the fact that the committee of ladies reside in the district. The school-room itself is cheerful, with texts such as "Let the Scriptures be the foundation of all instruction," and prints of the heroes of the Old Testament. I was glad to see a large doll's house and other toys. In all the Hornbrook Schools it is the practice to devote a certain afternoon in the week to play, this being a reward of good boys and girls. This school is well off for toys. Some little gardens outside, small selections, about a yard square, are given as prizes to the boys to cultivate. There is a very fair library of tale books, which are lent out from the Friday till the Monday, and a pile of patchwork and old clothes, which I saw being re-made into children's garments. Little girls are taught to make their own garments, which are then sold to them for a few pence each, which sum goes towards paying for needles and cotton. The principle, however, of making the child independent and above charity is always inculcated in the Hornbrook Schools, and at each of the schools there is a fiction of selling garments for a trifling sum, to preserve this idea. There is no doubt that, at these schools, the girls are likely to learn more useful work than at the State Schools, and one of the foremost rules of the Association appears to be well carried out. In every respect the Prahran School seemed equal to any ordinary public school in Australia, England, or America. With the exception of the re-made piles of clothes, there was nothing at all suggestive of ragged-ness about it. I asked my *cicerone*, "What class of children attend this school?" She had the answer glib—"Oh, all gutter children, sir!" "What do you mean by gutter children?" "Oh, children of poor people, who play about in the gutter." I afterwards walked about Prahran, in-terviewed several policemen and other citizens, and, from all I could see and hear, the Eastbourne-street School is a capital institution, as what it hails to be—a "Scripture Reading School," but has no more claim to be called a "Ragged School" than the Scotch College has.

Rokeby-street, Collingwood, is not a savoury locality, and it is the residence of a good many of the roughest of Mr. Langridge's constitu-ents. The school-house here is a dingy wooden building, bearing the name "Bible School." The children here seemed to me to be exactly of the same class as those to be met with at the adjacent State School. They were all well clothed, and, the teacher told me, were the children of working people. Nothing of the "street arab" or "guttersnipe" about them. Here there was the same amount of texts and needlework, the foundation of the Hornbrook system of education. A few minutes' walk across the Flats brought me to Sydney-street, where there is a nice little brick building, attended by some twenty-five children. One little girl, with a precocious knowledge of the power of her charms, made eyes at me, and was evidently highly delighted at the presence of a visitor to break the tedium of the afternoon. This seemed a well-managed little school, the children being of respectable parentage. Harmsworth-street, parallel with Sydney-street, contains the newly-opened Children's Church, a building erected by the Association out of funds collected to erect a Hornbrook School in Smith-street, Colling-wood, but which was rendered unnecessary by the opening of additional State Schools in that neighbourhood. The services there are of the simple kind suited, as far as such can be suited, to the intelligence of

Effect of state education on neglected children

children. The good little children of Collingwood Flat will, no doubt, be collected there; but I myself would rather see such a building in Little Bourke-street. The last school which I visited was the one in Cumberland-place, off Little Lonsdale-street east. As elsewhere, on asking for the Ragged School, I had a difficulty in finding this. Some children, however, at last discovered that I meant the school they attended, and marched me to the building, and introduced me to the teacher. The schoolhouse is an ordinary red brick building, the whole ground floor being converted into a schoolroom, the teacher's quarters being above. There was nothing in this school to distinguish it from the rest. There were the usual texts on the walls, and piles of needlework, of which I began to get rather tired. Although this is just on the outskirts of a rather bad quarter, the immediate neighbourhood is a good one, and the scholars, I was told, were the children of working people. They were of all ages, from three to fifteen, and of all sects, even including Jews and Roman Catholics. As an example of the strange manner in which the local committees of the Hornbrook Schools are formed, one of the principal ladies managing the establishment in Little Lonsdale-street resides in Prahran. To counterbalance this, however, the Sydney-street School in Collingwood is efficiently managed by ladies from Collins-street . . .

The system of instruction and management appears to be that of the old "dame school," combined with a goodly amount of Scripture teaching. The features of this which I like best are the facilities given for cleanliness, the recognition of the need of amusement by the introduction of toys, and the yearly treat to the children. The latter, I think, might be made a feature of each State School. But as the present schools of the Hornbrook Association now exist, they cannot be called "ragged," but are mere religious ones. Unsectarian they certainly are; but still the pervading spirit is, unintentionally, perhaps, as hostile to the State School system as that manifested by the Catholic Church, and without the same show of reason . . . The Hornbrook Association is worked on the idea that, without a certain amount of Scripture teaching, education is of no avail. The fact, too, that they have deserted the worst portion of the town—that Little Bourke-street and its purlieus are abandoned by them—is rather an argument against the prosperity of any great social work carried on entirely by committees of ladies. If a Ragged School is wanted anywhere; if the avowed objects of this association should anywhere be able to benefit the community, it is in Little Bourke-street. Yet the Gospel-hall, which it once rented, is now given over to the "godless" State School. Still, if, as the report of the association says, the State School is not efficiently doing the work of reclaiming gutter children, there is yet time for a change of front. A

Hornbrook School may be started in the worst position of Little Bourke-street, and the experiment made as to the comparative merits of religious and State instruction. In any case, I would advise the Association to concentrate its forces in the head-quarters of Melbourne vice and crime. There is little need for Collins-street ladies to go to Prahran and Collingwood when the work lies at their back doors . . .

20

State Baby-Farming

THE Boarding-Out system—Baby Farming by the State—which is at the present moment attracting so much attention, and is the subject of so much controversy, is an endeavour to rear orphan and deserted pauper children by giving them what they have either lost or never enjoyed—a kindly home, and parental training. To exchange the dull routine of a school life, and often dangerous associations, for the kindly influence of a genial home. To give children a foster parent instead of a schoolmaster or mistress. To train up a child in that condition of existence which is the foundation of all society—the family . . .

But my province is not to write a treatise on "boarding-out," but to give a report of personal investigations into the practical working of "The Neglected and Criminal Children's Act, 1874," authorizing and regulating the boarding-out of children from industrial and reformatory schools. This Act would be a dead letter without the personal assistance and voluntary aid of the ladies of the various "visiting committees," no child, unless with the special authority of the Chief Secretary, being allowed to be boarded-out with any person not residing within a district under the supervision of such a committee. Three ladies, representing, as far as practicable, all the denominations established in the district over which they propose to exercise supervision, may form a committee. Every boarded-out child must be visited at the home of its "foster parent" at least once in every six weeks by a member of the committee, who sends in a quarterly report, in writing, to the Inspector of Industrial and Reformatory Schools, as to the bodily condition of the child, the sleeping accommodation, attendance at church, Sunday and day school, &c. All foster parents have in their written applications for children to obtain a clergyman's certificate stating—"I am acquainted with the above-named applicant, her husband and family. I consider the family is one to which the Government may safely entrust the physical and moral training of either male or female children." This is again endorsed by the Boarding-out Committee, who certify that "due inquiry has been made concerning the within-named applicant and her family; and her home, and the accommodation she proposes to provide for the child, have been inspected. We are satisfied that she and her husband are suitable persons to be entrusted with the care of a child, and that they and their children are of good moral character. We therefore recommend that the application be granted. We also undertake, should a child be entrusted to the applicant, to exercise supervision over them in accordance with the conditions and the regulations that may from time to time be in force; to endeavour by counsel, and, when necessary, by the exercise of the authority conferred upon us, to preserve the child from evil and immoral influences and example, and to report regularly to the Inspector of Industrial and Reformatory Schools concerning their physical and moral welfare." This is signed by the lady who acts as "Correspondent" for the district, who is the recognized medium of communication between the Department and the foster-parents, and who, in many cases. I imagine, has a pretty hard and thankless task.

A medical officer is appointed for each district in which children are boarded out. Besides attending them in illness and supplying medicines, his duty is to visit them not less than once in every three months, and report any deficiency of accommodation, any defects in the sanitary condition of the residence, insufficient supply of food or clothing, or absence of cleanliness. For such attendance and supervision he is paid at the munificent rate of £1 per child per annum. It will be seen that the State has jealously guarded the farmed-out child, but that almost the entire burden of responsibility is placed upon the ladies of the different committees. The whole success of the system depends upon the volunteer and praiseworthy efforts of these ladies, and, as Mr. Duncan, the Inspector General, says in his last report, "in the care that is exercised in the selection of foster-parents and constant supervision maintained after children are placed in the homes."

There are now in Victoria more than one hundred districts and committees of ladies, and at the end of 1875 there were 866 children boarded out in various homes. Of the metropolitan districts, Richmond is one of the largest, and this has furnished me with my first experience of "State Baby-Farming." On the second Monday of each month the foster-parents assemble with their charges at the Richmond Town Hall, and are paid by the committee, which sits in judgment as to the appearance of the children. One committee day a "young man from *The Argus*" humbly put in an appearance, and for a time was accommodated with a seat outside the door of the Council Chamber. That "young man" was the "Vagabond." I was amused, but did not for a moment imagine the committee was engaged on any secret business, like the conspirators in "La Fille de Madame Angot" or the sub-committees of the Alfred Hospital. I recognized the fact that, where ladies meet each other once a month, they have little confidences and conversations to exchange which "a young man from *The Argus*" should not hear. Besides, in my Lazarus-like position, I saw all the children pass in, and Miss Henty, the "correspondent," who, with her sister, appears "to run" the district, kindly gave me information respecting them. I suppose, however, I looked so meek and harmless, that after a time Miss Henty said, "Won't you come inside?" I said I thought I would, and humbly took my seat amongst the ten ladies present. There are twenty ladies on the committee, of all denominations. The number of children boarded out is sixty-two, with thirteen licensed as servants, also under their supervision. I expect, however, some of the ladies are only honorary members, and that the real work of visiting and supervision is done by a few. I enjoyed the half hour which I thus spent in the pleasant Council Chamber on the upper floor of the Richmond Town Hall. As the foster-parents and their charges trooped in, they were all recognized by Miss Henty and the ladies under whose special care the children might be. The little ones generally seemed delighted with the attention they received. "Ah! those are my boys," a lady would say, and, after a little laugh at the joke, the children would be passed round and inspected, and their personal appearance, points, and improvement canvassed with all that loving zest and attention to detail which a man only lavishes on a horse. "Wonderful for his age!" "What a fine boy!" "They are wonderfully improved." "What splendid legs the child's got!" In this way, the maternal instinct strong within them, the ladies crowed and delighted over these orphans, and the loving tenderness they displayed touched the battered cinder which does duty as the "Vagabond's" heart. One lady knelt down, and nursed and petted some of the children, till I began to wish I was a "neglected child" boarded out in the Richmond district. The foster-parents were all well dressed, comfortable-looking women, and the children were the same. Some were very nicely attired, and their general appearance and looks would have done credit to a far higher social position than the foster-parents can boast of. "Dolly," who was kissed all round, except by "the young man from *The Argus*," who dare not so presume, was a dear little child any one might have been proud of. One could hardly realize that these were neglected pauper children, whose only heritage was vice and shame.

Whilst Miss Henty counted out the money due to the foster parents, the lady "correspondent" and others closely questioned the children and their guardians. There were not many complaints against the children and their guardians. One woman said "David ran off to the races, and she could not keep him out of the streets." I recognized a kindred vagabond spirit in David. Another said, "The're verra guid boys, but Maister Tom wipit his slate on his troosers," at which grave charge the ladies laughed and Tom hung his head guiltily. Some contumacious little girls were complained of, and Miss Henty talked gently to them. The ladies made inquiries as to the schooling of the children, and in this they have the reports of the State schoolmasters to guide them, as these furnish Miss Henty with lists of the attendance of boarded-out children. A child who was brought in with sore eyes received an order for the doctor—at least, its foster-mother did. One little girl sang a hymn in a weak treble, painful to listen to, but which precocious performance was generally approved of. To the query, "I hope you are good boys?" the answer was, of course, "Yes," although some of the children—a second generation of young Australia I should imagine—looked rather sulky at being shown around and questioned in this manner. On the shining faces of some there was a sense of injury at the infliction of yellow soap and coarse towels which had prepared them for "seeing the ladies."

One little girl, Clara "Kew," was a foundling, having been picked up in that township when she was a few days old. She is evidently far better off now than in the custody of her unnatural parents. Another pretty little girl had absolutely no name at all, but was called "Lily" by her foster-parent. "Never mind, she'll have a name some day," said one of the ladies present; and I hope she will, and a good husband with it. Some little gentlefolks had accompanied their mamma to see the show, and had brought sweets and bags of marbles, which they gave to some of the boys. Two boys went to return thanks to "the lady." One of them—a saucy young urchin—immediately got into difficulties. "Thank you, ma'am," said he. "Do you say your prayers?" asked the lady. "Yes, ma'am." "Can you say 'Our Father'?" "Our Father——" and there he stuck. I don't think he'll get any sweets next month . . . Some boys were brought out of school by their foster-parents, and their appearance, not being specially got up for the occasion, was most convincing as to the general health and well-cared-for state of these boarded-out children. They are mostly very healthy-looking, and the fact that during the last epidemic of scarlet fever only one child under the supervision of the committee died in the Richmond district is a very gratifying evidence of the care exercised in the selection of the homes. The ladies of the committee appeared to take the greatest interest in their work, and were about organizing a picnic for all the children and their foster-parents and families. The Misses Henty, whom I believe I have seen at the Alfred Hospital, are especially vigilant in the work of the committee, and to all the ladies great praise appears due. The amount of writing which the correspondent has to perform is, owing to the unnecessary red tape and formulæ required by the Department, something considerable.

All this is very well, written only of the children on show at the Richmond Town Hall, of their apparent condition when got up for inspection, and of the ladies' interest in them there. But it will be wisely objected that the fact of ladies once a month gushing over these children is not a convincing proof of the superiority of the boarding-out system. Certainly it would be hard to believe that these happy-looking, well-fed, well-clothed children would undergo any great metamorphosis in the homes of their foster-parents. But I determined to see them there; and being furnished with a few random addresses, I selected Saturday as a likely day on which to see things in their natural colours, and again made my way to Richmond, for the purpose of seeing these boarded-out ones at home.

At the railway station I chartered a cab, the driver of which was a venerable citizen, who knew all the numerous byeways of that borough. The first house I visited—a pleasant-looking semi-detached cottage—was in Swan-street. Passing through the garden, at the side-door I found two little children playing. They were well dressed, and looked healthy and happy. Questioning them, the eldest informed me, "Mammy's gone out." I tried to get into conversation with them, but at their tender years the stock of exchangeable ideas is limited; and after telling me their names and about the dog and fowls, they wanted to play hide and seek. I was perfectly satisfied that these children were well cared for, and when Mrs. —— came in she had no need to tell me they were "treated as if my own." This was one of those numerous cases in which a childless couple, with tender memories perchance of little ones gone before, are glad to take charge of these waifs of the State, and bring them up as their own, the pecuniary reward being a secondary inducement. In her pleasant parlour Mrs. —— confided to me many particulars respecting herself, her husband, and what she meant to do for the children, seeing, no doubt, that I am of a sympathetic disposition. She and her husband—who is in a situation in Melbourne—had got quite attached to the little ones. "They were such company." When they grow old enough they meant to send them to a private school. They should be brought up as their children; no common schools for them. Resisting hospitable offers of lemonade or tea, I escaped at last, kissing Jenny and Mary Ann, whose lines have, I fully believe, fallen in a pleasant place.

I was next driven to a side street, where the house I was in search of turned out to be a nice new six-roomed cottage, the property of the occupier, who is carpenter. Only one farmed-out child was here, and on my asking after her Mrs. —— said, aghast, "You ain't her father, are you"? I said I was not aware of the fact, and was conducted to the room where little Eva, three years old, lay asleep on the sofa. A pretty child is Eva. She was found under a tree in the Fitzroy-gardens when a few days old, and Mrs. —— has had charge of her ever since, and as they only have one boy of their own, they intend to always keep Eva. "Some may make a market of this," said Mrs. ——, "but I don't. It ain't the money I care about, though of course we may as well take it for the child's sake. Her clothes cost more than we get. You see we wanted a little girl." Mr. —— also informed me that he owned three houses besides the one he lived in, and I left very well satisfied as to the future of the child who lay sleeping, the picture of youthful happiness and innocence, on the sofa.

The next house I was driven to had not such favourable surroundings as the previous ones. Mrs. —— takes in washing, and her husband is a carter. As she has three children of her own, it is evident she takes boarders for what she can legitimately make. However, the place was equal to the majority of working-people's houses, and I daresay the children will be happy enough there. Mrs. —— seemed a kindly, if rather careless and slatternly, woman. She was very much frightened at my appearance, and shut the back-kitchen door, through which I was advancing, with the ready lie on her lip.

"Oh! the children are in the tub; I'm washing them, sir." Putting on official airs, I said, "I must see them." "Oh, but a gentleman would not want to see a naked child." Mrs. —— would not produce the children, but when I went out I saw them in the side-yard, playing about with a delicious *abandon* only possessed by those whose guardians have catholic views on the subject of dirt. One of these, named Gertrude May, was picked up in Singleton's Gardens, and given to Mrs. —— to nurse. As she thought it was dying, she sent for the priest, who received it into the fold of the Holy Roman and Apostolic Catholic Church. I trust the child will live to be a happy woman; and I myself am not particular as to the form of its creed. Mrs. —— had a baby to nurse, which she showed me. Twelve shillings a week for this, and 14s. for the two children, makes 26s. weekly, which Mrs. —— draws from the State. I think she does well out of that. I am sorry she would not let me see the children—it looked suspicious; but then, as the priest and the Boarding-out-Committee must have certified to her fitness, I suppose it was all right. "When will you be round again, sir? If I only knew when you'd be here, the children should be ready for you." I said I thought they would be, and she should receive a week's notice.

Driving across to Kent-street, my Jehu said, "You're looking after the baby-farming, are you, sir?" I said, "Yes; do you know anything about it? How do they treat them?" "Well," said he, "there's some of 'em treats 'em very well indeed—couldn't be better; and there's others drinks too much to look after their own, let alone anybody else's children." I record this as an impartial outside statement. In Kent-street, I found a milliner's shop kept by an old lady and her widowed daughter. Jane and May, three and two years of age respectively, were playing about in the yard. They were dressed plainly, but comfortably, and looked well fed and happy. The next house was that of the widow who had charge of the child with the sore eyes. The little one was playing in the kitchen with some flowers, and was perfectly happy and well, bar its eyes. "Have you seen the doctor?" I asked. "Well, no, sir. I had to go into town to see the lawyer about my property; but I shall take the little dear to-morrow." There was a little neglect in this, but not more, I think, than if the child had been her own; and in other respects she was well cared for.

My last visit was to Murphy-street, an eligible thoroughfare which figures beautifully on the map of Melbourne. In reality it is as great a fraud as the roads delineated on the plans of many American land agents. It is still in its primal condition of undrained bog, although several cottages have been erected on each side. An attempt has been made at the formation of a footpath, but it is a failure. As we drove along the "street," the cars wheels sank up to the axles, and my driver loudly lamented the bad job he had taken, when he "might have had the chance of going to St. Kilda." The cottage I was in search of was pleasant outside, with roses and creepers growing in Australian luxuriance. Here I found two little girls, of nine and ten years of age—Bessie and Minnie. Another sister had, so the foster-father said, "gone into town with the missis." They were quite as well dressed and looked heartier than the man's own children—a boy and girl. The place was clean and comfortable, and these foundlings were evidently happier than they would have been in a large asylum. The man—an old sailor—was an *employé* of the Hobson's Bay Railway Company, a good sample of the class with whom it is desirable State children should be boarded out.

In the half-dozen visits I paid to the homes of these farmed-out children, I found, with one exception, nothing to cavil at; and I am confident that they were far healthier and happier than if mewed up in some great school or reformatory, where their individual consciousness would be crushed out. I think, however, that the rule "A member of the committee shall visit the home of each child at least once in every six weeks," should be "at least once a month." I made particular inquiries as to when "the ladies" came round, and although Miss Henty, the correspondent, appears to be very diligent in going around the district for which she is responsible, still I found in two cases that no visitor had called for more than a month. The ladies of the different committees have great responsibilities thrown upon them, and, especially in the case of infants, I think frequent visits at the homes of the foster-parents desirable.

My experiences are a confirmation that the boarding-out system is a success; that many foster-parents have proved themselves well qualified to fulfil the duties they have undertaken, and that the children are generally well cared for, properly fed, clothed, and educated. The regulations framed by the authorities are very comprehensive in apparently protecting the children from all chance of ill-treatment. In some things, perhaps, the Act is too comprehensive, and does not leave sufficient discretionary power to the committees. A law of adoption, as in France, seems to me badly wanted in Victoria. Great complaint is made of the fact that parents will often claim their children when they arrive at an age that they will be useful to them, and after the foster-parents have had all the trouble of rearing, and have become attached to their charges. Of course, it will be held that it is unnatural to separate a child from its parents; but when, from the fault, vice, or crime of such parents, children have become charges of the State, I think they should remain so, and be legally transferred to the sole care of foster-parents. This, however, is a subject for discussion. On the other hand, the authorities do not allow children to be boarded-out with a surviving parent, and cases I think might arise where this would be advisable. An esteemed correspondent sends me the following instance:.. "In the neighbourhood of Fryerstown a poor woman lately lost her husband —a hard-working and industrious man, who died very suddenly, without making any provision for his family. There were six children left, ranging in ages from six months to nine or ten years. These children, up to the present time, have been principally supported by local subscriptions, and assistance from neighbours and friends, the mother being unable to enter into any employment outside her own home whereby a subsistence could be gained. To follow any employment indoors is next to impracticable, as her whole time and attention must necessarily be devoted to her children. In a case like this, the children must eventually be sent to the Industrial School, to be cared for by the State, and subsequently transferred to foster-parents, who will be remunerated for their trouble and responsibility. Hence the children are deprived of the society and companionship of their natural parent and consigned to strangers, when such a necessity would not exist if a provision could be made whereby the natural could occupy the same position as the foster-parent." It may be rightly urged that abuses might creep in if this principle was generally admitted. Still, in this and in other cases I think a rigorous departmental rule should at times be relaxed, and that the committees should, under authority of the inspector, have certain powers. At the present moment the whole working and responsibility of the boarding-out system rest with the various committees of ladies, and they should be trusted and endowed with discretionary privileges.

PART FIVE

Manly Sports

21

A Brutal Football Match

(From 'Manly Sports')

In Victoria . . . like every athletic sport, football is followed by all—larrikins, mechanics, clerks, and (self-esteemed) young aristocrats. It seems, amongst a certain class, to be even more popular than cricket. The favourite amusements of a people are signs of the times well worth studying. When I go to a new country, I make it a rule to read the newspapers (if I am master of the language), and to attend the churches and places of public amusement. I have learnt much from the press here; the churches have told me no new thing; and the amusements have principally bored me . . . But football, as it is carried out here, is a new study, and it has given me some curious ideas as to the civilization and humanity of the coming Victorian race.

I am not going to indulge in a tirade against athletic sports, although I have a suspicion that the tendency of the age here, as in England, is to the excessive cultivation of the bodily powers to the neglect of the mental. It is, no doubt, a good thing to be able to jump a five-barred gate, to run a mile in five minutes, and throw fifty-sixes over your head until further notice. But all virtue does not consist in training, and the country will not be saved by such gifts . . . *Mens sana in corpore sano* I believe to be generally true, but the principle may be carried to excess, and a healthy mind certainly does not exist where cruel and brutal sports are indulged in. Football, as now carried on here, is not only often rough and brutal between the combatants, but seems to me to have a decided moral lowering and brutalizing effect upon the spectators. The records of the past season show that several promising young men have been crippled for life in this "manly sport;" others have received serious temporary injuries, and laid the foundations of future ill-health, the luckiest getting off with scars which they will bear with them to their graves. Now, is the general good derived from the encouragement of physical endurance in the players, and the amusement given to the spectators, worth all this? I think not, and hold that the evil does not stop here, but that society is demoralized by such public exhibitions as the "last match of the season" between the Melbourne and Carlton Football Clubs, which I witnessed. I arrived early at the spacious piece of ground which has been given to our Catholic friends for religious purposes, and has been let by them for the highly religious performances of Blondin, football matches, &c. . . .

The six or seven thousand spectators comprised representatives of nearly all classes. It was a truly democratic crowd. Ex-Cabinet Ministers and their families, members of Parliament, professional and tradesmen, free selectors and squatters, clerks, shopmen, bagmen, mechanics, larrikins, betting men, publicans, barmaids (very strongly represented), working-girls, and the half world, all were there. From the want of reserved seats, or any special accommodation for ladies, the mixture all round the ground was as heterogeneous as well might be. I mingled with the throng everywhere, and had a good chance of arriving at the popular verdict respecting football, as at present played. The Carlton Club were playing on their own ground, and the feeling of the majority was in their favour, and from the commencement was so expressed rather offensively towards the Melbourne Club, which is considered, I believe, to be a little more high-toned, and consequently antagonistic to democratic Carlton. At the commencement I got a position at the rails between a seedy but highly respectable-looking old gentleman, a commercial traveller, and several hardy sons of toil . . .

If an intelligent foreigner had been present, watching these young men clad in parti-coloured garments, running after an inflated piece of leather, kicking it and wrestling for it, receiving and giving hard blows and falls, he must have thought it the amusement of madmen. The spectators, who howled, and shrieked, and applauded, he would have thought equally mad. It is true that, as a spectacle of bodily activity and endurance, the show was a fine one, but the cruelty and brutality intermixed with it, and which the crowd loudly applauded, and appeared to consider the principal attraction, was anything but a promising evidence of a high civilization. I was told by several that it would be a pretty rough game, and they gloated in the fact. As the play went on, and men got heavy falls, and rose limping or bleeding, the applause was immense. "Well played, sir," always greeted a successful throw. "That's the way to smash 'em," said one of my neighbours. "Pitch him over!" and such cries were frequent, and the whole interest and applause seem centred in such work. It was no fair conflict either; a man running after another who has the ball, seizing him by the neck, and throwing him down, does not, to my mind, do a particularly manly thing. It inculcates bad blood, as the victim is sure to spot his oppressor, and be down on him when occasion offers. Early in the game it was apparent that a bad feeling existed between the players. There was a dispute as to the first goal kicked by the Melbourne club: Was it a "free kick" or not? The umpire's decision was loudly canvassed, and angry players congregated in the middle of the ground. "There's going to be a scrap," said a Carltonite, delightedly, and called out to one of the players, "Go into the ——, Jim." Indeed, it seemed to me as if hostilities had already commenced. There was a squaring of shoulders, and the central mass heaved and surged for a minute, and then the would-be combatants were separated. Shortly after this, the umpire took up his stick, and walked off the ground, and the game was suddenly stopped. I asked this gentleman what was the matter, and he said the Carlton players used such blackguard language to him that he would not stand it; and in this, I think, he was right. One friend said, however, that he was wrong. "The umpire always has a hard time of it," said he; "the only thing he can do is to wear several brass rings, if he hasn't got gold ones, and let the first man who disputes his decision have it straight." This idea was received with great favour by the crowd, and is an instance of the good feeling generally engendered by this "manly sport."

After a fresh umpire was procured, the game became as rough as it well could be, without absolute fighting. Luckily the Rugby game, in which a man who holds the ball can be kicked until he releases it, is not played here. Still "hacking" was sometimes indulged in under cover of play, and I was not at all surprised to hear that a man had his eye kicked out at this very ground a short time back. The "scrimmages" were frequent, and altogether the violence used was often totally unnecessary and gratuitous. I watched several individual players. One man would throw or push another down after he had kicked the ball, and without, as far as the play was concerned, any excuse or provocation. The aggrieved one would "spot" his antagonist and repay in like manner. This system of aggression was altogether, to my mind, cowardly and uncalled for, and yet was loudly applauded by the spectators. Towards the end of the game one man fainted; several must be lame for weeks, and every man must have been bleeding or scarred. The gentleman who played in spectacles was plucky, but I would advise him to relinquish the game before he receives further injuries. The victory of the Melbourne Club proved unpopular with the larrikins, who commenced stoning the players outside the gates. One offender, however, received a good thrashing for his pains. I consider that football, as played at this match, is a disgrace to our civilization . . .

22

Boxing with Skin Gloves

(From 'Manly Sports')

... I have seen several prize-fights which, except for the surroundings, were far less brutal than a rough football match, and much fairer and more manly. When two clever boxers meet in the ring, there is really little damage done. A man's face may get knocked about a little, and his nose put out of shape; but, as a rule, they will spar and hit away until one is completely exhausted—cannot "come up to time." Hence, prize-fights were so often mere tests of physical endurance, and training was all-important. After a great fight, an English pugilist would be walking about the next day receiving the congratulations or condolences of his friends. He might be slightly disfigured, but was not crippled; seldom, indeed, did any serious injury follow a fight. At all times a blackguardly amusement, the ring in England is now only followed by the very lowest class ... Here, I believe, the ring has had good and evil days, but it seems to be looking up lately. Boxing with "skin gloves" is only another name for fighting, and yet it is becoming highly popular. Whilst I was in the Government service at Kew, such a performance came off at the Princess' Theatre, which I lamented that I could not attend. A fight with skin-gloves, for £50 a-side, also took place between two jewellers, in a room in a public-house opposite the County Court. Of this the police were fully cognizant, an inspector and detectives being present, and no doubt enjoying the sport. Harry Sellars trained a young gentleman belonging to one of the public schools, for a boxing match, with a professional, for £20 a-side. Harry is much more popular with the boys than the Dean; it is rumoured that they toss up to settle their hours of visitation. The future of the P.R. [prize ring], therefore, looks promising. It is a good thing to learn how to defend oneself with Nature's weapons; but ... here amateur boxing seems to have a tendency to public competition and display, a taste for which easily degenerates into encouragement for the P.R. It is the same, however, with every class of sport; young men appear to go in for rowing, cricket, or football, not for the good they get out of it, or real enjoyment, but for the purpose of public display and the satisfaction of beating some one else. In our sports, as in our moral code, it seems that we do not follow anything for love of it *per se*, but chiefly in hopes of present or future reward. It will be an evil much to be lamented if boxing-matches, with "skin gloves," are allowed to be carried on. Such are an encouragement to the ring, the followers of which range from the aristocracy of betting men and publicans, to "prigs" and larrikins, the majority being of the criminal class. It was to investigate the lowest grade of the P.R. that I went to the Polytechnic, and patronized the benefit of "Young Cavanagh," who, according to the public announcements, was going to America. I wish the States joy of the accession to their population.

"Tickets, one shilling, half-a-crown, and five shillings," said the doorkeeper. I went in with the gods. This hall in its pristine glory must have been a pretty one, but has now fallen upon evil days, and is seldom utilized for any respectable amusement. The shilling seats were crowded, the occupants thieves, larrikins, and loafing working-men. The half-crown seats contained two detectives, two attendants from the Kew Asylum, picking up hints before they thrash "the Vagabond" —as some have threatened— a publican, and a few strangers. The five-shilling gallery held a police inspector, a sergeant, another "trap," and a pressman. Altogether young Cavanagh's benefit did not appear to be a very successful one. The entertainment commenced by two seedy young men, seated on two chairs in front of the stage, playing the "Marseillaise" on piccolos. It was frightful! If they had played "Tommy, make room for your Uncle," I would not have minded; but all through the performance, with a strange appreciation of the fitness of things, they played operatic music, "Sweet spirit, hear my prayer" following a smart rally. After the overture three men came on to the stage, two clad in dirty singlets and pants, the third (the M.C.) armed with a towel. "Two friends, gentlemen," said he, "Young Travers, who fought ——, and ——, and ——, and a hamachure. Time." Then young Travers and the "hamachure" went at it, and danced about the stage, and feinted, and countered, and got in well with the right or left, and landed on the &c, &c. All, however, in pretty good humour, little damage being done. I made inquiries as to the character of these gentlemen. The M.C., a short, merry, good-humoured little fellow, who was in his glory all the evening, was known as the "Buffer." He was described to me as having been at one time "the biggest —— thief in the country," but now was keeping "square." Young Travers was a convicted thief. The Buffer was very amusing; when the combatants were in full swing he would waltz in between, often receiving a blow or two himself, and called out, "Go to your corners," and then he would proceed to fan and wipe them down with the towel, which, with the exception of the gloves and rope in front of the stage, was the only "property" of the entertainment. That towel was a sight before the evening closed. "Now, then, finish this round with a rally, my boys; give 'em a hand, gentlemen," said the Buffer. A rally consists in the boxers striking out blindly right and left at close quarters, without any attempt to guard each other's blows. Such always brought down the house. There was a weary round of boxers, "Novice Joe," "Liverpool Bill," "Young Gallagher," "A Hamachure," &c. They were always introduced by the Buffer as having "fought so and so"; and in nearly every case they were known thieves. The Buffer himself put on the gloves once, and got knocked off the stage; falling lightly, however, he bolted through a door underneath, hoping to find a trap and escape criticism; but after being a prisoner there for some time, had to sneak out amidst much laughter.

The audience appeared well acquainted with the performers, and my neighbours confided to me "how much" certain individuals had "done," and when they "came out." They would encourage their friends in language not always polite. "Pass no remarks, gentlemen," said the Buffer, and a youth named "John" shook his fist at a friend in the pit, shouting, "You shut up, or I'll come and make you." Altogether, good humour prevailed throughout the evening, the Buffer being the life and soul of the entertainment. Between the sets-to there was some singing by "hamachures." A gentleman, who had been several times convicted of larceny, asked us, "How could we wonder at crime?" Whilst he and his pals were around, I certainly would not wonder: his appearance alone was enough to get him "six months." He, however, thought that if the rich gave all their wealth to the poor—meaning no doubt himself—the thing would be square, and crime cease. Then the Buffer, by particular request, sang the "Shadows on the Wall"; and I was pleased to see the intimate and friendly manner with which he enforced his criticisms on the police by pointing at the detectives. A fellow of infinite jest was the Buffer, who caused much amusement by announcing "A hinterval of five minutes, gentlemen, whilst the M.C. gets a booze."

The saddest sight of the evening to me was the spectacle of two boys, ten or twelve years of age, who, with an equally juvenile attendant, appeared on the stage striped to the waist, and boxed in imitation of their superiors. The lads themselves enjoyed the sport, but the training and tastes which such association must give them will have the worst effect upon their future. They were two nice-looking boys, I believe belonging to the Gospel Hall School. "The Boneless Boy" sadly went through a series of contortions. He is a mulatto, his father a thief, his mother what Othello called Desdemona. Crime is hereditary with him, and he has already graduated at the gaol. Two factory boys, who danced some jigs, were very clever, and their performance was much appreciated. If it be true that the rudest and most brutal nature is bettered by any exhibition into which the art spirit, in however small a degree, enters, then these dances were the redeeming point of the performance.

The wind-up was between the *beneficiaire*, Young Cavanagh, and another "pug." Buffer led Cavanagh to the front and introduced him to the audience describing his prowess. "He says, gentlemen, he's sorry his friends didn't support him better, as he hisself always supported every benefit in Melbourne. He's going to America to better hisself; but before he goes he wishes to say a few words. He'll fight anything in Australia at eight stone and a half. There!" After hurling this defiance at everything, the Buffer called "Time," and some really good boxing wound up the entertainment, which, but for its surroundings, was innocent enough, and in itself, I believe, not so demoralizing to the lookers-on as a football match. But the P.R. is the main amusement of thieves and rowdies, and boxing-matches innocent enough in themselves, gather together the lowest of the community . . . it is by this lower class that the ring is mainly supported, and from it that its fighting-men are recruited. They commence by being prigs, and end as publicans and bookmakers; not, I believe, being any the more savoury or useful members of society by their advanced prosperity. It is for this reason that I trust amateur boxing-matches with skin gloves will cease to be encouraged by gentlemen, and that the ring will be left to its natural supporters—of the class present at Young Cavanagh's benefit. Let Young Australia learn boxing by all means; but let it be fully recognized in this, and in football, that brutality is not a necessary accompaniment of a manly sport.

23

Bare Knuckle Bouts

MELBOURNE
(From 'A Prize-Fight')

... There was a good deal of steady drinking going on, whilst the hours slowly slipped away and brought us nearer the dawn which was to decide who was the best man, in a pugilistic sense—James M. Christie, or John Thompson. It was rumoured that the fight was off, or that the detectives were too hot on the track of the men, for whose arrest they held warrants, to allow it to be safe for them to leave their hiding places and bring matters to an issue. Persons who, it was suspected, would take part in the proceedings were "shadowed" by the police; and the Chief Commissioner himself devoted some attention to "The Vagabond." But Victorian detectives, as a body, are notoriously inefficient, and they maintained their reputation in this instance. It was not until late in the evening that I got "the office" to wait at a well-known hotel, and remain there till five in the morning. At that hour the place of combat was to be named. Then the fiery cross was sent round by the gentleman who had charge of this part of the programme, and the principals, and their seconds and backers, were advised of the *locale*. In this respect every precaution was used; but if the detectives had only "shadowed" thoroughly certain prominent individuals who were bound to be present, or had kept guard on the main outlets from the city, the little game would have been spoilt. According to the "articles," only six persons on each side were to receive "the office" and be told of the scene of action. Making allowances for privileged beings, such as myself, who would not be denied, I imagined that, at the utmost, not more than two dozen people would be present. I was admitted into the secret as a great favour, and I had to give my word that I would not reveal the time of meeting to anyone, and that I would trust myself to my "guide, philosopher, and friend," to put me through without any question as to whither we were going. I was perfectly content. I took an amused interest in the amount of secrecy and caution exercised by my *cicerone*. He had a great deal of work to do in the early morning, and although, at a quarter past five, messengers were despatched from our hostelry, it was not until a quarter to seven that we mounted our buggy and trotted down Swanston-street.

It was a lovely, balmy morning; the first grey tints of dawn were succeeded by others of crimson and opal hue, presaging the rising of the sun. The air was pure, and not too chilly; and as we made good time along the St. Kilda-road, the sense of healthy exhilaration made me feel quite virtuous. Certain things are good in themselves, *per se*, and are not affected by the motives which cause them. A drive on a fine morning is healthy, and the lungs of a pugilist or bookmaker are as much revivified by pure air, as those of a bishop or dean. Nature is quite democratic in her treatment. Going to a "brutal prize-fight," I suppose, one ought to have moralized, and have "sickened at heart," at the morbid instincts which led others thither. In real truth, I did nothing of the sort; but enjoyed my ride muchly, and gaily chatted to my companion of other lands we had travelled in, far over the sea. One of our horses was restive, and amused himself by "shying" violently at every object we passed; but one of the best whips in the world, John Wilson, of circus renown, held the reins, and we got along in safety. A mounted messenger had told us that the members of this picnic party, in several cabs and carriages, were a-head, and that they had gone through Windsor and Prahran. We accordingly took the Brighton-road, to avoid suspicion, and then turned to the left, towards Mordialloc. Filing into this from a cross road, we saw a string of cabs and buggies. "Gracious Powers!" said my companion, "is this a funeral? You know how particular I have been to keep this thing quiet, yet it's been given away to all this lot already. Such a procession as that is enough to raise all the troopers in the country on to us." I agreed with him, and thought there was little chance of the fight coming off.

One by one we overhauled the vehicles, and had a chance of inspecting the occupants. Bookmakers—large and small—and some rough-looking customers, graduates of Thompson's sparring academy, formed the majority. There was certainly a lack of honour or discretion amongst some who had thus brought the crowd together contrary to agreement. Turning to the right we trotted over the beach, and cutting down the field, horsemen and all, we arrived at the appointed place at the same time as the party which had left nearly an hour before us. Near to Red Bluff, a level piece of heath, separated by a line of scrub from the cliffs which overhang the sands, the waters of Hobson's Bay glittering in the rising sun, the white-winged seabirds skimming the waves, two or three distant sails suggesting thoughts of home and friends—this was a scene for a poet to dilate on: the peaceful surroundings did not seem to fit in with the purpose to which the place was to be put. Two men were going to batter and bruise each other's heads and bodies until one of them was exhausted, and admitted himself defeated. But man is so seldom in accord with the poet's idea of Nature ...

One after the other, the vehicles and horsemen arrived at the spot. "The King of the Ring," in a handsome waggonette, drawn by a pair of fine horses, and several disreputable hangers-on of the Ring in most disreputable "jingles." There was Harry Edwards, the most popular host of a most popular hotel, other publicans, a sporting writer, trainers, and jockeys, a distinguished visitor from England (late in the pugilistic line of business himself), runners, clowns, and one of the golden-haired youth of Australia, who, sleeping at the Retreat, was rejoiced at being awakened by the passing multitude, and hence enabled to see the fight. There were between sixty and seventy present in all; the supporters of Thompson being in a majority of three to one . . . The principals, attended by their seconds, were closely wrapped up and guarded from the cold. The vehicles being hitched to the fence, business was at once proceeded with. The backers named each an umpire, but there was a little dispute as to the election of a referee, several bookmakers interfering, as if each particular one was running the machine. A referee was at last appointed, whose name was a guarantee of fairness. A level piece of ground was selected, and the large tufts of grass were carefully pulled up or cut away by industrious bookmakers. The four corners of the "Ring" were marked by walking-canes stuck in the ground, and my malacca being borrowed for the purpose, I suppose I at once rendered myself *particeps criminis*. There was not much time lost in getting to work. Thompson left his cab where he had been gaily singing "Just before the Battle, Mother," a *souvenir* of his military career; for he is an ex-Union soldier, and old enemy of mine. Claiming American citizenship as he does, and as one who has fought in our war (even on the wrong side), I rather like Jack Thompson. He marched into the Ring, clad in an ordinary pair of merino drawers, and, throwing in his cap, was rewarded by a cheer. He was followed by Christie, clad in regular fighting costume, who was also cheered. Then there commenced a rubbing down and shampooing of the gladiators by their seconds. The King of the Ring, regardless of his bank balance and the splendours of his home, stripped off his coat and rubbed his brother energetically, all throughout seconding him in a manner which showed he had not forgotten his early career. Indeed, at times, he was reproved by his own side for his too great and offensive demonstrativeness. The veteran, Tom Curran was Christie's principal supporter.

A bare knuckle fight of earlier days

"Time" being called, the two men stepped into the Ring, and, after shaking hands, faced each other at nine o'clock exactly. There was a great difference between them. Christie, well known as an ex-detective, has a reputation as an amateur athlete, and is generally liked as a gentlemanly, nice fellow. He seemed in splendid condition, the muscles standing out prominent, and with not an ounce of superfluous flesh: the question is, if he was not over-trained. Since his tour with Mace, he was considered to have improved greatly in science, and to be a very good boxer. Thompson—his opponent—is a much heavier man, taller, and with a longer reach of arm. He seemed to be in nothing like the condition Christie was, having a blister on his loins and a plaster on his wrist, and did not show so much muscle. As a bookmaker and keeper of a "sparring academy," Thompson is well known. Both the men are, to an extent, amateurs. For two years there has been rivalry and ill-blood between them, which culminated at last in this fight— a duel, in fact, between two enemies.

"£100 to 1 my brother wins," cried Joe Thompson, fraternally. No takers. One or two feints, and a straight-forward blow knocked Christie off his legs. Intense cheers and hooting by the Thompson party, the seconds picking up their man and carrying him in triumph to his corner, Christie's seconds doing the like good offices by him. "Round the first, knock down to Thompson!" said a bookmaker, who was industriously taking notes for an up-country journal. In the corners the men were fanned and sponged; then "Time!" again was called. Why go into hideous details? In each round Christie was knocked down by his opponent, in whose hands he appeared like a child. He was severely bruised, and his lips much cut, and was bespattered with blood from thence and his nostrils. It was not a pretty sight, and the thud of hard blows on human flesh is not a pleasant sound. Christie came up gallantly, however, and took his punishment "like a man," although throughout there appeared a dogged astonished look on his face, as if he himself could not understand it. Thompson was always smiling, cool, and confident, as if on parade, and, both as a fighter and boxer, completely overmatched his opponent. Only once did Christie mark him; and the end was that after nine or ten rounds, fought in twenty minutes, when it was quite evident that Christie was completely "knocked out of time," the sponge was thrown up, and, amidst great cheering, Thompson was declared the winner. It is to the credit of many of the spectators that, as Christie came up to the last two rounds, his condition being so palpable, cries of "shame," and "throw up the sponge," were directed at his seconds. Joe Thompson, even with a few adjectives, expressed his opinion that it was "cruelty and murder." Everything was conducted in the fairest manner throughout, and, taking it as a duel between two men, the affair ended satisfactorily, but the yelling and hooting by a portion of the crowd, the fierce delight they took in the sight of blood was a most obnoxious adjunct. Joe Thompson and one or two other individuals were particularly offensive. The one thing to be said in favour of such a contest is, that a personal difficulty is settled in a few minutes, without anyone being much hurt, as Christie was able to walk about nearly right in a day's time. A "champion" football match is more dangerous to the competitors than a Prize-fight, and, under certain rules, I think quite as brutal. It is in the debasing influences which too often surround it that the prize-ring does harm. I don't think, however, that anyone at this fight was made any worse by witnessing it.

After the third round, a couple of horsemen in plain clothes rode up. I thought they were farmers, but they forced their way into the Ring, and one said "You must stop this." He had ridden his horse in front of me, so I said, "Who are you?" "I'm a constable!" "How do I know; you're not in uniform. Where's your authority?" "This is my authority," said the man, showing a pistol in holster round his waist. Now, that's an argument we understand in America, if used; but its display we don't value a cent. In the States, the veriest tyro would not have been guilty of such an act of folly as this. The idea of a man threatening me with a pistol was a good joke. If he had shown any authority to act, I would have been the first to respect law and order; but to ride in and bail up a crowd at the pistol's mouth won't do in Australia. I thought of Power's tale of his treatment by the troopers, and I believe it more than ever. Being entreated to let the men "finish it," the *soi-disant* troopers left the Ring, and looked on for a time with interest. Aroused to a sense of duty, however, the senior said, "I must exercise my authority, and arrest these men." "What authority can you show?" said I again. "I'll do it on this," said he, again flashing his pistol. "I don't believe you are a constable," said I, "you threaten me with your pistol, do you? If you are a constable, I'll report you to the Chief Commissioner." To that functionary I accordingly recommend the consideration of this case. Some bookmakers spoke these men fairly, and begged me to be quiet, and I have no doubt they thought I was one of the biggest rowdies of the Ring; whereas I was only inspired by a zeal for law and order, which the servants thereof should be the first to respect. The men took several names; and if the whole crowd—myself included—had got six months each, I should have been happy.

I never write anything without a moral. I attended this prize-fight as a public duty. I didn't like it; and, but for the drive, I would have preferred being in bed. The tendency of the age is to athleticism, to vaunt the supremacy of muscle over brain. Boxing is a favourite amusement of our youth; indeed fair maidens and matrons, I am sorry to say, also "put on the gloves," and pommel each other's lovely features. In all our sports and exercises, the element of public display and competition is too largely introducd. No one appears to think he is good at anything till he has beaten somebody else . . .

Besides a moral this story has a sequel, which came off at the City Police Court, where I, in company with racing-men, bookmakers, circus people, rowdies, and gaol-birds, was charged with "riotously and routously assembling to offend the peace of our Sovereign Lady the Queen." Although legally, I suppose, I was as guilty as the rest, still, morally, engaged as I was on a public duty, I think it an outrage that I should have been summoned. Not that it mattered. Serjeant Sleigh, my talented deliverer, safely pulled me through, and again demonstrated the inefficiency of Victorian officials. In justice to the constables (who were genuine after all), I must say that they gave their evidence fairly. The Crown Solicitor, however, showed his total ignorance of law when he called Jem Mace as a witness, who, of course, refused to give evidence, on the ground that he would criminate himself. I like Mr Gurner, however, for the good service he did to the Confederate States in the matter of the *Shenandoah*, and I have no ill-feeling towards him for his second futile attempt to imprison me.

SYDNEY

(From 'Trial of Skill')

"Mind you, it's only a friendly trial of skill," said my informant, the Colorado Beetle*; and he winked cunningly, a wink which I returned. Then we laughed, and evidently thought each other very facetious and knowing dogs indeed. I had been sitting in company with the Premier of this great colony, and a Police Magistrate, trying hard to discover some loop-hole by which I might creep into a knowledge of the land laws of New South Wales, when I was mysteriously called on one side, and asked if I would like to see a fight. In pursuance of my mission to explore every phase of Sydney society, I, although against my "liking," assented, and was then jesuitically told that it was only "a friendly trial of skill." I have reason to believe, however, that this was in every respect a real prize fight, the stakes being £50 a-side. When I returned to the company of the law-maker and the law administrator I did not feel guilty, but I wondered if any sign of my criminal intent was perceptible in the slackened interest I took in the land question. I

---

* The Colorado beetle, *Doryphora decemlineata*, was a potato pest introduced from the U.S.A. which was beginning to give serious trouble in Australia. Defined by the *Sydney Morning Herald* (3 November 1877) as 'a persistent intruder,' it was soon applied as a slang term to human beings.

knew nothing at all about this fight, who it was between, or where it was to take place; but I concluded the preliminaries were arranged with all due regard to secrecy, and every precaution taken to avoid interference on behalf of the police . . .

I suppose I had about an hour's sleep, hardly enough to work the land laws off my brain, and then at half-past two I dressed, and, like a thief or a Tarquin, crept softly down stairs. A cup of tea refreshed us, and then we entered the cab and were driven slowly through the streets of the city. This early rising gives one a most disreputable sensation; it is quite as bad as stopping out late. The sight of the night-houses still plying their trade encouraged the idea that we had been out all night. Muffled in my Ulster I dozed in the corner of the cab until fairly out in the Randwick Road, when, turning sharply to the right through the tollbar, I was aroused to interest in the location of the proposed fight. Now, too, I discovered that the fog was lying low on the scrub or heath around Randwick. It was quite a new sensation this damp atmosphere. We drove on for about a mile and a half, and then sighted the red lamps of a cab ahead. Shortly we overtook this, and when it stopped, perforce halted as well. Then through the darkness and fog a man rode by, giving the order, "Put out the lights!" which was done. Leaving our vehicle and walking along the track, we found a number of hansoms, whose occupants indulged in whispered conclave, and suspiciously queried at strangers through the gloom. As the darkness turned to grey dawn, faces became visible. The horseman turned out to be a distinguished ex-prize-fighter, who was the general of the proceedings, and who, like many other generals, enforced his words of command with strong adjectives. There was a keeper of a night-house, two or three sporting gentlemen, five "Georgias," and a crowd of the "fancy" and "rats." A mean-enough looking throng altogether, but with money enough to pay for the hire of hansoms. A council of war shortly took place, when the general issued his instructions to go ahead past the place where "the cock-fighting is," and also said, "We must look sharp, for fear the traps will be on us." We shortly halted again near an open piece of ground at the side of the road, and another council was held. Men stretched their legs and yawned, and cigars and flasks were handed around. The Georgias, of course, made themselves obnoxiously conspicuous; and my disgust at the whole proceedings was enhanced by the thought that two white men were about to pommel each other for the amusement of negro rowdies. These "original coloured minstrels" have as their only attraction the fact that they were "originally slaves." I think they would have been far more useful members of society if they had remained in bondage.

Suddenly Nature's voice was heard—a quiet, clear, sweet note of a ground lark, or other song-bird, giving out its morning carol of thankfulness for life and liberty. Then in a few moments the warbling was taken up by other songsters, and "Around! around! flew each sweet sound." Could we but listen to the voice and moral! . . .

I was thinking of these things when there was a sudden rush to the vehicles. "The traps! the traps!" was the cry. Four policemen ran swiftly towards the front. Conscience made cowards of a great many; and the manner in which a noted publican made tracks through the scrub was most amusing. Others followed his example, hiding from the gaze of the officers of the law. And this was an easy matter, as in the fog figures could not be distinguished at a distance of twenty paces. The negroes took their cabs and fled back to town. Others followed suit, and the whole affair seemed to be over. I was thankful, and thought of home and bed. Whilst awaiting events the police returned, and hastened after some of the departing vehicles. When they were out of sight we drove towards the front, and came up with the General and half-a-dozen others, who had all fled into the scrub, and hidden from the police. These latter were evidently in search of the principals, one of whom, Hurley, was in front. Had the traps entirely gone? That was the question. The General rode back to reconnoitre.

In a few minutes, looking through the fog, I saw a horse's legs coming towards us at a tremendous speed. Then through the mist loomed the body, and the rider. The General was riding like Sheridan at the battle of Winchester. "The copperman! the copperman!" he yelled. The Beetle made a rush up the bank. "What's the matter?" "Don't run away," I cried. "The copperman!" was his reply, a panic at the strange slang having seized him. I believe he thought it was a new kind of wild beast. The General gave up his horse to Hurley, with instructions to ride across country if the police appeared; and then, recognizing me as a fellow criminal, he shouted "Come on, or they'll nab you," and darted through the scrub. The whole thing was so ridiculous that I suffocated with laughter, but followed the rest as well as my age and infirmities would permit me.

I think some of the sporting youths began to wish themselves safe at home. I did, but felt bound to see the thing through. The police were evidently masters of the ground, and no fight could take place there. Another hurried consultation, and it was arranged that Hurley and his backers should go across country, whilst we drove by cab to a new rendezvous, at "Shep. Smith's," at Waverley. By the time we got to the Randwick toll-bar it was broad daylight. A sergeant and constable of police closely inspected each cab and its inmates, and took notes of the numbers. The sun came out strong and powerful before we reached Waverley. Outside the public-house kept by Shep. Smith there were a number of hansom cabs and a collection of ruffians. These had retreated at the first panic caused by "the traps," and had followed the other principal, Oxley, in his flight to this head-quarters. After waiting a little, "the office" was given that the fight would take place on the beach at Bondi, two miles away. And now my punishment began. No cabs were allowed to leave the public-house, and by different routes the disreputable crowd started for the beach. This was an infliction I had little recked of. Nothing but a stern sense of public duty supported me through that weary tramp under a blazing January sun. The inhabitants of the peaceful suburb of Bondi were fast asleep as we passed their pleasant homes, although I am afraid they must have been disturbed by the oaths and fierce language which went up to heaven from the congregation of roughs. I loathed them more than ever, doubtless from the personal discomfort which I was experiencing. The bay at Bondi is not the sort of place which one would couple with the idea of a prize-fight, yet here, on a level plateau in the scrub above the sands, screened by the banks of the road, is a place which, as one "rat" said, "might have been made a-purpose." The glories of nature, of sun, sea, sky, and shore were all around us—but his only thoughts were to apply this spot to a degrading and disgraceful exhibition.

Wrangling, oaths, disputes, and the fight began. It is not to be supposed that I am going to particularize any of the hideous details. It is sufficient to draw the moral! Enough that these two youths, put up to fight for money by others, mere instruments of gambling in their hands, fought for one hour and a half under a blazing sun. They were neither of them very strong, or in good condition, and did not severely damage each other. But the surroundings were hideous. Amongst the fifty or sixty people present there were hardly half-a-dozen who could be called respectable. By sunlight these "rats" and roughs looked more disreputable than ever. One of the combatants being from Melbourne and the other from Sydney, provincial jealousy was aroused, and from the different "corners" compliments were freely bandied. Men shouted, and yelled, and snarled, like wild beasts, and cursed each other with the most opprobrious and abominable terms, and made the welkin ring with their hideous oaths and screams. It was a Babel of Hell. Faces were furious, disfigured by passion. Money at first was freely staked, and the supporters of the different men loudly cheered and threw up their caps at any successful hit or throw. The backers quarrelled and fought, and struggled around the combatants. Even according to the rules of the prize ring there was no fair play shown. Some men were particularly obnoxious. A big one-eyed Jew was especially so. "Yah! look—he's split his hye, s'help me!" cried this man, pointing with his finger, and dancing with delight. Then he turned his one eye to heaven, and joyously repeating the phrase, pantomimically appeared to call down the attention of the Almighty to this great deed. When I sleep ill at nights in the future, I shall dream of this one-eyed Barabbas, and his "Yah! he's split his hye!" The delight in blood, and the punishment which the two poor wretches gave and received, was abominable. The Anglo-Saxon race has within it as great a strain of brutality as the Spaniard; and a bull fight is, after all, not more degrading than a prize-fight.

I could not stand the near neighbourhood of this abomination, and retreated to the bank. Looking down, one saw a confused crowd of ruffians; in the centre the pink bodies of the fighters, their faces distorted with passion, at which I could hardly wonder, as one can scarcely feel charitable towards the man who has been knocking your face out of shape for an hour. One man, it was apparent, was nearly beaten; but he was continually sent into the ring by his backers, to be knocked, or thrown, or slip down. Poor devil! he was not his own master, but, like a racehorse, must go on straining every nerve to win money for his supporters. As long as he could stand on his legs, he would be sent into the ring, as some chance might yet occur in his favour. And the only possible thing did happen. As if a shell had fallen in their midst, the crowd suddenly scattered in all directions, leaving the miserable gladiators in the clutches of the sergeant and officer whom we had last seen at Randwick toll-bar. These had followed on our track, and crept quietly through the scrub until they appeared in the centre of proceedings. It was a very neat and clever capture. Up the banks, through the scrub, the cowardly mob fled like sheep. A young sporting gent and a trainer rode off on their fast horses. An ex-prize-fighter admitted to me, as he hurried past, that "it was the most disgraceful thing he had ever seen; and if this was fighting now-a-days, the sooner it was stopped the better."

The two poor wretches, for whom a few minutes before such cheers had been raised, but who were now deserted by seconds and backers and supporters, came slowly up the road, supported by the arms of their captors. I do not think that the custody was a harsh one. The officers had done their duty well and efficiently; but I believe they had a sort of sneaking regard for the men who had fought so hard. Anyhow, I was glad I had my flask with me to administer, as a medicine, a dram to each of these poor devils, who, the excitement of combat being over, trembled in every limb. The good-natured sergeant, when I expressed to him my professional opinion that the men must have a stimulant to enable them to bear the walk through the scorching sun, said, "It'll do them no harm, sir; give them a good dose." I shall remember that sergeant with pleasure.

These two poor wretches will, I suppose, be either bound over to keep the peace, or fined, or imprisoned. They have fought without obtaining any reward. If the fight had been concluded, the winner would have received a present from his backers, and a collection would have been made for the beaten man. But now they have had nothing except hard knocks and punishment. It is quite right they should bear the penalty of law-breaking, but they are not the worst. The men who "backed" them, who bet on them, who made them slaves to win money, who would make them fight to the death to put a few pounds in their own pockets—these are those who should be really punished. "A trial of skill" would not attract the crowd of "rats." It may be hard to prove the existence of stakes, of a battle for money, but the detectives should be able to do so. Punishment of those who are mere tools will never put a stop to such exhibitions—a disgrace to our civilization.

PART SIX

The Demi-Monde

24

The Theatre Vestibules

In the centre of this city of Melbourne exists a disgraceful, flagrant, heinous scandal, flaunting boldly and shamelessly in the face of decent society!—an outrageous insult to our wives and daughters!—an infamy hardly equalled in any civilized city in the world!—a reproach which should cover with ignominy those who instituted, and now profit by its continuance! "What is the matter with this vagabond, and why these adjectives?" you ask, in surprise. Who will dare to say that this denunciation is unmerited? I write of an immorality open as the day and known to all, of the places where vice meets, and chaffers, and makes its bargains under the very eyes of "respectability," of the chief marts of Melbourne prostitution—the Theatre Vestibules.

Let us first give a glance at the Theatre Royal. A stranger, used to the arrangement in London theatres, will naturally, if he wishes to obtain a good seat, ask his way to the stalls. At the gate of entrance there is a drinking bar; within a stone's throw there are scores of others. But, to his surprise, inside the shabby, dirty Vestibule, he sees two other bars, running right and left, almost the full length of the hall. There is also an entrance to the bar fronting the street. The doors of these are all wide open, and attractive-looking barmaids are in attendance to minister to thirsty souls. The sights and sounds they see and hear must conduce to a liberal view of the moral code, and I am not surprised to have had pointed out to me two frail sisters who were formerly barmaids in the Vestibules. Between the bar on the right and the entrance to the stalls, the stranger will perceive two mysterious closed doors. Surprised, no doubt, at the extremely liberal preparations for the supply of liquors, he will pass on to his seat, leaving further investigations till the *entr'actes*. Inside the Theatre, he finds the "stalls" are uncomfortable forms, crowded too closely. It is strange that Australian managers have not yet recognized the fact, now thoroughly

The Theatre Royal, Melbourne, showing the vestibule

appreciated in Europe and America, that this part of the house is the best. Before the curtain rises, the occupants of the stalls will be seen to be chiefly respectable people of the middle class—fathers with their families, and lovers with their sweethearts, including many who, according to the fashion of this time, may be called ladies and gentlemen. But, after the performance has commenced, considerable interruption will be experienced by the noisy entry of a number of women. There is no mistaking what class they belong to—no need that they should wear saffron, as of old. Their startling dresses and painted faces, without reference to their manner, stamp them as lorettes. They "make up" the part well. There is a notable difference in this class of women in France. There you may take your wife or daughter to any public place, and may sit next to the most notorious member of the demi-monde without perceiving, by her dress or manner, that she is different from the rest of the world. The fact is, that, in France, where these women are under police supervision, they, when they mix with the general world, take care not to be guilty, by their dress or manners, of any "offence against public decency," a charge which is very elastic, and is severely punished. How different in Melbourne! Flaunting in their dress, bold and vulgar in their manners, they flounce in and out of the stalls during the performance, causing in this alone a positive nuisance and annoyance. And whilst sitting down, their conduct is little better. They laugh and talk amongst themselves, or with some of their male friends, Melbourne "cads," who ("dressed to kill," with slouched hats, à la larrikin, and paget coats) crowd and crush decent people in a manner which would not be tolerated in England or America.

The conduct of these women in the stalls is really so bad, that audible cries of "shame" are sometimes raised by other occupants. They care little about any play, but come here to be seen, and to scrutinize the occupants of the dress circle, looking out everywhere for "friends," whom they will afterwards meet in "the paddock." From twenty to thirty of these women will often be present, and, in the course of the year, their contributions to the treasury will amount to a good sum; but that, for the sake of this, the lessees should tolerate (if not encourage) the presence of these women, is a disgrace to them and an insult to society, which should be resented by the decent portion of the public. It is not alone that the occupants of the stalls are annoyed, although to them it is a serious evil; and there is no more reason why they should be afflicted with the presence of these women than the visitors to the dress-circle. There is often little social difference between the occupants of the stalls and the circle. To a married man, wishing to treat his family to the play, the difference in the price will, if he pays many visits in the year, mount up considerably. He would, perchance, go often to the stalls, but there his wife and daughters are outraged by the presence of lorettes; and, if he goes to the dress-circle, the increased cost will lessen the number of his visits. But admitted, as they are, to the most prominent parts of the house, the vagaries of these women are seen by all. If they must be admitted, let them have a gallery to themselves, where they may show less publicly. "The management will never turn away three shillings," I am told; but if I could have my will, they should lose a good many three shillings as long as they admitted these soiled doves to annoy the audience. I remember that, twenty years ago, in Liverpool, the condition of the Ampitheatre (then leased by Mr. Copeland, and the only decent Theatre open in the town), was in this respect alike shameful. The members of the demi-monde were admitted to the side-boxes, and their presence there and in the passages was considered so scandalous that hardly any lady would attend the Theatre until they were banished. If the ladies of Melbourne would decline to patronize the Royal until this scandal is done away with, I think the lessees would soon find it to their interest to follow the example of the Opera-house management, and close their doors in the face of the demi-monde.

I have done with the inside of the house. Every frequenter of the Royal knows that I have mildly drawn the scenes witnessed there. Astonished at these, the stranger, strolling out during an *entr'acte*, would be still more surprised at Melbourne manners and customs, as witnessed in the Vestibule. This is generally crowded with men and larrikins, smoking and chaffing the loose women who pass in and out. The drinking bars are thronged, but only by men. The stranger sees that the women, possibly picking up a male companion, all enter the apartment which was previously closed, and which is now guarded by swing doors. Curiosity will doubtless prompt him to enter, and he will find himself in the far-famed "saddling paddock" of the Royal. It is a small bar, presided over by a man: the proceedings here are too unpleasant for a barmaid to witness. Here the most notorious women of Melbourne nightly throng, and run in the companions they have caught in the stalls or in the Vestibules. Here is Lais, in her drunken old age, the wealthy proprietor of a notorious house. Here is Phryne, of lowly origin, born in a right-of-way, and educated in an Industrial School, now loudly dressed in scarlet satin, and sparkling with gold and jewels. Here is *not* Aspasia, of wit and knowledge, redeeming her lack of morality by the wonderful use of her talents; for if one thing in these women is more conspicuous than another, it is their lack of grammar and utter vulgarity of speech and soul. Bah! it is an insult to the memories of those glorious women of Greece to mention their names in connexion with such as these.

Seven o'clock outside the Theatre Royal

After the Theatre is over, it is high change in the "paddocks." The men are of all classes—"gentlemen," betting men, sharpers, clerks, junior officers of merchant vessels, and new chums. The women are very anxious to be treated, and also bring a number of "lady friends" to join in a drink. The new chum, whose naturally weak brains have not been improved by two or three months at sea, falls into the toils, and spends his money foolishly. One or two come here now whose finery and jewellery have vanished, bit by bit, who have little money left "to treat," but who still cannot, apparently keep away from the scenes of vice and folly. Poor devils! I have my eye on two, who, I am afraid, will become brother vagabonds before long. One cannot literally describe the doings and the language here. Everything is low, coarse, and vulgar—emphatically "bad form!" and I cannot imagine how any one, with any pretension to the title of "gentleman," can frequent such a place. Melbourne vice is of a very poor kind. In London, at Cremorne or the Argyle, and in Paris, at Mabille, there is a certain amount of enjoyment to be obtained without actual vice; but in Melbourne, *roués* merely delight in visiting the "paddocks," and having drinks and vulgar talk with these wretched women. In this respect your young colonials are very "bad form," which is not improved by a tendency to Mohawkism amongst some of the wealthiest of them.

We have, as yet, only seen the doings of the demi-monde in the stalls, vestibules, and "paddock" of the Theatre Royal. There vice is most prominent, as lately these women have been refused admission to the stalls at the Opera-house. But the stranger crossing to that establishment will see little difference in the Vestibule. There are bars here likewise, and a private room partitioned off from these. Inside this the scenes are worse, if anything, than at the Royal. Many of the women pass the evening between the two Vestibules, but most of the frequenters at the Opera are of a very low class. The difference is only one of degree, when all are coarse and vulgar. Still there is a difference. In both the Vestibules there are experienced police officers on duty; but, as they are on private property, I presume their presence must be paid for by the lessees. They do their duty, keep out young thieves, and prevent any great disorder; but they cannot interfere with the women in the Vestibules or in the "paddocks." These ladies know that they have, according to the ideas of the proprietors, a right to be there. The management of the Opera-house has done well to keep these women out of the stalls. Why do not the proprietors, or lessee, insist upon the closing of the "paddock"? If we must meet these women in the street, there is no reason that they should elbow our wives and daughters in the entrance to a Theatre, or make assignations under their very eyes. We read in the papers that "the police are making great efforts to grapple with the moral and social evils of Melbourne." Why do they not summon the lessees of both the Theatres, and the proprietors of the bars, for keeping disorderly houses? To all intents and purposes, they commit this offence, as they "are frequented," &c., according to the Act.

Many will say that I am making a great deal to do about nothing—that there is no criminality or gross offence likely to arise from the presence of these women in the Vestibules . . . They will show that, if these women are debarred from the Theatres, they will congregate elsewhere, and that "isolation makes little hells." They will maintain, perhaps, that the mixing with respectable society keeps them, to a great extent, in order, and that it is better, as I have before written, that they should have healthy amusements. There is reason in all this. Healthy amusements for the people are sadly wanted here . . . I have no objection to the presence of the thief or outcast in the gallery, or even to Magdalen in the stalls, if, like her French sister, she will, for the nonce, behave herself. But the lorette of Melbourne frequents the Theatres and Vestibules—not for amusement, but to ply her trade; and even granting that it is hard to shut the door in her face, the existence of the "saddling paddocks" is a scandal established with a forethought for the courtezan's benefit which is an eternal disgrace to their promoters. There are people who believe that good always comes out of evil, and who may think that the scenes in the Vestibules act as a warning to modest young women, and will deter them from entering on a career of vice . . . these scenes cannot but have an evil effect upon the morals of society. Virtue sees Sin in the stalls, clothed in rich garments and sparkling with jewels; whilst she, in the pit, wears homespun. She sees that Sin enjoys herself in the Vestibules and in the "paddocks," and altogether appears to have a good time of it. It seems as if Vice had floated over the barriers which kept it apart, and is elbowing Virtue out of the field. It may be argued that, according to this doctrine, society is being injured through the representation of the amours of the Duchess of Gerolstein, Mdlle. Lange, and other stage heroines. But, after all, a stage play has little immediate influence on the morals of a generation. It indicates what they are, but does not originate them. Half-a-dozen abandoned women plying their trade in the company, or presence, of the virtuous of their sex, do more harm than the representation on the stage of a hundred immoralities; and this, besides the annoyance and insult to decent society, is the evil which I denounce . . .

25

The Magdalen Asylum

This article is not written for boys and girls. I intend to call a spade a spade, and not an agricultural implement. The "unco' guid," who have been reviling me for the last two months because I advocated Sunday excursions for the people, will, no doubt, be highly shocked at my manner of speaking of fallen women. I give them fair warning, and they had better pass. The social evil is, I believe, as strong in Melbourne as in any city of the world; and it is flaunted boldly and shamelessly in the face of society. Added to this, there is a general public immorality as glaring as that of Paris under the Empire, without the refinement of French vice. For graver sins, the coroners and members of the medical profession can vouch. Human nature seems particularly strong in Australia, and respectable society is full of "whited sepulchres." In a lower social stage there is not even a pretence of keeping virtuous. Girls "go wrong" with their eyes open; and it is useless to gush over them . . .

But immorality alone does not make what is generally known as a "fallen woman." I know that very good people—principally those of milk-and-water temperaments—hold that the slightest *discovered* breach of society's moral code makes a woman "fallen," and one to be shunned by her sex, and socially outlawed. Man does not usually condemn the offender; woman alone, forgetting what was written by His finger on the dust of the Temple pavement, casts stones at her erring sister. And this want of charity too often drives a weak girl into the ranks of the unfortunate and the outcast. Man's wayward passion may bring some to ruin, but woman's anger and venom too often complete the work. A strange instance of this came under my notice the other night.

I was wandering late in West Melbourne, when I was accosted in the dreary gay tones of a female outcast. Men of the world are used to this sort of thing; it neither shocks nor surprises us, and I was passing without heed when the gleams of the gas lamp fell upon the face of the speaker. I was certainly startled, for a countenance picturing more young, innocent purity, I have seldom seen. "How long have you been at this game, my child?" "Three days, sir," was the answer. "And do you know what this will end in: have you no idea of anything better for your life than this?" I asked. The girl burst out crying—"Oh God! I wish I was dead, sir. Oh! If I could only get something to do. But my mother turned me out of doors, and I had to come to the streets." The grief seemed genuine, and it touched me. A good dinner and copious libations of Bourbon whisky had perhaps obscured my intelligence; at least, I felt charitable, and inclined to play the Samaritan. The girl's story was soon told. She had been a barmaid, had been tempted and had gone "crooked;" the child was dead, but her mother, enraged by neighbours' sneers, had turned her out of doors. She was not what chapel people would call a good girl, nor particularly clear on the moral code; but her true womanly instinct, not yet lost, revolted at the abominations of her trade. "Oh! if I could only get a situation, and get away from this sort of life," sobbed the girl. Worldly wisdom told me that this very likely was "a put-up game," and that I was a fool to waste my time listening to the plaints of a young hussy. But Bourbon whisky, warming the cockles of my heart, told me that the story might be true, and that as a "Vagabond" I was bound to test it. I took out my notebook and wrote down the address of her mother, and promised the girl that, if what she said was true, I would get her a situation. Through the kindness of the public in buying up the first series of *The Vagabond Papers*, I had a few shillings in my pocket; so giving the girl money, I told her to go to her lodgings, and stop there till she heard from me. "If you go outside the door, or don't keep quite straight, I shall hear of it, and nothing will be done for you," said I, austerely. "I'm only too glad to keep off the streets, sir. Are you a magistrate, sir?" I intimated in a severe tone that I was something in that line, and the girl crept away to her dismal lodging, whilst I walked towards the Eastern-hill, thinking what a particularly thundering fool I was, and vowing in the future not to take more than five glasses of Bourbon after dining at the White Hart.

I woke in the morning with a headache, and a disagreeable impression that I had undertaken a duty. (I hate duties!) . . . "Bother the girl," I said whilst dressing, "why couldn't she keep out of my way?" However, I had passed my word, and I was curious to see if her tale was true, so I called at her mother's address. It was quite correct; the mother was a "respectable" woman, keeping a shop. Yes, her daughter had "gone wrong," and the neighbours talked about it. Her presence at

Theatricals of the period

home was a disgrace, and there was a young sister growing up. It is true they had a row, and she told Annie to clear out. She could not be disgraced with her in the house any longer. She had made her bed, and must lie in it. Thus said the mother. I spoke a few plain truths to that lady, which I am afraid only made her more bitter against her daughter. "I suppose you're one of her gentlemen, come here to gammon me to keep her for you," said the woman, firing up. Indignant, I left; but a few moments after I had a hearty laugh at my own foolishness, and I felt that I deserved all I got. "Whatever foolish people may say, I must keep my own self-respect in this case," said I, and so I enlisted the services of a good charitable lady, a friend of mine, to call on my new *protégée*. She went, and came back highly indignant. The girl was a wicked little thing; she wasn't penitent a bit, and wouldn't listen to any prayers. "She got quite impertinent at last, and said she was only civil because she thought I was your mother, Mr. Vagabond." Here was a pretty state of things. My new Magdalen was going it with a vengeance. "I wouldn't trouble my head about it any more," said Mrs. ———. "Madame," said I, "you know me; I'm a particularly bad egg. I drink, and smoke, and go down the Bay on a Sunday. I've no morals nor character—nary shred. *Vide* the religious newspapers. I'm a champion liar. I can look one clean in the eyes, and deny him ten times thrice, and nothing brings compunction to me. But I never yet promised a thing to a man or woman and broke my word. I'm going to get that girl a situation, though I wish she was at the bottom of the Red Sea." Following out this line, I had to make influence amongst my connections. I have an extensive acquaintance, from the highest in the land to a convicted thief in Little Bourke-street. I set to work, and in two days got a situation as waitress and barmaid at a country tavern for my *protégée*. I went and saw the mother again, and persuaded her to give her daughter a small outfit, and see her off by the train. This is some weeks back, and I hear the girl is doing well and giving satisfaction, and she may live to be a happy wife and mother. I never saw her after the first time I met her; and hope I shall never hear of her again, as I find the new Magdalen of fact remarkably troublesome.

Why spin this long tedious yarn? Well, only to show how the forces of society work against the weak, and as an example of how many stray ones there are who, with a little charitable feeling, may be kept from sinking lower, and, warned by the past, may keep straight for the future. For the few days that I had this girl on my mind, I had thought of persuading her to go to the Magdalen Asylum. I did not know anything about that institution, although from the lady superior, Miss Curtain, I had received a very kind invitation (which I did not deserve) to visit it. But I concluded rightly that it must be intended for the reception of women fallen to the very lowest depths, whom a long course of discipline and work would alone reclaim to the right path, and make useful members of society. There are gradations even in vice, and such a girl as the one I have described would have been degraded and made worse by association with the female ghouls of Little Bourke-street and its purlieus. These latter are a great sore, scandal, and evil to society, and if they can be aroused to repentance and reform, a moral and social benefit will be effected. This is entirely apart from the religious question. I was satisfied in my own mind that the Magdalen Asylum at Abbotsford, under the direction of the nuns of the Good Shepherd, was doing good work; although I have heard of wealthy bigots who refuse to give subscriptions to the institution because "it is conducted by Roman Catholics." I think the readers of *The Argus* are well satisfied that I am no friend to the Church of Rome, and that any compliments I may pay to the nuns at Abbotsford are forced from me by admiration of the true spirit of Christian charity with which they go about their work. To me it matters not if they are Catholics, Jews, infidels, or heretics. To comfort the sick, to raise up the fallen, are Heaven-ordained duties superior to all petty distinctions of sect or creed. If people would only bear this in mind, the world would be happier and better. It was with this thought in my heart that, the other afternoon, I took cab to Abbotsford ... The Convent of the Good Shepherd is situated on the south side of Johnston-street, the Yarra forming an irregular boundary around two sides, it being walled in on the others. Knocking at the door, the little-barred window therein is opened, and a female face, bandaged and hooded in white serge, appears thereat. "Can I see Miss Curtain?" I ask. "Who is that?" "Miss Curtain." "Do you mean the Reverend Mother?" Reproved, I confess that I wish to see the "Reverend Mother," and I am at once admitted. My first glance is towards the door. I see that inside it is not locked, and that it is possible during the day for anyone to get out without troubling the sister who acts as janitor, and that in this respect liberty of action is not controlled.

Many good Protestants believe that a Convent is a place of locks, and bolts, and bars; of *oubliettes* and dreary cells; of fasting, penance, and mortification, varied occasionally by a little active immorality—for there are people who credit the abominable lies of "Maria Monk" and the "Baron de Camin." On the Continent, I have seen Nunneries which outwardly might come up to the popular idea, but the high walls, and many locks were, I believe, principally designed to *keep out* intruders. At Abbotsford, however, all these ideas are upset. The Convent Proper is merely a spacious one-storied wooden cottage, with a broad verandah running around two sides. All the rooms are furnished with French windows, which are used as entrances, and through one of these I am shown into the Convent reception room. I send a card inscribed "The Vagabond" to the Reverend Mother, and await her coming. The room is neatly furnished, with nothing, except the extreme neatness and primness and the religious pictures, to distinguish it from an ordinary citizen's. The chromos on the walls are good, but the oil paintings are not of the highest order of art. I afterwards hear that they are painted by one of the sisters, and I give her every credit for her endeavours. Looking out of the window beyond the well-kept gravel path, I see that the garden slopes gently down to the river, the wooded heights of Studley Park on the other side confining the view, and giving an air of seclusion to the place. But I have not long to wait. The door opens, and two ladies enter, attired like the Portress, in long robes of white serge, and hoods and bandages of the same material. There is nothing in dress to distinguish the Superiors from an ordinary sister. Falling from the throat they all wear a broad white serge band, underneath which they can incessantly tell their beads without ostentatious display. They all have hung round the neck a chased silver locket, heart-shaped, and bearing the monogram V.J.M., which I afterwards find means *"Vive Jesu et Marie!"*

I explain that I want to see the institution, and that, although a depraved heretic, I have an interest in social reforms. "Yes," says the Reverend Mother, smiling gravely upon me, "we know you very well; you are very fond of writing in *The Argus.*" I admit the fact, and the lady, who speaks with a charming accent, the faintest *soupçon* of Irish brogue with a French veneer, expresses the pleasure they would feel in showing me everything. "We are always glad to see visitors, and let them judge for themselves," said she. After a little more ordinary conversation we start out and proceed along the path to some dismal bluestone buildings, separated from the Convent by a low, broken-down wooden paling. These are the wards of the Magdalen Asylum.

We first enter a yard where a shed is being erected, to be used as a temporary refectory, the present one not being half large enough for the requirements of the establishment. Next there is a room devoted to mangling and folding washed clothes, the principal industry here being laundry work. From this we proceed to the ironing-room, a particularly hot place on a summer's day, where I see men's shirts and mysterious female garments shining with a white brilliancy . . . From the ironing-room we pass into the washing-room, where the hot water is supplied from a large boiler. In all these rooms I see "penitent fallen women" working under the eyes and superintendence of a few nuns. Their dress is of the plainest, any attempt at personal adornment being apparently discouraged. They are of all ages, but the majority are old women. On some there is a settled look of despair and discontent; they have not yet found peace. Others, and especially the younger ones, look cheerful, happy, and contented with their lot. Except during the hour of silence, they sing at their work, French *chansons* and Welsh odes being heard; for many nationalities are gathered here, and many creeds, for it is the boast of the good nuns that they open their gates freely to females of all denominations.

The Reverend Mother tells me they will not attempt to influence the religious faith of any penitent, they will not press them to go to Chapel, or ask them to read religious works. If they do proselytize, I, for one, should hold them blameless. The fallen woman, rescued and reformed by Catholic hands, is likely, logically, to embrace that faith. Amongst these women there are to be seen many with a collar round their necks embroidered with the motto *"Marie est ma mère."* These are called "Children of Mary," and are those who have specially distinguished themselves by their good conduct, and have devoted themselves to a life of repentance. A higher stage is when they become, with the aid of Holy Church, consecrated penitents, being a sort of lay sisterhood. These wear a black dress and stiff white cap, and have, I presume, some slight authority over new comers.

We inspect a hot-air drying-room, to be used in wet weather, but now the clothes are all hung out in the yard. There we see the little gasometer and retort which supplies the institution with gas. This is entirely managed by one of the "Children of Mary," and I am told that the cost is very trifling. Then upstairs we march through rows of dormitories, spotlessly clean, but very crowded. In a room attached to each ward one or two sisters sleep. Night and day the penitents are watched and cared for. Everywhere there are little altars, and figures of the Blessed Virgin, to whom these fallen ones pray for grace to resist temptation. Down stairs again, we pass into the work-rooms, where all the clothes, including the shoes, used by every one in the institution, from the Reverend Mother to the latest penitent, are made. Sisters are in charge of the different departments, and when we enter the workers all rise with respect. I question Miss Curtain as to the inmates. There are at present 136 in the Asylum, some of whom have been there for many years. Last year the total number received was 244. Of these 48 were placed in service or restored to their friends; others were discharged for misconduct, or sent to the hospital, and 5 died. The receipts from all sources, including the Parliamentary grant of £950, and £2,045 realized by the penitents' labour, were £4,807. The expenditure was £5,400, or not £25 *per capita*. Over £860 was expended in building, repairs, fittings, and furniture. New buildings are, in fact, sadly needed for the health and comfort of the inmates.

The only thing requisite to obtain admission is an acknowledgment of penitence, and an agreement to abide by the rules of the institution. Any poor woman knocking at the door can, if there is room, be admitted on these terms. Some come here in this manner, others are sent by the worthy Catholic ladies who visit the hospitals. Many of the old women here cannot properly be said to now come under the scope of this institution. They are ruined, it may be by indulgence in strong drink, and are only fit for some such place as the Benevolent Asylum.

But, as the Reverend Mother says, "We cannot turn them into the streets to starve." Work and prayer are the means used to bring fallen ones to repentance. They work hard, which keeps down the devil, and pray some, which arouses softer feelings in their hearts. But they are fed well, and have their hours of ease and relaxation, when they can take exercise in the paddock, or read the good books provided for them. It is a discipline, and a hard one perchance—one likely to test the true repentance of any penitent. Every inmate has to remain in the institution for a certain length of time, and fully satisfy the nuns of her reform before she is recommended for a situation. But this discipline is softened by the kind womanly sympathy of the nuns, who look on the fallen ones—not as lost souls, but as strayed sheep, whom it is their duty and pleasure to gather to the fold of the Good Shepherd, for here and hereafter.

Leaving the Asylum, which is kept by strict moral boundaries from the other parts of the Convent, we visit the Church dedicated to the "Immaculate Conception." This is divided into four parts. In the central nave the nuns worship. On one side, partitioned off by a wooden screen, the inmates of the Magdalen Asylum sit. Opposite, also divided from the space allotted to the nuns, the general public are admitted. Above this there is a gallery for children. It is a pretty little church; nothing, however, very striking about it. A nun is praying kneeling on the bare stone, and in the vestry we find another sister . . . From the Church we go into the School-room. There are now 238 Catholic children in the institution, chiefly sent from the State Industrial and Reformatory Schools, and some few by their parents. The Government pays 5s. a week for each child, but to obtain this the nuns must show that they expend 7s. 6d. The difference is made up by donations from the charitable. The children are of all ages, from infancy to adolescence. The Industrial and Reformatory children are separated, and all strictly kept from communication with the "penitents" of the Magdalen Asylum. The elder girls are in working rooms, some doing needlework, others assisting in the kitchen and about household work. They are well trained by the sisters, and, when of sufficient age, readily find employment as domestic servants. In the School-room we find all the

Landlords and tenants
(a) Pray

Landlords and tenants
(b) Prey

younger children assembled. Some are sewing, the very little ones only nurse dolls. As we enter they are singing what at first I thought was a hymn, but it turns out to be a nursery rhyme. The little ones highly enjoy the fun, and the Reverend Mother and the sister accompanying her smile their acknowledgments to the bobs and looks of recognition given them. Sister —— is evidently particularly fond of children, and it is very evident that the rule here is one of love. Upstairs we visit the dormitories; from these the children can obtain admission into the Church gallery. Downstairs we see the children's refectory and the kitchen, in which jam-making, on an extensive scale, is going on, which promises hopefully for the future material wants of the little ones. Then we pass into the bakery and store. I taste the bread, which is very good, and see the mystic wafer in its initial state. Nuns are working in every place, and cleanliness and order are visible everywhere.

The School buildings are close to the sisters' quarters. As we walk around the verandah the Reverend Mother shows me the dwelling-rooms of the nuns. The "community-room" is simply a nice dining-room. It contains an old Broadwood's piano, and a photograph of the parent Convent *Du Bon Pasteur*, at Angers, in France. There the late and present Reverend Mother were reared, and came out to Australia to establish the existing institution. The Order especially devotes itself to the care and education of children. It has branches in every part of the world—in the Fifth Avenue, New York, close to the new St. Patrick's Cathedral, there is a very large establishment belonging to this Order. It is what is commonly known as an "enclosed Order," the nuns, from the time of their profession, never leaving the Convent grounds, unless by a dispensation to found new Branches. In a corner of the grounds I am shown a little cemetery, where seven sisters lie buried—all those who have died since this place was founded, in 1863. In death, as well as in life, they must remain here. Their only bonds are moral ones, for anyone wanting to leave could walk out of the front gate at any hour of the day . . .

There are at present thirty-seven nuns in the institution, and they really have a vast amount of work to do. "We want a few more sisters," said the Reverend Mother. "We do not object to the work, but as nuns we want time to pray, and we have not sufficient now." I think myself that these good ladies are praying best by their works. I have an idea that at the finish deeds will count for more than prayers. After leaving the community room we inspect the surgery, and then visit the garden. Out of this there is the farm-yard, where we find, in the stalls, a dozen patient kine, being milked by a sister, whose costume looks rather incongruous, who has charge of this department. A half-caste girl, from the Reformatory, is sweeping up the place. In the styes we see some fine black Berkshire pigs; and a brown retriever, which welcomes us, makes it appear more home-like. Near here are the cottages of the gardeners, who live on the premises. There are four male servants, three gardeners, and the man who drives the laundry-van. These have all been in the Convent service for some years.

The Reverend Mother and Sister—— kindly walk with me around the pleasant gardens, which are chiefly devoted to the culture of useful vegetables. A quantity of lucerne and maize is also grown for the cattle. Here there are some fine mulberry trees, the luscious fruit of which is being picked by a number of the children, who, I have no doubt, relish the employment. This is for jam-making purposes. Nuns have always been renowned as makers of excellent conserves and simples; indeed, there is a cunning medicine, originally compounded by them, called Chartreuse, which has a world-wide reputation. So I have no doubt capital jam is made at Abbotsford. In the garden we come upon a little grove of willows, circling an open space where formerly a fountain played. Here, however, now rises the gentle image of the Mother of Heaven. In the garden the useful has not been sacrificed to the ornamental, but there are some fine geranium and rose bushes, and I am honoured by having a bouquet for my buttonhole, picked for me by Sister —— under the Reverend Mother's instructions. These ladies are really so good and kind to me that I am afraid they will have to do some penance for it hereafter. In my day I have tasted all the sweets of success and popularity. In the old world and the new I have been feasted and *fêted*, but I consider the greatest compliment ever paid me was by the Reverend Mother, when she said, "We always look at *The Argus* on a Saturday to see your writings, and we think you have done a great deal of good." This was heaping coals of fire on my head with a vengeance! I am glad that my whole impressions of Abbotsford are favourable, so that I am not forced to hurt their feelings.

Refreshed by kindly hospitality, displayed in the form of cake and wine, I hold pleasant converse with these ladies for some time, they display a not unfeminine interest in the affairs of the outside world. At parting, I amuse the Reverend Mother by asking if they are allowed to shake hands with me; and I leave thoroughly pleased with my long visit, chastened by converse with two pure ladies, and satisfied that really good work is being done by the nuns of the Good Shepherd. They are reclaiming the lowest and worst kind of outcasts, the old miserable "man-eaters" of society. As regards other unfortunates, gradually sinking through the depths, charity displayed in time may prevent their falling so low as to make it necessary for them to lose their last atom of self-respect by associating with the fallen ones at Abbotsford. If you can reclaim the new Magdalen without publicly proclaiming her shame, so much the better; but where that is not possible, this Asylum steps in, and the work being done there deserves and requires the sympathy and support of all classes and all creeds in Victoria.

26

The Protestant Female Refuge

(From 'A Refuge')

... The "social evil" is an outcome of civilization which has been, is, and, I am afraid, ever will be, and which flourishes as a protest against many of the restrictions which society binds around the sexes. But all evils, necessary or inevitable—and I class this amongst the latter—may be curtailed. It is an unfortunate fact that this vice flourishes here in Melbourne in most undue proportions. The ranks of the fallen ones are full, and new recruits are always on hand. Taken *en masse*, the rising generation of young women, who should be the mothers of the Australian of the future, are neither physically nor morally adapted for the position they should naturally fill. And studying the status of the working girls of Melbourne, I cannot but think that it would have been better both for their minds and bodies if Elias Howe had not invented the sewing-machine, which seems a Juggernaut, crushing much youthful innocence beneath its evil sway. The life of a factory girl is, physically, almost as unnatural as that of the harlot. At present, however, we care little about this; we reck not of the injurious social influences working all around us; we refuse to see the Upas plant of "larrikinism" and female vice springing up, which may yet bear deadly fruit in the future.

All the exertions of law, religion, and philanthropy should be brought to bear on this great question. The law, by its highly moral and *un*corrupt police and detective force, will sometimes imprison and fine some poor outcast, or close some house in the suburbs. Yet the law and its astute paid magistrates wink at, and even defend, the proceedings in the theatre vestibules, and license the bars in the "paddocks" there. Very impartial indeed are the keepers of law and order in Victoria, as is instanced by the fact that weekly some poor publican in the wilds of Collingwood or Carlton is fined for Sunday trading, whilst the large houses in the centre of the city do a roaring trade, as before the passing of the late Act.

In this country it appears to me that the influences of religion do not extend much beyond the churches. Private philanthropy or volunteer missionary work is also, I am afraid, of small avail in dealing with the "social evil." I say so, as lately, since I was reformed by my visit to Abbotsford, I have, disguised as a Scripture reader, been doing a little missionary business amongst the fallen women of Melbourne. I am bound to admit that my success is about *nil*. The members of the aristocracy of the *demi-monde*, who so freely bleed our gilded or woolly youth (serve them right for their folly), laughed at me. "Do you think I'm a fool?" said one girl, who has, until you look between the lines, a face like a vestal, and a heart like the daughter of the horse-leech. "It's better to be as I am when you make lots of money at it. What have I got to repent of? I'm bad! All right! It pays, don't it? You bet I make them pay. They say I've got no heart or feeling. What feeling did any man ever have for me? It's the way we are treated at first that makes us what we are at last." There was a good deal of truth in this. A woman's heart will get early hardened by the faithlessness or bad treatment of her first lovers, and the successors have to suffer for it. This girl clothed in silk and jewels, glorying in her beauty and iniquity, was certainly in better case than if scrubbing floors or running a sewing machine. I was forced to admit to myself that it was a folly to talk to her now of the virtues of chastity, poverty, and hard work. "You had better wait till I'm old and ugly, or you should have come preaching when I was a chicken, five years ago. You're as bad as the 'Vagabond,' who hates all us women, and would stop us going into the theatres. I should like to horsewhip him, and if ever he says anything about me, I'll find him out and do it." Thus this handsome and vicious young party, one of the many who glory in their life, and whom it is useless attempting to reform. If, however, they will keep out of the theatres, and not flaunt their saffron to the temptation of poor working girls, I don't know that they do much positive harm; and, although they help to ruin the ignorant and callow heirs to countless bullocks and sheep, they have some good qualities in being charitable to their poorer sisters. I think, too, that a beggar stands a better chance of obtaining relief from them than from our clergy. It amused me, however, to note the spiteful way in which they would stop my "preaching" to hint something unfavourable of so-and-so in the next house. "If you are going there you'll only be insulted; she's an awfully bad girl." I have lived long enough to be generally very sceptical of the opinion of one woman about another.

All, however, who strut in the bravery of sin, satin, and furs, are not hardened. There are many who repent, and would abandon their life if they could. But the millstone of debt is round most of them. The Jews, who supply them with their finery, charge a few hundred per cent. above legitimate prices, and are in league with the "bossees" of the "gay houses," in keeping their victims under their control. "Do you think I like this life?" said a girl to me. "I hate it, and would leave to-morrow if I could; but I'm always in debt. I owe over a hundred pounds." "Why should that stop you?" I asked. "Well, I owe the money, and it would not be honourable to cut away without paying. Besides, if I got a respectable situation, I should be sure to be found out, and 'given away' by some of them. I know that all you've been preaching to me is quite true. I did try to get away from this once. A friend of mine got me a place as barmaid in a respectable hotel up the country. I worked hard, and was never so happy in my life. I was happy; oh! so happy"—and the tears stood in the girl's soft eyes as she spoke. "Why did you not remain there?" I asked. "Why?" said she fiercely, "I was put away by a man. You come here, sir, and preach to us girls. Why don't you preach to the men? ——, you know his name, perhaps, found me out, and said he'd split on me. I wouldn't have anything to say to him—you know. So then he told the people, and I had to leave, and come to this again. I should like to kill him. What sort of a man do you call that?" "I call him an infernal scoundrel" (forgetting, for the moment, my reverend character, and sorrowing at the grains of good seed in his girl's heart, which are rapidly being choked up by the tares). As, however, I am neither rich enough nor foolish enough to pay a Magdalen's debts on the chance of her reformation, I could only give this girl good advice and good wishes, both of which, I daresay, are thrown away.

Another also expressed a dislike for her present mode of existence. "But what can I do—I can't do hard work. I might get a barmaid's place, perhaps, but in many houses that isn't much better than this, unless it was in a respectable house, and I couldn't get in there, known as I am." "No," said I, austerely; "you, none of you want to work. You prefer idleness, and fine dress, and the indulgence of your passions, following out your natural instincts, and going to perdition wilfully. The devil's tail, which seems to be particularly long in Australia, is coiled around you. But if you have no sense of religion, nor fear of your future state, think what you will be in a few years. Your beauty will be gone, old before your time, disease and drink will do their work, and you will become like many of these 'low women' you now despise, who pass their lives between Little Bourke-street, the police court, and the gaol. Some of you who now flaunt about so gaily will return to the gutters from which you sprang." "I would die before I would come to that," said one. "Don't think I'm as bad as that," said the second girl, who had large Juno eyes, and a lazy, imperious manner, but who looked too good for her trade; "you don't know how I came here. When I had my little baby, I had nowhere to go after coming out of the Lying-in Hospital. I must keep it, and I had to take to this. If there had been anywhere I could have gone with my baby I would not have been here," and the woman shed soft tears for the memory of her dead child. The maternal instinct is generally strong even in these "fallen ones," and their love for children the one touch of nature which makes them akin to all womanhood.

I was not a success in beating up recruits for Abbotsford, although I have hopes that one girl—a Catholic—will yet go there. I do not, however, quite despair of the results of my missionary work . . .

The other morning, reading *The Argus* whilst lying in bed, as is my wont, I perused a sub-leader advocating the claims of the Protestant Female Refuge . . . But of a "Protestant" or other Refuge I had never heard. So I made inquiries, and was first told this institution was at Emerald-hill, but afterwards discovered that it was in Carlton. I took cab thither, and was landed at the top of Madeline-street, where an irregular block of ground is fenced off from the inspection of the curious, the only outward sign being a blank cottage wall and a doorway, bearing above it in plain letters, "The Refuge." After ringing, the door was opened by a good-natured-looking young woman, who admitted me on my claiming to have business with the matron. I noticed that she locked the door and carried away the key with her. This is contrary to the practice at Abbotsford, but goes for nothing, as any active girl could easily get over the fence. The cottage is apparently meant as a porter's lodge, and is fenced off from the front yard or garden. Entering this, I found the Refuge to consist of a low range of one-storey brick buildings containing numerous small windows in the walls. My guide took me to the entrance door, and then asked my name. "The Vagabond," written on a slip of paper, procured me admission to the modest parlour of the matron, Mrs. Hurry, a kind, pleasant, charitable-looking old lady, whose manner prepossessed me at once. One of the ladies of the committee was present, but retreated immediately, being either frightened at, or unwilling to countenance, the visit of the notorious "Vagabond." I present my compliments and apologies to her. I expressed a wish to go through the buildings, and Mrs. Hurry kindly volunteered to show me everything, not, apparently, being afraid of any evil consequences likely to accrue from my sudden and unexpected inroad.

To the right of the entrance door is the day-room and refectory. On the other side is the kitchen, which gave out to the olfactory organs

HUMANE PROPRIETOR OF SEWING MACHINES—Well, if you don't like it, you'd better go and order your coffins.

some very assuring evidence of the quality of the approaching dinner. Running parallel with the front line of the building is a long narrow passage, on each side of which are a number of small rooms, twenty-seven in number, the sleeping apartments of the inmates. At the ends of the passage are the bedrooms of the matron and sub-matrons, who are the only officers in the Institution. The practice of giving each woman a separate room is a very good one, and, although extra expense is incurred in the building, it is justified by Mrs. Hurry's statement that women sleeping in an associated dormitory are very apt to quarrel, and that here they have not, as at Abbotsford, a number of nuns, with religious authority to control any outbreak. The rooms, not so large as a cell at Pentridge, each contain an iron bedstead, a good bed, clean sheets, and warm blankets. On a shelf in the corner there is a water jug and basin, and a small table holds a looking-glass—generally considered an indispensable article of furniture to a woman, although at Abbotsford there is only one mirror in the whole establishment, and that is in the sacristy of the chapel for the benefit of *Monsieur le Prétre*—a few books, and generally a little workbox. Some of the books I saw were of a very good standard, far superior to the *Dairyman's Daughter* style of literature, which is too often considered sufficient for the mental wants of the inmates of charitable institutions. Whilst inspecting the dormitories I could hear sweet female voices singing joyously one of the new American hymns.

Opening a door we were in the ironing-room, where some twenty-five girls were at work, their voices ringing out cheerfully above the clattering of the irons. "Hush!" said Mrs. Hurry, reprovingly. "You see they are not used to visitors, sir." "I like to hear it; let them sing, by all means; it shows they are happy," said I. I was surprised at the youth of most of the inmates. They were nearly all between the ages of fifteen and twenty. There was no stamp of vice nor degradation on any of them. In their neat linseys and tweeds they presented all the attractions of youth, good looks, cleanliness, and content. One of the sub-matrons bossed this room, where all hands were working, it being the end of the week's ironing. Adjoining is the washing-room, which, if not so well-appointed as that at Abbotsford or Kew Asylum, still contains every requisite for getting through work. In another room the "sorting" takes place. We then inspected the drying ground, from which a good view of Kew, Hawthorn, and the ranges is obtained. "Now," said Mrs. Hurry, "we'll go and see the babies." An old cottage is used as the day nursery; and, in the verandah of this, eleven infants, from two to twelve months old, were lying in cradles and on cushions and pillows. They crowed merrily and lustily, happily unconscious of the stigma which society has placed upon their birth. One of the inmates was in charge of the nursery, but whilst I was there the dinner hour occurred, and I was pleased to see the mothers rushing for their babes, and, clasping them lovingly to their breasts, bear them off triumphantly to the day-room.

Returning to Mrs. Hurry's room, I peeped in on the inmates at their dinner. The sub-matrons presided, and they were all seated round the table, aparently enjoying a good meal, chatting and laughing merrily, the babies taking their dinners after the usual fashion. Then I interviewed Mrs. Hurry as to the objects, working, and success of the Refuge. The rules say:.. "The objects of the institution shall be—1. To provide a refuge for females who have fallen into vice, and who are desirous to return to the paths of virtue. 2. To reclaim them from their evil courses, and fit them to become useful members of society. 3. To assist in procuring them situations, or otherwise providing for them on leaving the institution. III. The institution shall be conducted on Protestant evangelical principles. IV. Applicants shall be admissible without regard to country or creed." As at Abbotsford, there is free trade in the matters of religion. The rule is that no one shall be admitted who is over thirty years of age, and that girls are allowed to keep their babies with them until they are twelve months old. The Institution is managed by an evangelical coterie, comprising two committees (of both sexes) and numerous honorary officers. Although the Dean and seven other clergymen are office-bearers, the last report says:—"The committee cannot refrain from expressing their regret that greater assistance has not been afforded by clergymen in carrying out the objects of the institution." This is not as it should be. The Refuge principally lays itself out for taking young girls after the birth of their first illegitimate child, before they are hardened or demoralized. Many of them come from the Lying-in Hospital, on leaving which they have, as I have before shown, too often no resource but the streets. A great number are graduates of the Industrial Schools; when they go out into the world, either the revulsion against their former seclusion, or the abnormally strong passions of Australian youth leading them crooked.

On entering the Refuge, they have to give a promise to stop twelve months—a term of probation which it is considered will ensure the breaking-off of all old connexions. During this time they have careful training and supervision, and are generally turned out capable of doing all domestic work. It is a gratifying fact that a very large proportion of those who have left the Refuge are known to be doing well, and Mrs. Hurry speaks in high terms of the conduct of the girls now in the house. Although the regulations are not hard, a residence of twelve months in the Refuge certainly requires patience, endurance, and self-denial. The inmates rise in the morning at six o'clock, work till eight, when there is a cessation for breakfast of tea and bread and butter. At eleven the same refection is given for lunch. At one, there is dinner of soup, meal, vegetables, and often pudding. Tea at six, same as breakfast, and from thence, until ten o'clock, when they have all to be in bed, the inmates can make their clothes, read, chat, or listen to some of the ladies of the committee, who come and read and talk to them. Morning and evening prayer is read by the matron; and on Sundays, a chance Church of England or Presbyterian clergyman may come and perform the service. Besides reading, the only recreation the inmates have is keeping the little plots of garden ground, which are divided out to each; but I can't say much for the results I saw, the grounds of the Refuge being generally in a very dreary condition.

Although there are many things in the report which I might cavil at, still, on the whole, I am pleased with the Refuge, and think it is doing a very good work. At the present time funds are greatly needed to complete the erection of twelve more rooms, the building being crowded, and applicants having been turned away. There is little doubt but what the amount will soon be raised—indeed, I do not see why the buildings should not be greatly enlarged. There is ample room both for this institution and for the Magdalen Asylum at Abbotsford, irrespective of any question as to creed. The great fault I have to find with the number of "deadheads" who are on the committee is that, not taking sufficient interest in the Institution themselves, they have not invited public attention thereto, but have allowed it to become, like so many of the charities of Victoria, a semi-private affair. The "Romans," after all, understand how to manage these things better than Protestants. Still, if not in the actual letter, in the spirit I heartily endorse the conclusion of the last report of the Committee:—

"It is, no doubt, very satisfactory that the actual labour of the inmates should do so much to make the Institution self-supporting; but not the less on that account should it draw to itself the active sympathy of Christians who believe that it is trying to do a good work in an efficient and practical manner; for if to save the lost is truly a divine work, while it is also in the truest sense a high work of humanity—and this is the work the Refuge endeavours to do, this is the service which it offers to the Redeemer of mankind—and if the manner of its work be both practical and sensible, then, surely, to increase its power, to enlarge its capacity for receiving inmates, to equip it more thoroughly for its good work, ought to be the constant aim and the earnest desire of the liberal expenditure and of the wise thoughtfulness of those who believe that, in helping the Refuge, they are working the works of Christ."

A 'VAGABOND' BIBLIOGRAPHY

ARTICLES BY 'THE VAGABOND'

Dates of original publication of most of Stanley James's Australian articles have been traced and are listed below. They provide a reasonably accurate guide to his movements.

Melbourne Punch
    Notes on Current Events: 21 October 1875 to 13 December 1877.

Argus
    A Night in the Model Lodging House: 15 April 1876.

Australasian
    A Night in the Model Lodging House (reprinted): 22 April 1876.
    Cinderella: 22 April 1876.

Argus
    A Day in the Immigrants' Home: 29 April 1876.
    The Outcasts of Melbourne: 20 May 1876.
    Sixpenny Restaurants: 27 May 1876.
    Three Days in the Benevolent Asylum: No. I, 3 June 1876; No. II, 10 June 1876.
    In a Fashionable Church: 17 June 1876.
    The Theatre Vestibules: 1 July 1876.
    A Month in Kew Asylum and Yarra Bend: No. I, 22 July 1876; No. II, 29 July 1876; No. III, 5 August 1876; No. IV, 12 August 1876; No. V, 19 August 1876; No. VI, 26 August 1876.
    Impressions in Parliament: 29 August and 5 September 1876.
    The Davenports' Seance: 8 September 1876.
    At the Sailors' Home, No. I, 9 September 1876; No. II, 16 September 1876.
    Ragged Schools: No. I, 23 September 1876; No. II, 28 October 1876.

Manly Sports: 30 September 1876.
Morning at Flemington: 30 October 1876.
Three Weeks in the Alfred Hospital: No. I, 4 November 1876; No. II, 11 November 1876; No. III, 18 November 1876.
The Cup Day: 8 November 1876.
Settling Day: 8 November 1876.
Boarding-Out in Practice (published in *The Vagabond Papers* as 'State Baby-Farming'): 25 November 1876.
Sunday in the Royal Park: 2 December 1876.
Sunday Excursions: 9 December 1876.
A Suburban Church: 16 December 1876.
The Kew Asylum Inquiry: 22 December 1876.
Hospital Funerals (published in *The Vagabond Papers* as 'Pauper Funerals'): 23 December 1876.
The Magdalen Asylum: 27 January 1877.
At a Show: 3 February 1877.
A Month in Pentridge: No. I, 24 February 1877; No. II, 3 March 1877; No. III, 10 March 1877; No. IV, 17 March 1877; No. V, 7 April 1877; No. VI, 14 April 1877; No. VII, 28 April 1877; No. VIII, 23 June 1877.
A Country Race Meeting: 24 March 1877.
Electioneering at Home and Abroad: 12 May 1877.
A Victorian Vintage: 19 May 1877.
Fenianism: 2 June 1877.
A Peep at "The Blacks": 7 July 1877.
The Chinese Question in Queensland: 12 October 1877.
Six Hours in a Dark Cell: 15 December 1877.
An Embryo City: 22 December 1877.
Impressions of Cooktown: 29 December 1877.

Sydney Morning Herald

Impressions of Sydney: 25 September 1877.
The Waifs and Strays of Sydney: No. I, 25 January 1878; No. II, 1 February 1878.
The Common Lodging-Houses of Sydney: 8 February 1878.
At Newcastle: 22 February 1878.
Down in a Coal-Mine: 22 March 1878.
In the Hunter Valley: 29 March 1878.
New Colonists: 17 May 1878.
The Immigrant Depot: 24 May 1878.
With the Immigrants: No. I, 14 June 1878; No. II, 15 June 1878; No. III, 21 June 1878; No. IV, 22 June 1878; No. V, 25 June 1878; No. VI, 29 June 1878; No. VII, 6 July 1878.
At Berrima [Gaol]: No. I, 13 July 1878; No. II, 16 July 1878; No. III, 18 July 1878; No. IV, 20 July 1878.
New Caledonia. En Voyage: 3 September 1878.
The War in New Caledonia. Bouloupari, 1 August: 4 September 1878. Bouloupari, 5 August: 5 September 1878. Noumea, 30 August: 13 Sep-

tember 1878. Bouloupari, 8 August: 5 October 1878. The Causes of the Revolt: 12 October 1878. The Past and Present Situation: 15 October 1878. Penitencier Agricole de Fouwharii, 10 August: 25 October 1878.

Australian
People As They Are: October 1878-March 1879, pp. 393-400, 541-51, 618-29, 758-67.
Colonial Critics: pp. 565-70.

Argus
A Cruise in a Collier: No. I, 20 August 1881; No. II, 27 August 1881; No. III, 3 September 1881; No. IV, 10 September 1881.
Chinese Sketches: No. I, 17 September 1881; No. II, 8 October 1881; No. III, 29 October 1881; No. IV, 26 November 1881; No. V, 3 December 1881; No. VI, 10 December 1881; No. VII, 17 December 1881; No. VIII, 24 December 1881; No. IX, 31 December 1881.
Notes from Japan: No. I, 7 January 1882; No. II, 14 January 1882; No. III, 21 January 1882; No. IV, 28 January 1882; No. V, 4 February 1882; No. VI, 11 February 1882; No. VII, 18 February 1882; No. VIII, 25 February 1882.
In British Columbia: No. I, 4 March 1882; No. II, 11 March 1882; No. III, 18 March 1882; No. IV, 25 March 1882; No. V, 1 April 1882; No. VI, 8 April 1882; No. VII, 15 April 1882; No. VIII, 22 April 1882; No. IX, 29 April 1882.
San Francisco Revisited: No. I, 6 May 1882; No. II, 13 May 1882; No. III, 20 May 1882; No. IV, 27 May 1882; No. V, 3 June 1882.
At Honolulu: 10 June 1882.
"Swiftly Flying South": 17 June 1882.
A Cruise in a Collier. Epilogue: 24 June 1882.

Victorian Review
The Salvation Army in South Australia: 1 December 1882.
An Australian Order: 1 January 1883.
An Embarrassment of Strikes: 1 February 1883.
On the War-Path in New Caledonia: 1 February 1883.

Argus
The New Hebrides. With the Natives: 8 December 1883. The Volcano of Yasur: 15 December 1883. The Mission Station at Aneiteum: 22 December 1883. Out Recruiting: 5 January 1884. Smart Recruiting; 12 January 1884.
Life on Board a "Labour Vessel": No. I, 19 January 1884; No. II, 26 January 1884; No. III, 2 February 1884; No. IV, 9 February 1884.
In Northern Queensland. At Townsville: 16 February 1884. Townsville to the Herbert: 23 February 1884. On the Lower Herbert: 1 March 1884. The Sugar Industry: No. I, 8 March 1884; No. II, 15 March 1884.
Pentridge Revisited: 22 March 1884.
A Trip to New Guinea. Townsville to Thursday Island: 29 March 1884.

At Thursday Island: 5 April 1884. In Torres Straits: 12 April 1884. The Voyage of the Elsea: 19 April 1884. Along the Coast: 26 April 1884. At Port Moresby: No. I, 3 May 1884; No. II, 10 May 1884. Missions and Mission Work: No. I, 17 May 1884; No. II, 24 May 1884; No. III, 31 May 1884; No. IV, 7 June 1884. Retreat from Port Moresby: 14 June 1884. Goodbye to Papua!: 21 June 1884. Homeward Bound: 28 June 1884.

Some Lecture Experiences: No. I, 5 July 1884; No. II, 12 July 1884.

Picturesque Victoria. Kilmore: 19 July 1884. About Wangaratta: 26 July 1884. Beechworth: No. I, 2 August 1884; No. II, 8 August 1884; No. III, 9 August 1884. Myrtleford to Wandiligong: 16 August 1884. Around Harrietville: 23 August 1884. Mid-winter on the Alps: 30 August 1884. The Goulburn Valley: No. I, 3 September 1884; No. II, 6 September 1884; No. III, 13 September 1884; No. IV, 20 September 1884; No. V, 27 September 1884. Nathalia to Echuca: 4 October 1884. In Gunbower Country: 11 October 1884. On the Murray: No. 1, 18 October 1884; No. II, 25 October 1884; No. III, 1 November 1884; No. IV, 8 November 1884. The Cradle of Victoria: No. I, 15 November 1884; No. II, 18 November 1884. Excursions from Portland: No. I, 22 November 1884; No. II, 26 November 1884. Warrnambool: No. I, 29 November 1884; No. II, 6 December 1884. About Warrnambool: No. I, 13 December 1884; No. II, 20 December 1884; No. III, 27 December 1884; No. IV, 3 January 1885. At Wentworth: No. I, 10 January 1885; No. II, 17 January 1885. Colac District: No. I, 24 January 1885; No. II, 31 January 1885; No. III, 7 February 1885. The Otway Forest: 14 February 1885. Camperdown: 21 February 1885. Around Camperdown: 28 February 1885. Camperdown to Belfast: 7 March 1885. At Belfast: 14 March 1885. Belfast to Hamilton: 21 March 1885. At Hamilton: 28 March 1885. Roundabout Hamilton: 4 April 1885. Dunkeld and Penshurst: 11 April 1885. Herrnhut: 18 April 1885. Coleraine: 25 April 1885. Casterton: 2 May 1885. Lilydale: 9 May 1885. To Healesville: 16 May 1885. Around Healesville: 23 May 1885. Fernshawe: No. I, 30 May 1885; No. II, 6 June 1885. Marysville: 13 June 1885. Marysville to Alexandra: 20 June 1885. Around Alexandra: 27 June 1885. Alexandra to Yea: 4 July 1885.

A Winter Tour in Queensland. Melbourne to Roma: 11 July 1885. To Roma: 18 July 1885. Roma to Mitchell: 25 July 1885. To Charleville: 1 August 1885. Charleville: 8 August 1885. Mount Morgan: 15 August 1885. Rockhampton: 22 August 1885. Clermont and Westward Ho!: 29 August 1895. A Railway Township (Jericho): No. I, 5 September 1885; No. II, 12 September 1885. The Central Railway: 19 September 1885. To "The Towers": 26 September 1885. At Charters Towers: 3 October 1885. To Ravenswood: 10 October 1885. Around Townsville: 17 October 1885. To the Johnstone: 24 October 1885. On the Johnstone: 31 October 1885. The Johnstone to Mackay: 7 November 1885. Around Mackay: 14 November 1885. Mackay to Maryborough: 21 November 1885.

Picturesque Victoria. Around Beaconsfield: 28 November 1885. To Sale: 5 December 1885. Sale: No. I, 12 December 1885; No. II, 19 December 1885. Around Sale: 26 December 1885. Ramahyuck: 2 January 1886. Stratford and Maffra: 9 January 1886. Port Albert: 16 January 1886. Bairnsdale: 23 January 1886. Around Bairnsdale: 30 January 1886. On the Lakes: 6 February 1886. Traralgon to Walhalla: 13 February 1886. Walhalla: No. I, 20 February 1886; No. II, 27 February 1886. Lakes Entrance: No. 1, 6 March 1886; No. II, 13 March 1886. Lake Tyers: No. I, 20 March 1886; No. II, 27 March 1886. Lake Tyers to the Snowy River: 3 April 1886. On the Snowy River: No. I, 10 April 1886; No. II, 17 April 1886. Croajingolong: No. I, 24 April 1886; No. II, 1 May 1886; No. III, 15 May 1886. To Bruthen: 22 May 1886.
Homeward Bound. To Albany: 5 June 1886. To Colombo: 12 June 1886. Two Days in Ceylon: No. I, 19 June 1886; No. II, 10 July 1886.
Australians at Home: 3 July 1886.
Homeward Bound. Ceylon to Aden: 17 July 1886. The Red Sea Passage: 24 July 1886. A Flight Across Egypt: No. I, 31 July 1886; No. II, 7 August 1886; No. III, 14 August 1886; No. IV, 21 August 1886; No. V, 28 August 1886.
Australians at Cambridge: 4 September 1886.
Australians at Home. Naval Fete at Portsmouth: 11 September 1886. Old Melbourne: No. I, 18 September 1886; No. II, 25 September 1886. A Trip to the North: 2 October 1886. A Trip to Ireland: 9 October 1886. A Trip to Grantham: 16 October 1886. At Liverpool, Manchester and Chester: 23 October 1886. In Scotland: No. 1, 30 October 1886; No. II, 6 November 1886. Bristol and Bath: 20 November 1886.
England Revisited. Devonshire: 18 December 1886.
Ocean to Ocean: 25 December 1886.
Through Canada. Quebec: No. I, 1 January 1887; No. II, 8 January 1887; No. III, 15 January 1887. To Montreal: 22 January 1887. Montreal: No. I, 5 February 1887; No. II, 12 February 1887; No. III, 26 February 1887. To Winnipeg: 19 March 1887. To Manitoba: No. I, 12 March 1887; No. II, 9 April 1887.*

Age

The Carnival of Labor: 22 April 1887.
By the Grace of God: 30 April 1887.
Country Sketches. A Quiet Sunday (Beaconsfield): 7 May 1887. Yan Yean and Whittlesea: No. I, 21 May 1887; No. II, 28 May 1887.
The Empire Is Saved: 14 May 1887.
A Rush Through Europe: No. I, 4 June 1887; No. II, 11 June 1887.
In a Studio: 18 June 1887.
In the South Seas. To Noumea: 25 June 1887. Life in New Caledonia: No. I, 2 July 1887; No. II, 9 July 1887. Windward Ho!: 3 September 1887. Goro to Port Villa: 10 September 1887. Sandwich Island: 17 September 1887. Havannah Harbor: 24 September 1887. Missionaries and

* This is apparently the last article the Vagabond ever wrote for the *Argus*.

Natives: 1 October 1887. Through the New Hebrides: 8 October 1887. More Mission Work: 15 October 1887. Beachcombers and Traders: 22 October 1887. Aurora and Aoba: 5 November 1887.
An English Derby: 29 October 1887.
A Lost Navigator: No. I, 12 November 1887; No. II, 19 November 1887; No. III, 26 November 1887.
"For My Sake": 3 December 1887.
From My Note Book. A Temperance Territory: 10 December 1887. Queensland to Queen's Gate: 17 December 1887. Christmas in Many Lands: 24 December 1887. The Old Folks: 31 December 1887. Some California Jottings: No. I, 7 January 1888; No. II, 14 January 1888; No. III, 21 January 1888; No. IV, 11 February 1888.
Centennial Notes: 4 February 1888.
Poor Jack: 18 February 1888.
From My Note Book. In a Paris Picture Gallery: 3 March 1888. "Night and Day": 10 March 1888.
Country Sketches. Lilydale: 17 March 1888. Healesville: 24 March 1888. The Don Track and Coranderrk: 31 March 1888. Warburton District: 7 April 1888. Warburton and Yarra Flats: 14 April 1888. The Warr's River Waterworks: 21 April 1888. To Anderson's Creek: 28 April 1888. The Caledonia Goldfields: 5 May 1888. Diamond Creek: 12 May 1888.
At Sea: 7 July 1888.
Through the Mediterranean: 18 August 1888.
The Paris Exhibition of 1889: 24 November 1888.
Outward Bound: No. I, 1 December 1888; No. II, 8 December 1888; No. III, 15 December 1888; No. IV, 22 December 1888.
The Immigrants' Home by Day: 25 December 1888.
The Immigrants' Home By Night: 27 December 1888.
Parisian Sketches: No. I, 29 December 1888; No. II, 5 January 1889; No. III, 12 January 1889.
In Belgium. Antwerp: 19 January 1889. To Spa: 26 January 1889. At Spa: No. I, 2 February 1889; No. II, 9 February 1889; No. III, 16 February 1889. At Brussels: 23 February 1889.
In Normandy: No. I, 2 March 1889; No. II, 9 March 1889.
In Brittany: No. I, 16 March 1889; No. II, 23 March 1889.
In Ireland: No. I, 30 March 1889; No. II, 6 April 1889; No. III, 13 April 1889.
Across the Australian Alps: 20 April 1889.
Across the Main Divide: No. I, 27 April 1889; No. II, 4 May 1889.
From My Note Book. At Naples: 11 May 1889.
Country Sketches. At Wangaratta: 18 May 1889.
At Geelong: No. I, 25 May 1889; No. II, 1 June 1889; No. III, 8 June 1889; No. IV, 15 June 1889; No. V, 22 June 1889.
Samoan Sketches. To Apia: 3 August 1889. Church and State: 24 August 1889. Men and Manners: 7 September 1889. Life in Apia: 14 September 1889. Past and Present: 21 September 1889. "Starving Samoa": 28 September 1889. Apia, 12th August: 5 October 1889. "A May Meet-

ing": 12 October 1889. After the May Meeting: 19 October 1889. Why Germany is Hated: 26 October 1889. De Mortuis: 2 November 1889. To Manona: 23 November 1889. To Apolima: 30 November 1889. The Samoan Difficulty. A Review of the Situation: 21 December 1889. Holy Tonga. To Nukualoga: 28 December 1889.

Leader

The V.R.C. New Year's Day Meeting: 4 January 1890.

Holy Tonga. King and People: 4 January 1890. Church and State: 11 January 1890. Nature and Law: 18 January 1890. To Haapaii: 25 January 1890. To Vavau: 1 February 1890.

In New Zealand. To Auckland: 15 February 1890. About Auckland: 22 February 1890. To the Hot Lakes: 8 March 1890. At Rotorua: 15 March 1890. Wonderland: 22 March 1890. Infernal Regions: 29 March 1890. The Poor Maori: 12 April 1890. The Bay of Islands: 26 April 1890. Around Russell: 3 May 1890.

Age

In the Name of the Prophet: 24 May 1890.
Henry M. Stanley. Personal Reminiscences: 26 July 1890.

Leader

New Bendigo: 10 June 1893.
At Maryborough: 24 June 1893.
Ballarat City: 22 July 1893.
Ballarat East: 5 August 1893.
About Geelong: No. I, 12 August 1893; No. II, 26 August 1893.
Around Echuca: 9 September 1893.
At Kyneton: No. I, 16 September 1893; No. II, 23 September 1893.
Castlemaine: 30 September 1893.
At Warrnambool: No. I, 14 October 1893; No. II, 21 October 1893.
Koroit and Port Fairy: 28 October 1893.
Portland: 18 November 1893.
Hamilton: 25 November 1893.
Queenscliff: 2 December 1893.
Healesville: 16 December 1893.
Lilydale and District: No. I, 30 December 1893; No. II, 6 January 1894.
Ararat and District: No. I, 13 January 1894; No. II, 20 January 1894.
At Great Western: 27 January 1894.
At Hopetoun: 10 February 1894.
At Horsham: 17 February 1894.
Warracknabeal: No. I, 24 February 1894; No. II, 3 March 1894.
Mildura. A Record of Six Years Progress (16-page supplement): 24 March 1894.
Fairfield [Rutherglen]: 14 April 1894.
Rutherglen: 21 April 1894.
Wangaratta: 28 April 1894.
Beechworth: 5 May 1894.
At Euroa: 12 May 1894.

Benalla: 19 May 1894.
The University High School: 26 May 1894.
Seymour: 2 June 1894.
Kilmore: 9 June 1894.
At an Engineering Works [O'Grady's, South Melbourne]: 23 June 1894.
Victorian Industries. Candles and Candle Making: 7 July 1894; Boots and Boot Making: 21 July 1894; Ropes and Rope Making: 4 August 1894; Confectionery Making: 18 August 1894; Messrs James Miller and Company's Rope Works: 8 September 1894; Hats and Hat Making: 22 September 1894; The Timber Trade: 17 November 1894; Nails and Nail Making: 19 January 1895.
Picturesque Tasmania (24-page supplement): 6 October 1894.
Picturesque Tasmania (16-page supplement): 27 October 1894.
The Wool Trade (8-page supplement): 3 November 1894.
Victorian Holiday Resorts: 22 December 1894.
Through Gippsland (8-page supplement): 12 January 1895.
Glass and Glass Making: 2 February 1895.
The Metropolitan Meat Supply (4-page supplement): 9 February 1895.
At Stawell: 2 March 1895.
St Albans: 6 April 1895.
Sights and Scenes in Collins Street (8-page supplement): 13 April 1895.
Sights and Scenes in Bourke Street (12-page supplement): 15 June 1895.
Sights and Scenes in Flinders Street and Lane: 21 September 1895.
Cup Day Past and Present: 2 November 1895.
Sights and Scenes in Swanston and Elizabeth Streets (8-page supplement): 16 November 1895.
Yachting (8-page supplement): 21 December 1895.
Western Australian Supplement: 30 May 1896.
Albury Supplement: 29 August 1896.

BOOKS AND PAMPHLETS BY 'THE VAGABOND'

1877-8 *The Vagabond Papers.* 5 vols. (George Robertson, Melbourne).
1877 *The "Vagabond" Annual.* (F. T. F. Keogh, Brisbane; Turner & Henderson, Sydney). A collection of stories, etc., mainly by other writers.
1879 *Mediums and Their Dupes* (Sydney).
1881 *South Sea Massacres* (Sydney).
1882 *Occident and Orient* (George Robertson, Melbourne).
1885 *Picturesque Victoria. Alexandra and Yea Districts* (Gordon and Co., Alexandra).
1886 *"The Vagabond's" Article on the Lakes Entrance, Gipps Land* (Arnall & Jackson, Melbourne).
1886 *Cannibals & Convicts* (Cassell & Company, Limited, London).
1889 *Australie, en avant! 1789-1889. Victoria en 1889.* (Government Printer, Melbourne).
1890? *Holy Tonga* (Melbourne, n.d.).

ARTICLES ABOUT 'THE VAGABOND'

1877 'Ultra-Vagabond': *Sixty Months in Pentridge. Geelong Advertiser,* 1 June 1877. A reply to the Vagabond's prison articles.
1879 Harold W. H. Stephen: *Vagabonds and Their Dupes.* Sydney, 1879. A reply to the Vagabond's articles on spiritualism.
1891 J. F. Kirk: *A Supplement to Allibone's Critical Dictionary of English Literature, Vol. II.* Philadelphia, 1891. Entry under THOMAS, Julian.
1896 Obituaries: *Age* and *Argus,* 5 September 1896. *Leader,* 12 September 1896. *Bulletin,* 17 October 1896. Each obituary contains much misleading information.
1897 *Leader,* 27 November 1897. Description and photograph of the Vagabond's tomb.
1912 J. B. Cooper: *Who Was "The Vagabond?" Life,* 1 January 1912.
1946 *Journalist and Botanist: 'The Vagabond' and 'The Baron' compared. Age,* 20 July 1946.
1955 L. Priday: *Thomas Was First Australian War Correspondent. West Australian,* 21 May 1955.
1958 *Australian Encyclopaedia* entry under JAMES, Stanley.
1968 H. Anderson: *Vagabond Journalist. Walkabout,* February 1968.

INDEX

ABC Radio National, iv
ABC TV, iv
Aborigines, lii, liii, li
'Across the Australian Alps', 14, 262
'Across the Main Divide', 14, 262
Adelaide, 171
Adriatic, s.s., xvi
'Advertising doctors', 24
Age, 11, 12, 13, 189, 261-3, 265
Aged, care of, *see* Benevolent Asylum, Charitable institutions, Immigrants' Home
Agricultural workers, 3; *see also* Farming
Ah Goon, 179-80, 183
Ah Sing, William, 179-80, 183
Albany, WA, 261
Albert William, 176
Albion Hotel, Sydney, 56
Albury Supplement, 264
Alexandra, Vic., 260, 264
Alfred Hospital, 66, 69, 112, 115, 197, 199
'Alfred Hospital, Three Weeks in the', 258
Allan, Edgar, xxxiii
Allbeury, John George, 169, 174-6 *passim*
Amusements for poor, 44, 165, 172-4, 207
Anderson, Hugh, xlviii, lvii, 265
Anderson's Creek, Vic., 262
'Aneiteum, the Mission Station at', 259
Anglo-Saxon characteristics, 27, 224
'Anglo-Virginians', xxxiv-xlii *passim*
Antwerp, Belgium, 262
Apia, Samoa, 262
Apolima, Samoa, 263
Appomattox, Virginia, xv, xxvi, xxviii
Ararat, Vic., 5, 263
Arch, Jospeh, xvii, xviii, xxxvi, 3

Argus, xvi, xlv, xlvi, xlviii, 5-13 *passim* 39, 126, 141, 145, 196, 240, 241, 247, 253, 257-61 *passim*, 265
Argus expedition to New Guinea, 12
Armit, W. E., 12
Art, 129, 261, 262
Ashenhurst, John J., xxii
Assault, 27, 30, 33, 86
'At a Bazaar', 119-23
'At a Show', 258
'At Sea', 252
Ataii, Chief, xlv
Ateliers, photographer, xxi
Auckland, NZ, 14, 263
Australasian, 5, 6, 257
Australia, 11
Australian, 11, 259
Australian Alps, 14, 260, 262
Australian Club, Melbourne, 13
Australian Encyclopaedia, 265
Australian Museum, Sydney, 126, 128-9
'Australian Order, an', 259
'Australians at Cambridge', 261
'Australians at Home', 13, 261
'*Australie, en avant!*', 264
Authors, amateur, 116

'Baby-farming, State', 195-203
Bairnsdale, Vic., 261
Baker, Rev. Shirley, 14
Ballarat, Vic., 145, 263
'Balleyram', *see* Gately, Michael
Bankers, 108; *see also* English & American Bank
'Banker's Club' at Pentridge, 89, 90, 98
Baptism, xxviii

Baptist Church, 36
Baptiste, Kanak chief, xlix
'Bare Knuckle Bouts', 214-25
Barmaids, 134, 208, 229-35 *passim*, 237, 239, 250
Barron, T. H., 77
Bath, England, 261
Bathing habits, 34, 146, 148, 153, 156, 170
Battersby, Robert, xxii
'Bay of Islands, The', 263
Bazaar, charity, 119-23
'Beachcombers and Traders', 262
Beaconsfield, Vic., 261
Beechworth, Vic., 90, 260, 263
Beggars, 55, 64,; *see also* Vagrants
Belfast, Vic., 260
'Belgium, In', 262
Benalla, Vic., 264
Bendigo, Vic., 263
Benevolent Asylum, Melbourne, 7, 34, 73, 149-67, 243
Benevolent Asylum, Sydney, 162
Bent Street, Sydney, 126
Berrima, NSW, 258
Bible Schools, *see* Hornbrook Ragged Schools
Billiard rooms, 30, 34, 37
Bishop of Melbourne, 130-1
'"Blacks", a Peep at the', 258
Blacksmiths, 128
Blindness, 150, 152, 156
Bliss, S. H., xxxiii
Blondin, Charles, 208
'Boarding-Out in Practice', 258
Boarding-out, *see* 'State Baby-Farming'
Boileau, S. H., xxi
Bondi, NSW, 223
Bookmakers, 134, 223; *see also* Gambling
'Boots and Boot Making', 264
Botanic Gardens, Sydney, 125
Botany, NSW, 124, 125
Boulouparis, New Caledonia, xlv, xlvi. lviii, 258-9
Bourke Street, Melbourne, 30, 33, 142, 264
Bowen, Sir George, 113, 114
Boxing, 145, 158, 210-25
'Boxing with Skin Gloves', 210-13
Boynton, Robert S., lvii
Bradley, Walter, 125
Bradshaw, Herbert C., xli
Brière, ex-convict, xlix, l, lv
Brighton Road, Melbourne, 215

Brisbane, Qld, ii; gaol, 77-83
Bristol, England, 261
British Association, Farmville, xviii
British colonial methods, xxxv, 11, 14; *see also* English
British Columbia, 11, 259
Brittany, 262
Bromby, Dr John Edward, 113-15 *passim*
Brussels, Belgium, 262
'Brutal Football Match, A', 207-9
Bruthen, Vic., 261
Buckingham County, Virginia, xv, xxiii, xxxvi
Builders, xv
Bulletin, Sydney, 4, 8, 265
Bugg, Chas., xxxiii
Bullard, Alice, lvii
Burke and Wills monument, 66
Burkeville, USA, xv
Bushmen, *see* Station hands
Bushrangers, 86
'By the Grace of God', 261

Cab drivers, 44, 45, 201
Cabbage tree hats, 91
Caledonia goldfields, Vic., 262
California, 11, 86; *see also* San Francisco
'California Jottings, Some', 262
'Cambridge, Australians at', 261
Camperdown, Vic., 260
Canada, xxxiv, xxxvi, 13, 261
Canaques, *see* Kanaks
'Candles and Candle Making', 264
Cannibals & Convicts, xlii, xlviii, xlix, l, lii, lvi, 12, 264
Cannon, Michael, iv, xxxvi, lvii
Capital punishment, 94; *see also* Gately, M.
Capitation tax, 9
Carlton Football Club, Vic., 208
'Carnival of Labour, The', 13, 261
Carpenters, 128
'Carpetbaggers', xv
Casey, J. J., 8
Casterton, Vic., 260
Castieu, John Buckley, 38
Castlemaine, Vic., 100, 263
Castlereagh Street, Sydney, 132
Casualty wards, 19, 22, 26
Cats, stray, 140
Cattle, xlv
Censorhip, xlvii
'Centennial Notes', 262

INDEX 269

'Ceylon to Aden', 261
'Ceylon, Two Days in', 261
Champ, Colonel W. T. N., 99
Charitable institutions, 5, 8, 73; *see also* Hospitals,; Orphanages; Poverty; Ragged schools
Charity, public attitude to, 21, 37, 110, 119-23, 195, 250
Charity, Royal Commission on, 14
Charleville, Qld, 260
Charlotte County, Virginia, xv, xxiii
Charters Towers, Qld, 10, 260
Chase City, Virginia, xxii-xxiv, xli
Chester, England, 261
'Chicken-hazard', 30
Children: as prostitutes, 1, 38, 40; illegitimate, 254-5; pauper, 7, 26, 34, 36-8 *passim*, 67, 70, 72, 148, 195-203 *passim*; working, 30, 60; *see also* Newsboys; 'Street arabs'
Children's Church, Collingwood, Vic., 191
China, 11
Chinese in Australia, xxx, 9, 24, 30, 38, 40, 64, 66, 96, 99, 124, 156, 159, 171, 179-80, 183, 227, 245, 358
'Chinese Sketches', 259
Christ Church, South Yarra, Vic., 112
Christie, James M., 214-20 *passim*
'Christmas in Many Lands', 262
Church of England, funerals, 66, 70-3 *passim; see also* Episcopalian
Churches, 36, 107; *see also* Religion
'Cinderella', 257
Cintra, 13
Civil Rights Bill, USA, xxx
Civil Service Hotel, Sydney, 4
Civil War, American, xv, xxx, xxxi, xxix, xxxvi, 4, 64, 66, 216
Clarence Street, Sydney, 46
Clarendon colony, Virginia, xxiv
Clarke, Jos., 86
Clarke, Lady Janet ,14
Clarke, Marcus, 91
Clarke, W. J., 120
Clayden, Arthur, xxxvi-xxxvii
Clermont, Qld, 260
Clohesy, police-inspector, 9
Clothing, xxxviiii-xl
'Coal-Mine, Down in a', 258
Coburg, Vic., 90; *see also* Pentridge
Cockatoo Island, Sydney, 52
Cock-fighting, 221

Colac, Vic., 260
Coleraine, Vic., 260
Collingwood, Vic., 185, 191-3
Collins Street, Melbourne, 264
Colombo, 261
Colonial and Indian Exhibition, 13
'Colonial Critics', 259
Colonialism, *see* British; French; German
'Colorado beetle, the' 134, 220
Colored Baptist Church, Virginia, xxii-xxiii
'Common Lodging-Houses of Sydney, The', 258
Commune of 1871, xxxi, xlv, 8
Concert halls, 29-30, 37; *see also* Theatres
'Confectionary Making', 264
Connecticut, USA, 124
Contagious Diseases Act, 26
Convent of the Good Shepherd, 240
Convicts, xlii-lvi *passim*, 5, 56, 158
Coogee, Sydney, 124
Cooktown, Qld, 9
'Cooktown, Impressions of', 258
Cooper, John Butler, xxxi, xlii, 2, 4, 11, 12, 265
Coranderrk, Vic., 258, 262
Corporal punishment, 183
Counter lunches, 65
'Country Race Meeting, A', 3n., 258
'Country Sketches', 14, 261, 262
Cox, Dr, 46, 49
Crane, Stephen, xliii
Crawford and Co., coaches, 14
Cricket, xxiv-xxv, 4, 207
Crime, prevention of, 36-8 *passim*
Criminals, 6, 30, 33, 34, 85-103 *passim*, 108; *see also* Assault; Pentridge; Prisons
Croajingolong, Vic., 261
Croquet, 156
'Cruise in a Collier, A', 259
Crute, H. J., xxxviii-xxxix
Cup Day, Melbourne, 258, 264
Curran, Tom, 216
Curtain, Mary C., 239
Cuzco 13

Dabney, Robert Louis, xx
Daily Telegraph, Sydney, 11
Dampier, Alfred, 11
Dancing, 30, 123, 213
Dandenong, 176-7
Darling Point, Sydney, 124
Darlinghurst, Sydney, 11

'Davenports' Seance, The', 257
Daves-Johnson, Alecia, xxvii
'Day in the Immigrants' Home, A', 7, 139-48, 257
Dead, burial of, 7, 66-73, 163, 246
Demi-monde, 31, 208, 227-56 *passim; see also* Prostitution
Denon, Professor William, 12
'Derby, An English', 262
Devonshire, England, 261
Diamond Creek, Vic., 262
Dickens, Charles, 174
Dickinson, R. M., xxxiii
Dilke, Ashton, 113
Dilke, Sir Charles, 113
Disorderly conduct, 27, 30
Dispenser, at Pentridge, 84, 95-6, 101-3
Divorce, 131
Doctors, 7, 19-26 *passim*, 87, 134, 149, 153, 158, 196, 236
Dogs, xxv, 65, 140
Domain, Sydney, 124, 125
Doré, Gustave, 47, 80
Drunkenness, 10, 24, 27, 30, 34, 35, 38, 43, 49, 56, 58, 60, 64, 65, 126, 132, 141, 155, 168, 175, 176, 179, 214, 229-35 *passim*
Duke of Edinburgh, 115
Duncan, G. O., 196
Dunkeld, Vic., 260
Durham, 162

Eastbourne Street, Prahran, Vic., 190
Eastern Market, Melbourne, 33
Echuca, Vic., 260, 263
Economic conditions, USA, xvii
Education, *see* Hornbrook Ragged Schools; Ragged schools; Roman Catholic schools; Stanley Park Academy; State schools
Edwards, Harry, 216
Eight Hours Day, 13
Eisenhuth, Susie, iv
'Electioneering at Home and Abroad', 258
Elizabeth Street, Melbourne, 21, 264
Elizabeth Street, Sydney, 54-6 *passim*
Elsea, 12, 260
'Embryo City, An', 258
Emerald Hill, Vic., 72, 119
'Empire Is Saved, The', 261
England and Russia or The White Hand, 11
English & American Bank, xx-xlii *passim*
English, as migrants, xiv-xlii *passim*
Episcopal Church, xxiii-xxiv, 113-18 *passim*

Euroa, Vic., 263
'Europe, A Rush Through', 261
Euthanasia, 7
Executions, *see* New Caledonia; Pentridge

Fancy fair, 121
Farming, xv, xxii, xxii, xxxii-xlii *passim*
Farmville College, Virginia, xxiii
Farmville Commonwealth, xxii
Farmville Mercury, xxii-xlii *passim*
Farmville, Virginia, xvi-xlii *passim*
'Fashionable Church, In a', 107-11, 257
Fellows, Mr Justice, 113
Fencing with foils, xxx, xl
'Fenianism', 258
Fernshawe, Vic., 260
Ferrero, Chantal, lvii
Fiji, 11
Fitzgerald, Colonel J. P., xxxviii
Fitzroy, Vic., 14
Fitzroy Gardens, 200
Flippen, Col., xviii
Flippen, Robert G., iv, xxvi
'Flemington, A Morning at', 258
Flinders Street and Lane, Melbourne, 264
Food, xv-xvi; *see also* Restaurants
Football, 207-9, 210, 213, 219
Forest & Stream Magazine, xxv
Forgery, 90
'"For My Sake"', 262
France, *see* New Caledonia; Paris
Franco-Prussian War, 3
Fraser, Miss, 185, 186
Freemasonry, xxv-xxvi, xli
French colonial methods, xliii-lviii *passim*, 9, 10, 12, 13
'Friendly Islands', 14
'From My Note Book', 13, 262
Furniture, xxxviiii-xxxix

Gambling, 30, 90, 120, 151, 169, 179, 180, 211, 223, 225; in mining shares, 90
Garibaldi, Ricciotti, 64
Gately, Michael, 101-3
'Gately the Hangman', 101-3
Gaunson, David, 5
Geelong, Vic., 87, 262, 263
Geelong Advertiser, 265
George I, King of Tonga, 14
George, Hugh, xlv, 5, 8, 9, 10, 13
George Washington University, The, iv
German colonial methods, 14, 263

INDEX

Gilbert, W. S., 174
Gillbody, Henry, 46
'Gippsland, Through', 264
'Glass and Glass Making', 264
Gospel halls, 36-7, 108, 188, 193, 213
Goulburn Valley, Vic., 260
Governor's Ball, 123
'Government billets', 14, 37, 84
Government House, Melbourne, 8, 139
Grand Lodge of Virginia, xxv, xl
Grange Hall, xxix
Grant, General Ulysses S., xxviii, xxxiv
'Grantham, A Trip to', 261
Great Revolt, New Caledonia, xliii-lviii *passim*
'Great Western, At', 263
Guinness, Rev. W. N., 113
Gunbower Country, Vic., 260
Gunga, xliv, 9
Gurner, Henry Field, 220

Haapaii, Tonga, 263
Haddon, Frederick, 12
Haines, W. C., 112
Halford, Professor G. B., 116
Hamilton, Vic., 260, 263
Hampden-Sidney College, xviii-xx
Hang-Hai, 180
'Hanging, A', xli, lv
Harmsworth Street, Collingwood, Vic., 191
Harrietville, Vic., 260
Hartsock, John, l, lvii
'Hats and Hat Making', 264
Healesville, Vic., 260, 262, 263
Heath, Dr Richard, 161
Henderson, Alexander, 122, 134
Henty, Misses, 198, 202
Herald, Melbourne, 179, 189
Herrnhut, Vic., 260
High Bridge Trail State Park, Virginia, iv
Hill, George, 31, 33, 37, 178
History of Freemasons, xxv-xxvi
Hobson's Bay Railway Company, 201
'Holy Tonga', 263, 264
Homer, Thomas, xxiii-xxiv, xxxiii
'Homeward Bound', 261
Homosexuality, at Pentridge, 91
'Honolulu, At', 259
Hooper, H. R., xxxiii
Hopetoun, Vic., 263
Hornbrook, Mrs Hester, 185

Hornbrook Ragged Schools, 182, 184-94
Horses, xxv
Horsham, Vic., 263
Hospitals, 7, 19, 66, 73, 84; *see also* Alfred Hospital; Melbourne Hospital
'Hospital Funerals', 258
Hotels, xviii, xxii, 4, 30, 33, 49, 56, 61, 65, 132, 155, 214, 222, 239
Howe Crescent, Emerald Hill, Vic. 119
'Hunter Valley, In the', 258
Hurd, Albert, xxxiii
Hurry, Mrs, 252-5 *passim*
Hyde Park, Sydney, 56, 128

Ile des Pins, xlv
Illness among poor, 43, 47, 68, 141, 156, 166; *see also* Benevolent Asylum; Doctors; Hospitals; Medicine; Outpatients
'Immersion journalism', xvi, xlvii
'Immigrant Depot, The', 258
Immigrants, xv-lvi *passim*, 24, 51; *see also* English
Immigrants' Aid Society, 141, 148
'Immigrants' Home by Day, The', 262
'Immigrants' Home by Night, The', 262
Immigrants' Home, Melbourne, 34, 139-48
'Immigrants, With the', 258
'Impressions of Sydney', 9, 258
'In the Name of the Prophet', 263
Independent Church, Melbourne, 188
Indians in Australia, 24
Industrial and Reform Schools, 37-8, 60, 98, 195, 202, 232, 243, 255
Insurance, xx, xxxii
Intemperance, *see* Drunkenness
International Association for Protecting Game and Fish, xxv, xli
Ionic, 14
'Ireland, A Trip to', 261
'Ireland, In', 262
Irish in Australia, 19, 26, 43, 61, 64, 67, 85, 143, 145, 158, 179, 180, 241
Irrigation, xlv

Jacob, Henry, xxiv
James, Mrs Caroline Lewis, xvi, xli-xliii
James, John Stanley, biography, 1-15; relations with father, xlvi, 1, 2, 4; as schoolboy, 1-2, 113; mixes with vagrants, 2; love affairs, xvi, 2, 3; in London, 2, 3; in Wales, 3, 4; arrested in Paris, 3; in Warwickshire, 3; in New York, 4, 117; in Virginia, xv-xlii

passim, 4; poses as 'Dr.', xxii-xlii *passim*; flees Virginia, xxx-xxxi *passim*; lies about origins, 4, 8; claims visit to Russia, 113; suicide attempts, 4; arrives in Australia, 4; writes for *Melbourne Punch* and *Argus*, 5-8; reasons for popularity, 6-8; methods of writing, 6-7, 12; farewelled from Melbourne, 9; writes for *Sydney Morning Herald*, 8-10, 130; visits Queensland, 9, 10, 77; visits China, 9, 11; visits New Caledonia, xliii-lviii *passim*; voyage on *Woodbine*, 11; writes plays, 11; visits New Hebrides, 12, 13; visits New Guinea, 12; returns to Melbourne, 12; sails to London, 12; visits Canada, 13; joins *Age*, 13; visits France again, 13; visits Samoa and Tonga, 14; secretary of royal commission, 14; writes for *Leader*, 14; dies, 14-15; views on death, 71; *see also* 'Thomas, Julian'; 'Vagabond'.
James, Joseph Green, 1, 2, 4
James River, Virginia, xv, xxv
Japan, 11
'Japan, Notes from', 259
Jewels, xl
Jews in Australia, xlviii, 24, 31, 103, 193, 223, 250
Jika Jika reform school, Vic. 98
Johns Memorial Church, Virginia, xxiii
Johns, Rt Rev. Bishop, xxiv, xli
Johnson, E. W., lviii
Johnson, Gordon, xxvii
Johnston Street, Abbotsford, Vic., 240
'Journalist and Botanist', 265

Kanaks, xliii-lviii
Kanaka trade, 9, 12, 259
Kelly, Pat, 51-60
Kent Street, Richmond, Vic., 201
'Kew Asylum and Yarra Bend, A Month in', 257
'Kew Asylum Inquiry, The', 258
Kew Lunatic Asylum, 7, 122, 210, 211
'Kilkenny Boarding-house', Sydney, 49
Kilmore, Vic., 260, 264
'King of the Cannibal Islands', xxviii
King Street, Sydney, 52, 54, 55, 132
Koroit, Vic., 263
Kyneton, Vic., 203

'"Labour Vessel": Life on Board a', 259
La Foa, New Caledonia, xlv, xlvii
'Lake Hill', Virginia, xx

Lakes Entrance, Vic., 261, 264
Lake Tyers, Vic., 261
Land dummying, 85
Landlords, slum, 31, 39, 131, 244; *see also* Lodging-houses; Slums
Larkins, Sergeant, 46
Larrikins, 29, 30, 32, 35, 37-8, 51, 59, 178, 186, 190, 207, 208, 211, 231, 249; *see also* 'Street arabs'
Laubarede, M. liv
Launceston, Tas., 145, 175
Lawyers, 1, 29, 38, 108, 116, 134, 158
Leader, 14, 263, 265
Lectures by John Stanley James, 9, 10, 260
Legislative Assembly of NSW, 46n., 126, 162
Legislative Council of NSW, 46
'Leo', xliv
Leonard, J. H., xliv
Lewis, Mrs Caroline, *see* James, C. L.
Libel, 14
Libraries, 126-8
Life, 265
Lilydale, Vic., 260, 262, 263
Lincolnshire, 175
'Literary journalism', iv, xliii-lviii
Literature, tastes in, 122, 128, 172, 254
Little Bourke Street, Melbourne, 33, 36, 171, 178, 179, 183, 185, 188, 193, 240, 250
Little Collins Street, Melbourne, 169, 170
Little Lonsdale Street, Melbourne, 19, 185, 188, 190
Liverpool, England, xvi, 261
Livingstone, Dr David, xxii
Lizzie, 12
Llandudno, Wales, 3
Lochlee, xlvi
Lodging-houses, Australian, 5, 6, 41-50, 168; English, 2; *see also* Hotels
Lodging-houses, NSW inquiry into, 46n.
London & North Wales Railway, 3
Lone Hand, 6n.
Longwood University, xxiii
Lonsdale Street, Melbourne, 30
'Lost Navigator, A', 262
Lotus Leaves, 122
Love, romantic, xxxii, 2, 3, 29, 122
Loyalty, xxxv-xlii *passim*
Lunatic asylums, xvi
Lying-in Hospital, Melbourne, 252, 255
McCulloch, Lady, 185

INDEX

McCutcheon, James, 150, 151, 159, 160
McDonald, Dr Willa, iv, xliii-lviii
McGrath, 'Tip', 143-4
Mace, Jem, 218, 220
Mackay, Qld, 260
McKinney Bros. & Co., xxxix
Mackinnon, Sir Lauchlan Charles, 13
Macquarie Street, Sydney, 126
Macquarie University, NSW, iv
Madeline Street, Carlton, Vic., 252
Maffra, Vic., 261
'Magdalen Asylum, The', 236-48, 252, 256, 258
Malden Island, 175-6
Manchester, England, 261
'Manitoba, To', 13, 261
Manly, NSW, 124
'Manly Sports', 207, 210, 258
Manona, Samoa, 263
'Maori, The Poor', 263
Maras, Steven, lviii
Margaret Street, Sydney, 46
Market Street, Sydney, 56
Maryborough, Qld, 260
Maryborough, Vic., 263
Marysville, Vic., 260
Massachusetts, USA, 124
Mazas Prison, Paris, 3
Media Hall of Fame, xvi
Medicine, 26, 95
'Mediterranean, Through the', 262
Mediums and their Dupes, 10, 264
Melbourne Bulletin, 8
Melbourne Church of England Grammar School, 114
Melbourne Cup, 123; *see also* Cup Day
Melbourne, England, 261
Melbourne Football Club, 208
Melbourne General Cemetery, 7, 14, 66
Melbourne Hospital, 19-26, 161, 163
Melbourne Punch, 5, 6, 8, 257
Merchants, 9, 21, 108, 134, 158
Metropolitan Hotel, Sydney, 51, 54, 134
'Metropolitan Meat Supply, The', 264
Middle class: James's attitude to, 1; popularity of his work among, 3, 6; morality of, 6-7, 29, 108, 122, 231, 236, 239; different in Sydney, 9, 10, 124; and charity, 21, 38, 40, 119-123, 149, 163, 165, 188, 195; as slum landlords, 31, 39; failures among, 34, 44-5, 65, 153-5, 158; as churchgoers, 36, 107-18 *passim*; *see also* Merchants

Mildura, Vic., 263
Military forces, xv, xliii-lviii *passim*, liii, liv
Mill, John Stuart, 108, 140
Miller, Hon. Henry, 39
Miller's Rope Works, 264
Mining, xlv
Missionaries, 14, 259, 260, 261-2
'Missions and Mission Work', 260
Mitchell, Qld, 260
Model Lodging-house Company, 44
Molloy, Dr W. T., 122
'Month in Pentridge Gaol, A', xlviii
'Montreal, To', 261
Moody and Sankey hymns, 168, 174, 175
Morality, Victorian, xvii, xlviii, 6, 29, 30, 122, 125, 130-1, 146, 207, 229, 236; *see also* Middle class
Mordaunt, Sir Charles, 3
Mordialloc, Vic., 215
'Morning at the Hospital, A', xlviii, 19
Morrison, George Ernest, 12
Moth, Alfred, xviii, xxxiii
Mount Morgan, Qld, 260
Mrs Macquarie's Chair, Sydney, 125
Munchhausen, Baron Karl, 10, 95
Murder, xvii, xlvi, 72, 95, 131
Murphy Street, Richmond, Vic., 201
Murray River, 260
Museums, *see* Australian Museum; University of Melbourne Museum
Music halls, *see* Concert halls
Muybridge, Eadweard J., xvii, 4, 131
'My Prison Experiences', 3
Myers, Francis, 13
Myrtleford, Vic., 260

'Nails and Nail Making', 264
Naples, Italy, 262
Nathalia, Vic., 260
National Agricultural Laborers' Union, xxxvi, 3
Native outrages and rebellions, 13, 14; *see also* New Caledonia
Naturalisation, xxii, xxxix
'Naval Fete at Portsmouth', 261
Neglected and Criminal Children's Act 1874, 195
Neglected Children's Aid Society, Melbourne, 14
Negroes, xv, xviii, xx, xxiv, xxviii, xxxii, xli, 4, 5, 30, 33, 39, 64, 79, 139, 142, 171, 221; *see also* Slavery

New Caledonia, xliii-lviii *passim*, 9, 261
'New Caledonia. En Voyage', 258
'New Caledonia, On the War-Path in', 259
'New Caledonia, The War in', 258
'New Colonists', 258
New Guinea, 12
'New Guinea, A Trip to', 259
New Hebrides, 12, 13, 259, 262
New Hebrides Company, 13
New York, xvi
New Zealand, xxxvi, 11, 263
Newcastle, NSW, 177, 258
Newsboys, 179, 189
'"Night and Day"', 262
'Night in the Model Lodging-House, A', 6, 41-5, 145, 257
Nightingale, Florence, 19
No Mercy, 11
Norfolk, Virginia, xl
Norfolk Island, 86, 91
Normandy, 262
'Notes on Current Events', 5, 8, 257
Nottoway County, Virginia, xv, xxv
Noumea, xliv, xlv, liv, lvi, 9, 13, 258, 261
Nurses, 19, 86, 150

'Oakland', Virginia, xxiv
Oakum picking, 140, 141, 144, 146, 148, 163
Obituaries, 265
O'Brien Lane, Melbourne, 36-7, 178
Occident and Orient, 9, 10n., 11, 264
'Ocean to Ocean', 261
O'Farrell, Henry James, 115
O'Grady's Engineering Works, 264
'Old Folks, The', 262
Oliver Twist, 174
'On the wallaby', 46, 171
Opera House, Melbourne, 232, 234
Ophthalmia, 152
Opium, 38, 179, 183
Orphanages, 60
Orphans, *see* Children, pauper
Orwell, George, xliii, lv, 6
Otway Forest, 260
'Ouida', 122
'Out Recruiting', 259
'Outcasts of Melbourne, The', 6, 27, 257
Outpatients, 19-26
'Outward Bound', 262
Palmer River goldfields, Qld, 9
Pantomime, 8, 60, 130

Panton, Joseph Anderson, 12
'Papua! Goodbye to', 260
Paris, 3, 13, 29, 34, 231; *see also* Commune
'Paris Picture Gallery, In a', 262
Parisian, 13
'Parisian Sketches', 14, 262
'Parliament, Impressions in', 257
Pasta Signora, 130
Patriotism, *see* Loyalty
Paulett, W. F., xxxii, xl
'Pauper Funerals', 66-73, 258
Pearce, Rev. William P., 113, 115-18 *passim*
'Peep at "The Blacks", A', xlii, 258
Penitencier Agricole de Fouwharii, 259
Penshurst, Vic., 260
Pentridge Gaol, 7, 12, 30, 38, 81, 84-103, 265
'Pentridge, A Month in', xlviii, 7, 84-100, 258
'Pentridge Revisited', 12, 259
'People As They Are', 259
Petre, Father, 58
Photography, xvii
Phrenology, 117, 153
'Picturesque Tasmania', 264
'Picturesque Victoria', 12, 13, 260, 261, 264
Pitt Street, Sydney, 50
Plantation owners: New Hebrides, 13; Queensland, 9, 12, 13; *see also* Virginia
Poe, Edgar Allan, 79
Police: NSW, 222, 224; Queensland, 12; Victoria, 29, 30, 33, 34, 38, 41, 143, 210, 211, 212, 214, 219, 234-5, 249
Police courts, Melbourne, 27, 30, 31, 37, 220
Polytechnic, Melbourne, 211
'Poor Jack', 262
Port Albert, Vic., 261
Port Fairy, Vic., 263
Port Moresby, 12, 260
Portland, Vic., 260, 263
Portland Bay, 86
'Portsmouth, Naval Fete at', 261
Potter's Field, Melbourne, 67
Potts Point, NSW, 124
Poverty, 3, 6, 24, 30, 56, 67, 108-9; *see also* Amusements; Charitable institutions; Children, pauper; Lodging-houses; Ragged schools; Slums
Powell, A. G., xxxiii
Power, Harry, 86-7, 90
Powys, Walter N., xxiv-xxv

INDEX

Prahran, Vic., 185, 190-1
Presbyterian Church, 110
Presbyterian Union Theological Seminary, xviii, xx
Price, John Giles, 99
Prince Edward County, Virginia, xv, xx, xxii, xxiv, xxxii, xlii
Princess Theatre, Melbourne, 210
Prisoners' Aid Society, 33, 38, 99
Prisons: Australian, xvi, 3, 7, 12, 30, 34, 38, 76-103, 257; English, 85; French, *see* Mazas; *see also* Brisbane gaol; Pentridge
'Prize-Fight, A', 214; *see also* Boxing
Prospect, Virginia, xxiv, xxvii
Prostitution, xvi, 6, 7, 24-6, 27, 29, 30, 31, 34, 38-40 *passim*, 52, 55, 132, 183, 229-56 *passim*; *see also* Children, as prostitutes
'Protestant Female Refuge, The', 249-56
Public Libraries: Melbourne, 127; Sydney, 126-9
Punt Road, South Yarra, Vic., 112

Quebec, Canada, 261
Queen Victoria, xxxiv
Queenscliff, Vic., 263
Queensland, 9, 10, 12, 262
'Queensland, A Winter Tour in', 12, 260
'Queensland, In Northern', 259
'Queensland, The Chinese Question in', 258

'Race Meeting, A Country', 258
Racism, xx, xlviii, l, liii, lvi; *see also* Negroes
Raffles, 120, 123
Ragged schools, 178-94, 257
Railways, xvii, xxii, xxiv, xxvi, xl, 135, 260
'Railway Township, A', 260
Ramahyuck, Vic., 261
'Rambler', xvii
Ramsay, James and Peter, 188
Randolph House, Farmville, xviii
Randwick, NSW, 221
Rathouis, M., xvii
Ravenswood, Qld, 260
Reade, Charles, 79
'Red Sea Passage, The', 261
'Refuge, A', 249
Religion, xv, xx, xxii-xxiv, xxviii, 34, 35, 37, 40, 45, 67, 85, 90, 92, 107-18, 120, 124-6, 130, 142, 144, 148, 151, 155, 157, 159, 162, 169, 175, 178, 184, 187-94 *passim*, 207, 208, 250, 255, 256, 259; *see also* Gos-

pel halls; individual churches
Rents, in Melbourne, 61
Republican Party, U.S., xxviii, xxxivii
Restaurants, xvii-xviii, 50, 52, 62; *see also* Food; Sixpenny restaurants
Revolt of the Field, xxxvi
Richmond, Vic., 196-201 *passim*
Richmond, Virginia, xvii, xxiv-xxv, xxxi, xl, 4, 8, 66
Riverina, NSW, 171
Rivière, Commandant Henri, xlvii, xl, lvii
Roads, xxii
Robertson, George, xvi
Rockhampton, Qld, 260
Rodgers, E. T., xxi
Rokeby Street, Collingwood, Vic., 191
Roma, Qld, 260
Roman Catholic Church: charities, 60, 236-48; education, 181, 190, 193, 243, 246; funerals, 67, 70; *see also* 'Magdalen Asylum'
Rome, 13
'Ropes and Rope Making', 264
Rotorua, N.Z., 263
Royal Commission on Charities, 14
'Royal Park, Sunday in the', 258
Royal Princess Theatre, Sandhurst, 11
Russell, N.Z., 263
Rutherglen, Vic., 263

Sabbatarian party, 126, 236, 249
'"Sabbath-Breaking" in Sydney', 124-9
'Saddling Paddocks, The', 231, 232, 234, 235, 249
Sailors, 128, 135, 158, 160, 163, 164, 234; *see also* 'Sailors' Home'
'Sailors' Home, At the', 7, 168-77, 257
Sailors' Union, 172
St Albans, Vic., 264
St Andrew, Joseph Andrew Horner, xviii-xxv *passim*
St Anne's Church, xxiii-xxiv
'St. David's Day', 3n.
St John's State School, Melbourne, 188
St Kilda Road, Melbourne, 140, 141, 215
St Luke's Church, Emerald Hill, Vic., 119
St Mary's schools, Sydney, 52, 58-60 *passim*
Sale, Vic., 261
'Salvation Army in South Australia, The', 259
Samoa, 14, 262-3
'Samoan Difficulty, The', 263

'Samoan Sketches', 262
Sandwich Island, 261
San Francisco, xvii, xl, 11, 131
'San Francisco Revisited', 259
Sandridge, Vic., 174, 175
Sanitation, 31, 44-5, 49, 196
Sappho, 128
Savings banks, 168
Scarlet fever, 141, 198
School of Arts, Brisbane, 9
Scott, Sir Walter, xxxiv
Scotland, 261
Scots Church, Melbourne, 107, 112, 118
'Scripture Reading School', 190
Seamen's bethel, Sandridge, Vic., 175
Sebastopol, Vic., 145
Sellars, Harry, 210
Sentimentality, 6, 29, 71, 236
Servants, female, 49, 134, 152-3, 162; *see also* 'Stanley Park'
'Settling Day', 258
Sewing machines, 249, 253
Seymour, Vic., 264
Shaw, Charlie, 55
Shop girls, 29, 124; *see also* Prostitution
Shrewsbury College, England, xxviii-xxx
'Sights and Scenes in Bourke Street', 264
'Sights and Scenes in Collins Street', 264
'Sights and Scenes in Flinders Street and Lane', 264
'Sights and Scenes in Swanston and Elizabeth Streets', 264
'Silent System', 81, 82, 92-3
Sims, Norman, lvii
Singleton's Gardens, 200
'Six Hours in a Dark Cell', 77, 258
'Sixpenny Restaurants', xvi, 5, 7, 61-5, 257
'Sixty Months in Pentridge', 265
Skittle alleys, 30, 169
Slavery, xxxvi, *see also* Virginia
Slayton, General James R., xvii, xxii, xli
Sleigh, Serjeant, 220
Slums, Melbourne, 6, 7, 30, 31, 36-7, 39; *see also* Lodging-houses
Slums, Sydney, 56-8 *passim*; *see also* 'Sydney Common Lodging-Houses'
'Smart Recruiting', 259
Smith, Shep., 222
Smith, Sydney, 111
Smoking, xxv, xxviii, 43-5 *passim*, 49, 55, 95, 99, 100, 125, 143, 151, 153, 157, 164
Snake-bite cure, 116

Snowy River, Vic., 261
Social classes, xxxv, xxxvi; *see also* Middle class
Solitary confinement, 82, 91, 93
South journal, New York, xvii
'South Australia, The Salvation Army in', 259
South Sea Massacres, 11, 264
'South Seas, In the', 261
Southside Virginia Immigration Society, xviii-xlii *passim*
Southside Virginian, xxii, xli
Spa, Blegium, 262
Spectator, 14
Spencer Street, Melbourne, 168, 169, 172
Spiers and Pond, 134
Spiritualism, 10, 80, 265
Sport, 207-25
Spurr, David, lii, liii, lviii
Squatters, 108, 134, 208
Stanley, Henry M., xxii, 263
Stanley, John, 179
'Stanley Park', xvi-xlii *passim*
Stanley Park Academy, xxviii-xxx, xlii
'Stanley-James, J. S.', *see* James, John Stanley
Stanton, J. H., 7
'Starving Samoa', 262
'State Baby-Farming', 195-203, 258
State schools, xx, xxiv, 36-7, 59, 178, 186-8 *passim*, 192, 198; *see also* Ragged schools
Station hands, 24, 86, 141, 171
Stawell, Vic., 264
Stephen, Harold W. H., 10, 265
Steerage immigrants, xvi
Stonebreaking, 96, 141, 146, 148
Stratford, Vic., 261
'Street arabs', 49, 51-60, 186
'Strikes, An Embarrassment of', 259
Strong, Rev. Charles, 109-11
'Studio, In a', 261
Studley Park, Melbourne, 241
'Suburban Church, A', 112-18, 258
'Sugar Industry, The', 259
Suicide, attempted, 4, 95
Sunbury, Vic., 161-2
'Sunday Excursions', 258
'Sunday in the Royal Park', 258
Sunday observance, *see* Sabbatarian party
Surry Hills, Sydney, 127
Sussex Street, Sydney, 46, 50
Swan Street, Richmond, Vic., 199

INDEX

Swanston Street, Melbourne, 139, 215, 264
'"Swiftly Flying South"', 259
Sydney, xxxviii, xliii, li, 9, 10, 11, 12, 124-35, 220-5; *see also* Slums, Sydney
'Sydney Common Lodging-Houses', 2n., 46, 258
'Sydney, Impressions of', 9. 258
Sydney Morning Herald, iv, xliii, xlv, xlvi, xlvii, xlviii, lii, lvi, lviii, 9, 10, 11, 220n., 258-9
Sydney Soup Kitchen, 48
Sydney Street, Collingwood, Vic., 191, 193
'Sydney Theatres and Bars', 130
'Sydney, The Waifs and Strays of', 258
Syme, David, 13, 14
Synagogue, Sydney, 56

Tanna, 12
'Tasmania, Picturesque', 264
Taylor, J. M. & Farnsworth, xxv
Telegraph, electric, xlvi, xlvii
'Telemachus', 13
Temperance Hall, Melbourne, 172
Temperance movement, xxiii, 168, 170, 175; *see also* Drunkenness
'Temperance Territory, A', 262
Texas Pacific Railway, 117
Thackston, W. W., xxxiii, xxxviii
'Theatre Vestibules, The', 229-35, 257
Theatre Royal, Melbourne, 11, 229-35
Theatre Royal, Sydney, 60, 130-4
Theatres, 11, 49, 51, 113, 130-3, 229-35 *passim*, 238, 250; *see also* Concert halls
Theft, 27, 29, 33, 34, 49, 180, 211
'Thomas, Julian': adopted as pseudonym, xvi, xxx, xl, xlii, xliii, lv, 4; name used in Australia, 5, 10; revealed as 'The Vagabond', 8; buried as, 14; *see also* James, John Stanley; 'Vagabond, The'
'Thomas Was First Australian War Correspondent', 265
Thompson, John, 214-20 *passim*
Thompson, Lydia, 122
'Three Days in the Benevolent Asylum', 149-67, 257
'Three Weeks in a Nunnery', 8
Thursday Island, 259-60
'Timber Trade, The', 264
Times on Sunday, iv
Tobacco, *see* Smoking
Tonga, 14, 263
Toorak Road, South Yarra, Vic., 112

Torres Straits, 260
Toth, Stephen A., lviii
Town Hall, Melbourne, 121
Townsville, Qld, 10, 12, 259, 260
'Townsville to the Herbert', 259
Traralgon, Vic., 261
'Trial of Skill', 220
'Trip to the North, A', 261
Trollope, Anthony, xxxiv-xxxvii
Turpin, Dick, 87
Twain, Mark, xliii
Twelvetrees, Frederick Harper, xxi, xxvi, xxxii

'Ultra-Vagabond', 265
Unemployment, xv, 6, 145; *se also* Poverty
Union Steamship Company, 11, 12
University High School, Melbourne, 264
University of Melbourne Museum, 128

'"Vagabond" Annual, The', 264
'Vagabond Journalist', 265
'Vagabond, The': adopted as pseudonum, 5; mystery of his identity, 8; *see also* James, John Stanley; 'Thomas, Julian'
Vagabond Papers, The, first series, xvi, xl, 4n., 237
Vagabond Papers, The, second series, xxx, xli, 12
Vagabond Papers, The, third series, xxxii, 3, 7
Vagabond Papers, The, fourth series, xxv, xlii, 3n.
Vagabond Papers, The fifth series, xvii, 2n., 4n.
Vagabonds and Their Dupes, 10, 265
Varnauld, M., liv, lv, lvi
Vagrants, 6, 7, 27, 29, 34, 60, 64
Vavau, Tonga, 263
Venable, N. E., xxxiii
Vermin, 146, 156, 163
Vice, *see* Drunkenness; Gambling; Prostitution
Victoria, xxxiv, xxxvi
'Victoria, Pictureque', 12, 13, 260, 261
'Victoria, The Cradle of', 260
'Victorian Holiday Resorts', 264
'Victorian Industries', 264
Victorian Review, 259
'Victorian Vintage, A', 258
Virginia, USA, iv, xv-xlii *passim*
Virginia Immigration Society, xv
'Volcano of Yasur', 259

'Voyage of the Elsea, The', 260
'V.R.C. New Year's Day Meeting, The', 263

'Waifs and Strays of Sydney, The', 4, 51, 130, 258
Wainui, 14
Waiters, 65
Waitresses, 61, 65
Walhalla, Vic., 261
Walkabout, 265
Walsall, England, 2, 4
Wandiligong, Vic., 260
Wangaratta, Vic., 260, 262, 263
Warburton, Vic., 262
Warders, prison, 84
Warracknabeal, Vic., 263
Warrnambool, Vic., 260, 263
'Warr's River Waterworks', 262
Warwickshire, England, 3
Watkins, James, 44
Waverley, NSW, 222
Weekly Dispatch, 113
Wentworth, NSW, 260
West Australian, 265
West Melbourne, 236
Western Australian Supplement, 264
Westward Ho!, Qld, 260
White Hart Hotel, Melbourne, 237
White Star Line, xvi
Whittlesea, Vic., 261
'Who Was "The Vagabond"?', xlii, 2n., 265
'Why Germany is Hated', 263
Wicker, O. T., xxi, xxxiii
Wildlife, xxiv
Williesburg, Virginia, xxiii
Wilson, John, 215
Wilton, Thomas Talbot, 11
Winnipeg, Canada, 261
Wolfe, Tom, lviii
Wolverhampton, England, 1
Womack, J. W., xxxviii
Women's wards: at Benevolent Asylum, 150, 152, 163; at Immigrants' Home, 146
Woodbine, 11, 259
'Wool Trade, The', 264
Woolloomooloo, Sydney, 124
Working girls, 29, 30, 38, 44, 61, 65, 124, 208, 249; *see also* Prostitution; Shop girls
Working men, 44, 47, 64, 124, 126-9

Yachting, 264
'Yarra Bankers', 28, 34
Yarra River, 34
'Yasur, the Volcano of', 259
Yea, Vic., 260, 264
Yorick Club, Melbourne, 9
'Young Cavanagh', 211

Zeehan & Dundas Herald, xlv, lviii
Zox, Ephraim, 14